William T. (William Thomas) Baird

Seventy Years of New Brunswick Life

Autobiographical Sketches

William T. (William Thomas) Baird

Seventy Years of New Brunswick Life
Autobiographical Sketches

ISBN/EAN: 9783337031039

Printed in Europe, USA, Canada, Australia, Japan

Cover: Foto ©ninafisch / pixelio.de

More available books at **www.hansebooks.com**

SEVENTY YEARS

OF

New Brunswick Life.

AUTOBIOGRAPHICAL SKETCHES

BY

WILLIAM T. BAIRD,

LIEUTENANT COLONEL,

Paymaster of Military District No. 8, Dominion of Canada, from the Confederation of the British Provinces to the year 1887, Superintendent of Stores at St. John, New Brunswick, from the year 1879 to the year 1887.

"This is mine own, my native land."

ST. JOHN, N. B.:
PRESS OF GEO. E. DAY, GERMAIN ST.
1890.

PREFACE.

THESE PAGES, prepared at different times in moments of leisure, were originally intended for perusal by my children, friends or others who, in later years, might have a desire to learn something of pioneer life in New Brunswick. At the request of friends, some portions of this book have already been given to the press. notably " *Sparks from a Camp - Fire* " and some of the *Historical Sketches*, and from their favorable reception by the public, they are, with other unpublished matter, now given in a more permanent form.

The experiences of a life extending over a period of more than three score years, obtained by contact with the ever - varying phases—social, commercial, political and military — incidental to the growth of a young Colony, should enable one tolerably observant, to present much that would be interesting and instructive to the general reader.

The training of a young mind in log cabin life in the back-woods has a tendency to mature and ripen the understanding and cause a higher appreciation of the blessings and enjoyments of a more cultivated society.

The foundation has ever much to do with the superstructure reared thereon; and whatever may be the result of an internecine struggle on this Continent (which will surely come), New Brunswickers will be recreant indeed if not found in the front rank in defence of the sacred trust committed to them by their fathers.

In the discharge of my duty as Paymaster in Military District No. 8, for nearly twenty years, I have met with men representing the

three arms of the service in the Dominion in
every section of the Province where assembled, and am fully satisfied it is not the pay,
the equipment, the readiness to meet at
Headquarters the reasonable demands of
either officers or men, that has supplied the
quota annually for drill, but the unflinching
loyalty of the New Brunswick soldier.

In my treatment of public men and their
acts I shall give a simple relation of facts
as bearing upon the individual or public
weal, which every unit in the mass electorate
has a right to do; and if but one atom be
removed from the political "Augean stable"
there will be an atom less in the general
cleansing.

Thrusting out my frail bark on the great
sea of literature, I can only say, " Waft,
gentle breezes."   W. T. B.

WOODSTOCK, N. B.,

    January 1st, 1890.

CONTENTS.

CHAPTER VI.

CHAPTER VII.

CHAPTER VIII.

CHAPTER IX.

CHAPTER X.

CHAPTER XI.

CHAPTER XII.

Chapter XIII.

Chapter XIV.

Chapter XV.

Chapter XVI.

Chapter XVII.

Chapter XVIII.

Chapter XIX.

Chapter XX.

PAGE

Chapter I.

The Baird Family.

IN 1870 a book was published in London for members of the Baird family, and reprinted from the original MS. of William Baird, Esq., now preserved in the *Advocates' Library*, Edinburgh, by which it seems that in 1578 a union of two families of Bairds took place, one representing, through the female line, the family of Ordinhnivas, an heiress, Lillias Baird, who married Gilbert Baird, the third of Auchmeddan. They had thirty-two sons and daughters. Three sons went to Ireland as adventurers in the beginning of the reign of James the First of England. Two of them settled in the Province of Ulster, north of Ireland, from whom are descended the families on the St. John River, other parts of Canada and the United States. The other son went to the south of Ireland and from him are descended those of the name in Westmorland, New Brunswick, Amherst and other parts of Nova Scotia.

In the death of John Baird, my great grandfather, terminated a three-lives' lease of land, in the County of Monaghan, town of Graffa.

He had seven sons, viz., John, William, David, George, Adam, Joseph and Thomas, who occupied seven houses and farms adjoining each other and were known as the Bairds of Graffa.

The period of possession—nearly two centuries—having lapsed, the land was taken into an estate and its occupants compelled to leave the home of their ancestors, and my grandfather accepted an invitation from my father and came to America.

He spent some of his time with us in Fredericton and died about the year 1840 in the Parish of Kent.

The fourth son of my great grandfather, George, came also to this country, bringing his family with him, excepting his eldest son, Henry, who preceded him, and settled on a farm purchased from my father in the Parish of Kent.

The old people found on their arrival a comfortable home and lived to see their children well and respectably settled in life.

Several farms adjoining, owned by the brothers, Henry (known as Squire Baird), Adam and George, form the well known settlement and Post Office station of "Bairdsville." George T. Baird, son of the last named, is now a member of the Local Parliament for the County of Victoria.

MY FATHER.

John, son of William Baird and Susan Teel, was born in the town of Graffa aforesaid in the year 1795.

He received his first instruction at the school of Mr. Farmer, in Graffa; and later attended a school in the town of Monaghan, three miles distant.

When by age and education sufficiently advanced, he entered the Seminary for School Masters in the County of Kildare.

Printed and written in my father's Prayer Book (Church of England) in my possession, may be found the following :

"The Association Incorporated for Discountenancing
"Vice and Promoting the Knowledge and Prac-
"tice of the Christian Religion,

"Adjudged this Premium

"to

"JOHN BAIRD,

"For superior merit at examination in the Principles of
"the Christian Religion and the Knowledge
"of the Gospel, held in

"THE SEMINARY FOR SCHOOL MASTERS,

"On the 13th day of March, 1816.

"The Rev. Samuel Jones, Examiner."

About this time the 74th Regiment quartered in Dublin,—with its ranks depleted by foreign,

active service,—the commander, Colonel French,
entered one day and the young men of the Seminary, being formed in line, the Colonel addressed
them as follows:—"I want a young man to join
"my Regiment and go out to America as a teach-
"er. He will have the rank and pay of a Ser-
"geant, with some perquisites, and in this case the
"term of service will be but seven (7) years, at
"the close of which he will be entitled to a grant
"of land from the crown of 200 acres, with some
"privileges thereto attached."

My father was the first to step to the front, and
being well recommended, was accepted and joined
the regiment.

Arriving safely in New Brunswick, the regiment was stationed at Fredericton, the Capital,
where he completed his term of service, having for
a time as his assistant teacher the late Robert
Cowan. He then proceeded to possess his land,
which was situated on the west bank of the River
St. John, about 100 miles above Fredericton.

After a residence of two years in the Parish of
Kent, he returned to Fredericton, where, as Principal of the National School, he continued to teach
during a period of twenty years. Children of
some of the most respectable families attended the
school ; and several, yet living, are occupying high
and honorable positions in public service.

A few years later he discontinued teaching, sold
his property in Fredericton, and removed with his

family to a newly purchased farm a few miles above the Tobique Village, where he resided until his death, which occurred in the year 1858. His remains lie in the Episcopal burying ground in Tobique Village.

MY MOTHER.

Annie Diggin was born in the city of Dublin in the year 1798. Her grandmother was a Quakeress, and her own mother retained a love for what was chaste and plain in language and dress. Her mother died when she was young. Her father held for many years an appointment as clerk in the Dublin Post Office, retiring on a superannuated allowance, which he lived to enjoy to the good old age of ninety-four years. I have often heard my mother speak of being kidnapped when a child going to school. An old woman met her in the street, and under the pretence of giving her some dolls' clothing and confectionery led her sev-eral blocks out of her way, thence into a dark alley, where she stripped her of most of her clothing, and was examining the rings in her ears when a gentleman passing, attracted by her shrieks, came to her relief, and happening to know her father, had her conveyed to her home.

My mother's brother, John Diggin, whose letters in my possession show him to have been a clerk on plantations in the islands of Grenada and

Caracoa, was last heard from as a lieutenant on the "Spanish Main." I remember hearing my mother speak of his joining the Columbian service under Bolivar in the struggle for independence, which he (Bolivar) eventually secured, both for Columbia and Peru.

The letters from my grandfather and uncle, with a miniature of the latter, are well preserved, and denote the writers to have possessed an intelligence and religious fervor which, I trust, will never be found wanting in their descendants.

I have been unable to obtain any information other than contained in these letters regarding my uncle, John Diggin, but the probabilities are that he was killed during the war or fell a victim to some of the malignant diseases that infest the cities and shores of South America.

In a Book of Common Prayer, in use by the Church of Ireland, is written:

"Samuel Diggin, No. 13."

Also:

"Anne Diggin,

"Born in Dublin, in Simpson's Court, Beresford Street,

"In the year of our Lord 1798.

"Married to John Baird on the 30th day of

"March, 1817."

This Prayer Book had evidently been used by my grandfather, and the "No. 13" referred to the pew occupied by his family.

I set much store by this book, which seems to bring me in direct contact with my dear mother and the scenes of her early life.

OUR HOME.

Our home and the place of my birth, was situated on Queen Street in Fredericton and near the residence of Mark Needham.

A portion of my mother's time was occupied in teaching some young ladies, among whom I remember the Misses Needham and Grosvenor, more especially as they would take me occasionally to their homes.

The long journey from Fredericton to the Parish of Kent in an open sleigh in the month of March, with two children under five years of age, must have been to my mother a trying one.

I remember, while we were occupying temporarily a small cabin on a steep bank of the river, nearly opposite the now " Muniac Station " of the N. B. Railway, seeing her weep bitterly while reading a letter received from her father.

To a sensitive mind, the contrast must have been painful in the extreme. My mother felt here the absence of what to her were necessaries of life. No near neighbour to break the dull monotony of forest life,—friendly interchanges with the Morehouses opposite was rendered difficult and at times impracticable by the rapid flowing river between,—no highway road above the River de

Chute, three miles below,—and no regular postal communication.

I well remember the courier of that time, Martin, a Frenchman. The trip to and from Quebec was made each month; in winter on snow-shoes, with dog and toboggan.

The next remove was to a small log house on our own place, and I have no doubt the protection it afforded, humble though it was, was a great relief to my mother.

Our nearest neighbor was a family named McDougal, whose kindness during our stay there was long after remembered.

The prospect of a return from the wilderness of that time to Fredericton, must have been truly gratifying to my mother; but the time spent in Kent was far from being a blank in our existence. Its lessons can never be lost!

In our new home on George Street, Fredericton, we enjoyed, for a few years, as much happiness as this world generally affords.

Among the kind friends who visited my mother during occasional illness was Mrs. Dr. Wood-forde, a good Christian woman and a type of the old New Brunswick stock of true nobility.

Our life was very quiet and retired. My mother saw very little society, and devoted herself entirely to the comfort and happiness of her family.

When her health permitted, she attended regularly the morning service in the old church, where the Cathedral now stands. A few years previous to her death she occasionally attended the evening meetings in the New Methodist Church. I generally accompanied her, and after a time, a pew being rented, my father did also.

The rules and usages of the Church of England were closely observed by my parents, in the partaking of the Sacrament, reading of prayers on stated festivals, etc.

I remember a serious conversation between them at a certain time with reference to my Confirmation; but which, for some reason that I cannot now explain, never took place. My sponsors, therefore, have never been relieved from the great responsibility which Bishop Mountain placed upon them.

My mother's health had become sadly impaired: a lingering cough, with hectic flush, showed but too plainly the terrible enemy with which she was struggling. Consumption! that ruthless disease, had marked her for its own.

The winter of 1836-37 was a dark and gloomy one to our family. Death made a sad inroad upon us, taking away the two youngest children, and our dear, dear mother.

Language fails to express the sense of loneliness we feel on our return from the burial of a loved one. Every object the eye rested upon, seemed to wring fresh anguish from the heart and stamp there indelibly, gone!—gone!—never again to see or speak with on earth.

As I write, and more than three score years
have passed away, I would not suppress the tears
that flow in memory of my mother ; and many,
many times, as in a dream, have I felt that dear
loving face to be near to mine and been comforted.

My mother died in February, A. D. 1836, and
was buried by the Rev. Mr. Sterling, in the old
burial-ground, Fredericton, a *few feet* to the *North-
East* of a tomb and vault in which rests the remains of the wife of the late Hon. Thomas
Baillie. ›

Chapter II.

Two Years in the Wilderness.

IN the month of March, 1823, my father having purchased a horse, sleigh and harness for the journey, with my mother, self, four-year-old and younger sisters, set out to explore the wilderness and endure for a time the hardships of pioneer life.

The only roadway was on the river, and marked out by fir bushes planted in the ice.

I have yet a recollection of some of the incidents of this journey, the cutting wind, the heavy snow-drifts, and breaking up of a fine fishing rod in urging the horse through them, the dangers of ice travel — often treacherously giving way and engulfing man and beast.

We at length reached the hospitable home of George Morehouse, Esquire, now Muniac Station, from which we could see at a distance of a few rods across the river the long looked for land.

Two teams loaded with furniture and necessaries, one of them driven by the owner, John Rierdon, arrived shortly after without serious mishap.

The summer was spent in clearing land and

making preparation for building on the new farm. A few miles farther up on the eastern side of the river, the country being more thickly settled, we occupied a house there, and my father taught school during the winter.

Occasional visits with my father and mother to Mr. Morehouse's barn, where was stored for a long time our furniture, and from some mysterious parts of which they would bring out raisins and nuts, must have been events deeply interesting, as they still linger in memory.

One of the most remarkable events of my life and providential escapes occurred while we occupied the hut on the front of the Glebe lot. A pathway led from thence through the forest to a creek on our place, over which we passed on a large tree, or windfall, flattened for the purpose. While one of the settlers, a Mr. Grant, and my father, were engaged in building the log house, it was my duty to pass through the woods, a distance of one-fourth of a mile, and call them to dinner. I was then about six years of age.

One day, following the pathway for this purpose, when about half way, I saw at my feet a small living black object, its hair coarse and straight, and as I stooped to examine it, it turned its head to one side with a whining noise. Its mouth being open, its tongue resembled a piece of scarlet flannel. While fondling it as a puppy dog, a peculiar rumbling noise caused me to rise up, when I saw a large, black object bounding towards me through the underbrush. I had heard many stories of bears and an intuitive fear prompted me to run instantly and with all possible speed in the direction of the men. I had almost reached the creek where it was necessary to turn to the left to cross on the tree already named, when looking over my shoulder, I saw the huge monster close upon me. Throwing myself into the stream to avoid instant seizure, I was carried down with the current amongst some brush, and had probably, in the meantime, made good use of my lungs, for the men came in haste to my rescue. A brace of dogs were soon on the scent, followed by the men with guns in pursuit. The bear with her cub got safely away, but Basto, a spaniel dog, brought back a severe mark from bruin's paw.

My father having purchased for me a small, narrow axe, I essayed to fall a tree. The one chosen by myself was a tall, dry cedar, the hardest kind to cut, about eight inches in diameter, and quite near to our hut. I spent some time mangling this tree, and, after many days, there was evidently a decrease in the circumference, which resembled the work of a beaver. After many repeated efforts, and blistering my hands, at length I heard a creaking noise, and looking up, saw the tree had actually commenced to fall. Dropping my axe, I ran at full speed for the house, which was just in the direction it had taken, and narrowly escaped injury, as the topmost branches were broken at my heels.

The removal to our new log-house, and within hailing distance of a neighbor, was an agreeable change.

There being no highway road, the appearance of a stranger was to the settlers an event, and the news as greedily seized upon as we now do our morning paper; with this difference, that *related* might have been several months old; that *read*, the event of yesterday.

I remember on one occasion studying a traveller at his luncheon, through the cracks of the floor above; and admiring, boy like, a new jack-knife he seemed to delight in exhibiting.

A partial clearing had been previously made by a squatter, of an acre or more, on the high bank of the river in front of the house.

In this space was a beautiful spring of water, to which I sometimes found my way.

Its Genii was a large, green frog, which, on my approach, shot leisurely across the bottom and became a thing of life, whose presence I gladly sought in my visits.

Incidents of these kinds, now considered so trifling, yet unobliterated by the graver events of more than half a century, startle one with the thought of the probable condition of a mind permitted to mature in such isolation and surroundings.

Soldiers disbanded from various British regiments were the principal settlers, and a less severe training than that endured by those veterans of "flood and field" would not have secured to them the same measure of success in overcoming all the obstacles presented as "pioneers of the wilderness."

The Indians — Melicites — were very numerous on the St. John river.

An old Scotch veteran, Archy McLean, well-known afterwards in Fredericton, where he died, who lived near us the first winter at a farm known as "Vinegar Hill," told me many years later, that in ascending the St. John river to a military station at Presque Isle in a tow-boat with troops, he had seen the islands fringed with their canoes. They were peaceable when not excited by the demon buc-ta-witch, or fire-water, and I never heard of any cruelties being practised by them on the settlers of the St. John, even in their palmiest days.

The names of the settlers known to me on the east side of the river during our stay in Kent are: George Morehouse, a retired officer, 104th Regiment, and William Hallet, Magistrates; McDonald, Grant, Marcheson, Inman, Donaho's, Jonas Fitzherbert (the only blacksmith within miles of our home), and others; on the west side: James and Joshua Bishop, McDougal, Larlee, Linen, Holmes, &c.

Two of Mr. McDonald's sons made each a mark beyond the limits of their early home : William, as a surveyor, well-known in Carleton County ; and Frank, merchant, and partner for a time of O. D. Smith in Woodstock ; later, president for several years of the "Portland (Maine) Albertine Oil Co." In this enterprise he was fortunate in making considerable money, and was generous in distributing patronage to the sons of former friends in Woodstock.

Many of the settlers, driven by necessity, soon became experts in the pursuit and capture of wild animals, salmon and other fish, with which the forests and streams abounded.

The adventures of one of those veterans, Dick Inman, a vigorous and resolute man, were numerous.

On one occasion a moose closely pursued by him through the deep snow leaped into the bed of a stream, its sandy bottom affording the animal firm footing for a distance of about one hundred yards. The walls of snow on either side prevented the exit of the now imprisoned animal, which raced madly up and down. Inman, watching his opportunity, leaped successfully astride the galloping beast, and maintained his seat uutil it became exhausted, when with his knife it was easily despatched.

Again, making with his axe a fierce attack upon a bear, she, with her cubs, was driven up a tree. Calling loudly to his wife, who went to his assistance, and placing her, axe in hand, to prevent their descent and escape, he hastened to procure his gun, and succeeded in killing two of them.

Three miles below our home was the "River de Chute" — Falling or Rapid River. On this stream was the only "grist mill" in this part of the country, owned by Hil. Kearney, whose hospitality to travellers was proverbial.

The River St. John was navigated by tow-boats, drawn by horses. All the lumber — square timber and logs — cut upon its banks or tributaries was floated to St. John. It was first made into joints or rafts, on which one or more men, according to the quantity of lumber, was put to pilot and run as far as Fredericton, where a number of rafts were put together and with a larger crew sent on to St. John.

The scull-oar in the hands of a raftsman is a powerful lever ; many large rafts are handled with this implement alone, but a sweep or rudder is often placed at the tail of the raft as a double security.

At certain pitches of water the swift currents and eddies demand skilled pilots, to which add an occasional gale of wind and the best and most successful pilot often comes to grief. At the highest spring freshet the current is over eight miles an hour, and rafts are run in the light of one day from Tobique to Fredericton.

Reverting to tow-boats as the only means of transporting freight in former times, the mouths of the rivers entering the St. John were crossed by the horses, bearing their riders gallantly through the deep or rapid water. I have seen them thus swimming, surrounded by running ice, the rider standing upon the saddle. To the horses was attached a long rope, united with two others connected with the centre and bottom of the mast in the boat, all of which were occasionally raised by means of a pulley on the mast, to escape in their progress objects of a higher level.

The boats had a carrying power of from 100 to 200 barrels, and were the only means of transport for supplying lumber operations on the St. John and its tributaries.

The ordinary mode of transport from Fredericton, where all supplies were obtained by the settlers, was the canoe; and many a weary man has lain down with a stone for his pillow and slept soundly, after shoving his load through tide and rapid with a spruce pole from early dawn.

The largest lumbering establishment of those early times was known as the "Concern Place," a few miles below the Tobique River and near the "Tobique Rocks." The firm was composed of Peters & Wilmot, the latter the father of the well-known and talented Judge Wilmot.

The pine tree grew to an enormous size, and was found in great abundance along the St. John and its tributaries, while white pine timber was for many years the staple of the Province,—its chief article of export.

In the early days of lumbering, when fine groves of pine were found on the banks of the St. John, fortunes should have been made; but drunkenness, extravagance and a waste of valuable time occasioned many failures.

The fur of wild animals was also an important item of export from this Province.

An old Scotch gentleman, Peter Fraser, whom I well remember in Fredericton, was a buyer and exporter of peltry, perhaps the principal one in the Province. The Indians had great confidence in him, and he is said to have treated them kindly.

How long before my time I know not, but I heard it said that in buying fur by weight from the unsuspecting native, the hand of the purchaser weighed one pound, and his foot two pounds. Some friend of the Indians, pointing out the fraud, they cut the hand from a dead man, the weight of which they found to be a pound. They had no means, however, of weighing the muscular pressure of the living hand.

Chapter iii.

Return to Fredericton.

THE crude state of society and the poor prospect of any speedy return from his labors, together with the absence of everything congenial to the tastes and habits of himself and my mother, prepared my father in the spring of 1825 to accept a proposition for his immediate return to Fredericton, to take charge of the National School.

The incident of our journey down was the tow-boat being swept by the current of a high spring freshet under overhanging trees, which brushed from the cabin's deck the steersman into the seething waters below. I remember, also, our stopping for a night at Colonel Ketchum's, a little above Woodstock, where we were kindly treated.

Again in Fredericton, my father at once resumed his former work of teaching.

The buildings, occupied as a residence and school-room, were situated opposite Wilmot's alley, just above the present stone barracks, and formed two sides of a square. We spent part of one year in this place and then removed our residence to a large two-story building, owned by a Mr. Wells, on King street, near the jail, occupying the half of an upper flat.

Before all our effects were removed, however, there occurred the great fire of 1825, which in the month of October, destroyed the greater part of the town of Fredericton ; also the forest and many dwellings on the Miramichi River, where several lives were lost.

The school being in session and the flames nearing the building, the school was dismissed. A large dictionary was given me to carry, and as I reached the street — now filled with smoke, burning cinders and retreating people — and crossed to the opposite side, I saw a horse coming down furiously ; he was attached to a cart on which was some bedding in flames. I ran into an alley leading into the yard of the Yerxa House, the horse took the same course. Having run the length of the alley, in turning the corner the left wheel came in contact with the building, swinging the shafts and horse suddenly round over a cellarway, down the steps of which I had retreated to the door, which was closed. Suspended above me was the horse, but I was soon relieved from the perilous position by the arrival of the men in charge.

The school was re-opened in the Market House, second flat, directly opposite to Taylor's Alley on Queen street. The other half of the flat, easterly, was the "Court Room," in which the Bible Society and other public meetings were held.

Many residents of Fredericton who have since

become solid men and women, often refer to their early training in the "Old Market House."

My father also taught a night school, where, to keep me out of mischief, I was frequently taken, and where I dozed away many a restless hour on the desks or benches. At the top of the stairway leading to the school-room, on the outside of the building, was a platform enclosed by balusters; where some of the latter were wanting, young children indulged in the dangerous amusement of passing through and along on the outside. My brother, John D., was the victim. One of the balusters giving way, he fell to the ground, breaking his leg, but from which he soon perfectly recovered.

Just above the Market House, and almost darkening the windows, were several large ships in course of building by merchants in Fredericton.

The site of the brick dwelling and garden owned by the late Judge Saunders was at that time a shipyard, and the sons of the builders or contractors — Dows & Hoopers — schoolmates.

My father, having purchased a comfortable one-story house on King street, above the range of the fire and just below the residence of Dr. Somerville, we removed thereto, where, on a first flat, with garden attached, we enjoyed many comforts hitherto unknown. I now, when in Fredericton, pause to look upon this unpretentious building, with which are connected so many associations of the long ago.

After a few years' residence on King street, my father rented from the Church Corporation of Fredericton an acre of land extending from Brunswick to George St., then the rearmost street in the town, on which latter he proceeded to erect a commodious two-story building, with barn, etc. These buildings are yet standing, in fair condition, a little above and opposite to St. Ann's Church.

A National School building having been erected on King street, a little above the Parliament buildings, with ample accommodation, and separate apartments for an African school, the school was removed thereto from the Market House. In this building a room had also been prepared for the books of the Fredericton library, of which my father was the librarian. I was frequently asked by lady and gentlemen subscribers to add to the catalogues, in a good round hand, the titles of new books received. I remember a kindly old gentleman, Judge Bliss, giving me for this service a silver half dollar.

Our removal to Fredericton was one of the great events of my life. Almost uninterrupted attendance at school, with free access to an excellent library, presented rare opportunities for study or recreation, and to these early advantages I owe the development of the powers which God had given me, the position and much of the happiness I have enjoyed in the world.

After being settled in our new home on George

street, there was a systematic arrangement of time for employment or recreation. Assisted by my father, the short afternoons from four o'clock were fully occupied during the winter in keeping the house supplied with fuel, frequently hard wood logs, or birch timber, cut with a cross-cut saw. Surrounding the table after supper, lessons invariably took precedence; after which, sketching with water colors—many of which we were taught to make, — or reading, often aloud, occupied the time till nine o'clock, when we retired. At early dawn, books were drawn from under the pillow, and in winter, with hands rolled up in the blankets, held before the eyes, to refresh the studies of the previous evening.

A cow, pig and poultry also occupied the time, so that little was left for outside amusement.

The enjoyment of a half hour's skate was intense. The river Nashwaaksis and "Government Pond," so called, afforded fine fields of ice, and good skaters were not wanting as models in this graceful and healthful exercise. Of these I would name Hon. J. A. Beckwith, Captain Hansard, Stephen Miller and Beverly Robinson.

On one occasion, a smaller boy and I were skating on the river; we had found a space of smooth, black ice unmarked. Presently, the first of the above-mentioned gentlemen entered, and seizing the smaller boy, held him out at arms' length, and made some almost perfect curves on the outside, backward and forward. Seeming to read my mind, as I looked on wonderingly, he said to me, "Sonny, can you do that?" I said, "No, sir." Then said he, "You must try; 'there's an upper part to everything.'"

The words were truly fitly spoken, and have been to me "as apples of gold in pictures of silver." The poise of mind and body I have found many times necessary to the accomplishment of what I considered great and good. If the highest and best objects of our pursuit are not always attained, we should at least be found struggling in the path of duty.

The Hon. J. A. B. set a good example in many ways to the youth of Fredericton as a lover of athletic sports.

I have had many faithful dogs in my life, to which I became warmly attached. When about twelve years old, I had a large black and tan Newfoundlander, which was well harnessed and trained to draw me, anywhere guided, on a sled. He was a powerful animal and would draw very heavy loads, and often hauled my brother and I to school, returning with as many boys as could pile on the sled. I enjoyed many merry and exciting rides after the brave and faithful "Danger."

Some half a mile back from our house, on the race-course and near the edge of the woods, carcasses of dead animals from the town were deposited. Dogs of all sorts and sizes would gather about these, and many a frosty morning, sitting on my sled, have I guided "Danger" for a chase. He understood the thing better than I; his tactics were good. As we approached near — the dogs being intently engaged — in a crouching and stealthy manner and taking advantage of cover, he drew slowly on, nearer and nearer, until with a dash and a yelp he struck terror into the hearts of the feasting canines. As they broke for the town the largest dog was selected; previous experience gave fleetness to their motions, and for a half mile or more the pace was terrific. As a rule the dogs were more scared than hurt, but the chase sometimes ended in disaster to sled and harness.

Early morning trips were also made to the woods on the crust, for pea sticks to be used in the garden in summer, selected from the tops of birch trees recently cut.

In the summer time an acre of ground, under cultivation as field or garden, occupied our time morning and evening. Duty being always the first consideration, then amusement.

For an hour's fishing in the morning, I have left home at early dawn, walked two miles to the second creek below Fredericton, caught a good basketful of smelt, and returned in time for school.

On wet days during the summer large flocks of English plover could be heard whistling as they circled around the open space or ran over the green sward of the race-course, directly in front of our residence. Thus tempted, I took my father's gun, which was loaded, and made my *debut* by bagging a few of these fine birds. From this time forth shooting and field sports became a passion, and in after years many mornings in summer have I disturbed the nighthawks on the streets of Fredericton on my way to the hills.

For my mother's amusement, when engaged with her needle, I read to her Washington Irving, Marryatt's writings, Doctor Syntax, etc.

I became deeply interested in the Memoirs of John Shipp, which aroused an inspiriting and military ardour, an effect produced also in others with whom I have conversed.

The provincial law at that time required but three days' military training in each year. Previous to the muster, the officers of companies met just opposite our residence for drill.

Being tall for my age, I was frequently selected to fill a blank in the rear rank — the initiatory step in the service of my country.

The veteran commander of the militia was Lieutenant Colonel Minchin, who had served in the royal artillery.

The knowledge obtained in battalion drill was very superficial, the volunteer companies only being supplied with arms.

The Royal African Corps, about 50 strong, was the centre of attraction, as it possessed a band.

Captain M——, of Douglas, with a nondescript uniform, was the commander. George Lawrence, late big drummer in the 104th Regiment (colored), ·was the drill instructor, and the half forgotten words of command, Africanised, afforded much amusement on parade.

Fronting on George street was a large open space, which extended from our residence downward to the Scotch kirk. Its circuit was nearly a mile, near the centre of which the exhibition· building of later days was erected. The open space above referred to was the race-course of those early days, where many races were hotly contested. The most notable horses were the "Rattler," the "Mark's Horse" (beating the "Cannon Ball" in a three mile race), "Silk Stockings," "Gipsy" and others.

It was also the scene of many brilliant "field days" and inspections of the "regulars" stationed in Fredericton. In the march home, plucky young urchins dared to grab from the aprons of the grim, bear skinned pioneers a handful of cartridges, gathered upon the field. Here, too, was the annual training and the preparatory drill of troop or company.

With all the improvements and modern appliances in the militia force of the present day, the conduct of our volunteers in field movements is no advance npon the practical and heroic of former times.

It was no uncommon thing to see a troop of cavalry in uniform galloping over the parade ground, and by cut and parry, eliciting applause; or sweeping down upon a battalion in square, through fire and smoke, re-form, with blood flowing from their horses from bayonet pricks received in the charge. On one occasion I saw more than one horse on its haunches, and another fall completely over backward upon its rider. Again, a charge was made upon a square, into which the artillerymen ran at the last moment. A trooper, dismounting, seized a drag rope and remounted, upon which a non-commissioned officer (Brannen) rushed out, administering from his rifle, at close quarters to the horse's tail, a depilatory powder, to the great astonishment of its rider and the amusement of the crowd.

At the rear of the race-course was an elevated earthwork called the " battery," into which many bullets from the old flint rifles entered in friendly contest. The crack shots of those days were L. A. Wilmot, George White, John Davis and others.

The presence of regular troops in the garrison at Fredericton, their personal neatness and precision in movement had much to do in framing the tastes and habits of our young men; but the miasma of immorality, floating from a thousand idle men and poisoning the atmosphere, makes questionable any advantages derived from their presence.

Chapter iv.

Choice of a Business.

BEING now nearly fourteen years of age, Dr. Emerson, our family physician, proposed that I should enter a dispensary opened by himself and Dr. George P. Peters, who had recently formed a co partnership.

There being no objection, the current of my thought was suddenly changed to obtaining a knowledge of the "Uses and Properties of Medicines," simple and compound.

Dr. Peters had just returned from "Edinburgh Medical College." His father was the Attorney General of this Province. Under the doctor's supervision and instruction I was to learn daily from the Dispensatory the use and properties of medicine contained in three of the bottles on the shelves.

Dr. Emerson was for many years the best known man in Fredericton. He had an extensive practice, and the impress of the large rings of his pattens indicated his presence in every street and alley throughout the town. He was a great lover of horses ; he owned the " Rattler," a race horse and the fastest of his time in America ; he also owned "Gipsy," a beautiful light bay mare, a winner in many races.

SMITH EXECUTED.

While here an execution by hanging took place of one Smith, on the highway near the gate of the old graveyard. He had been in prison some time before his trial for murdering two or three men by chopping them to pieces with a sharp axe while they lay asleep in a lumber camp on the Tobique River.

Returning from school one day I stood with another boy on the top of a greenhouse in the jail yard opposite the window of the cell in which he was confined. He looked savagely at us through a triple barred grating of iron,—the glass window was raised. Presently, without our having said a word, a piece of brick, accurately aimed by him through one of the narrow apertures of the grating, passed rapidly close by our heads.

He walked to the place of execution in his grave clothes, his arms pinioned behind him, between Sheriff Miller and his deputy. A large gathering surrounded the gallows to witness the unfortunate wretch pay the penalty of his terrible crime. He was buried outside the gate of the graveyard.

The execution took place shortly after my entering the dispensary, underneath which was a dark cellar with a stairway. Going down to the cellar one day I stumbled over a basket, which, on examination I found to contain a human head and portions of a dismembered body,—the remains of Smith exhumed by Drs. P. & L., the latter being surgeon of the Rifle Regiment, then lying in Fredericton.

The hangman of that time was a tall old colored man named Lowden ; he lived in an old house opposite Dr. Brown's residence, the corner of a large field extending back to the race-course. The boys all knew Lowden, as he made or repaired sleds, toboggans, axe-handles, ladders, etc. He had a team of six powerful well-trained fox hounds, which hauled very heavy loads and exceeded horses in swiftness.

I recollect a man being hung at Gagetown at which the hangman's life was threatened. Immediately after the execution he was conveyed by the authorities to the glare ice on the river, where his fleet hounds awaited him, and soon left his pursuers far behind.

ENTERS LATIN SCHOOL.

Finding, after a few months spent in the dispensary, that some knowledge of the Latin language was necessary to make the study of medicine, either as druggist or physician, a success, I found myself transferred to the Fredericton Grammar School, under the tuition of the Rev. Mr. Cowell, who was a curate of the Church of England, and a gentleman for whom I shall ever entertain the highest regard. The morning was devoted to the study of Latin, the afternoon to Algebra and Euclid.

L. P. Fisher, barrister, and late mayor of the town of Woodstock, went through with me the first and second books of Euclid, and there was some rivalry as to which should first be able to demonstrate a proposition.

George N Segee was my classmate in Latin, who also became a barrister, practising in Fredericton. As we had arrived at an age to feel the necessity of making the best use of our time, at the close of the first year we had passed through two of the lower classes in Latin.

Many of the boys were sons of the so-called aristocracy of that day, and Segee and myself were subjected to no small amount of taunts and sneers, at and after the competitive examinations which twice in each year were held on the hill at King's College. The sympathies of the professors and the examiners were, I am sure, with us, notably of the Rev. George McAuley, who resided in the college building. He gave me a book in which were the lessons of Henry Kirk White, and at his invitation I visited his private apartment on Saturday afternoon to repeat them to him.

I also attended for some time on Saturdays, at

the hall of the college, lectures on chemistry and natural philosophy by Drs. Robb and Grey.

Considerable rivalry had for several years existed as to muscular supremacy between the "National" and "Grammar" schools. Many large boys, sons of mechanics and others, attended the "National" in the winter time, when the battles occurred, and in which the "Nationals" were generally the victors. From the day of my attendance at the Grammar school I was marked as a "National," and a system of persecution commenced, which in a little while became intolerable. The school was divided by the scions of aristocracy — as by Romulus, the Romans — into two classes; and the Plebei thus proscribed were made to suffer many indignities. The yard of the Collegiate school was the scene of many combats.

I had been advised by my parents to avoid quarrelling with the boys of this school, which was wise and prudent teaching; but the repeated insults, from one boy in particular of about my own age, I could no longer endure. Segee, my classmate, was my second; my opponent and his second — we four only — were in the yard. The remainder of the school were looking through open places made by knives in the fence. The style was "as you please," or "rough and tumble." The sense of accumulated wrongs gave force to every blow.

I had little knowledge of what occurred until

the fray was over, when I saw prostrate (the fence had been climbed by friends on both sides) a number of bleeding Patricians and near and about them as many exultant and crowing Plebs.

Many years have since elapsed, but from that day forward my then opponent and myself have been on the most friendly terms.

I refer to this and similar events to show the spirit of the times, and feel that through influences or training of this kind latent energies are brought into action that might have remained dormant; but stimulated by success inspire to nobler achievements.

I have seen one of our late judges, when attending King's College, enter the Fredericton library and in a flood of tears relate to my father the indignities he was daily made to suffer from the class of young men above referred to.

INDENTED APPRENTICE TO THE DRUG BUSINESS.

The best drug establishment at this time in Fredericton was owned by James F. Gale. He was a St. John man and served his apprenticeship with Walker & Maccara of that place. He then went to London, England, and served two years in Apothecaries' Hall, prior to commencing his studies for the profession of M. D. A change in his father's circumstances, financially, compelled him to abandon this, and he returned to New

Brunswick.   He purchased the business and stand of Dr. George Baldwin, situated in Amasa Coy's brick building on Queen street, just below the officers' square.   He understood his business thoroughly as a chemist and druggist, and was most exacting in his demands as a master.

While attending the Latin school, I spent from four to six o'clock p. m. each day in this establishment, and during the second year, an opening being presented, was installed therein as an apprentice for four years to the drug business.

The hours in summer were from six a. m. to nine thirty p. m., often later; and many times aroused at night to put up prescriptions, when competent to do so.

For about a year I boarded at home, and my father provided me with clothing during the whole time of my apprenticeship.

On Mr. Gale's marriage my quarters were changed to his residence, and I was thus deprived of a good walk and being at home morning and evening.

I was expected to be in my room every night at ten o'clock.   A previous severe training had made obedience with me a first law and in this case was seldom violated.

From four to six a. m. were the only hours I could obtain for out-door exercise; and a mental apparition is often presented to me of old "Libby," the colored bellman, tapping from a ladder on the window at grey dawn and in an underbreath calling, "Massa Will'm, it's fo' o'clock!"

Wild pigeons were then very numerous. Maryland Hill, a spruce grove back of the race-course, and Hanwell, then a new settlement, were favorite places of resort. I have often visited the last named place (between two and three miles distant) in a brisk gallop on horseback, made a good bag and returned in time to have the shop open at six o'clock.

My gun was a flint-lock,—percussion-locks had not then been introduced. On one occasion covering some pigeons, I pulled the trigger. It seemed to miss fire; the birds flew. Following them with my eye, as I brought the butt of the gun to the ground, I was startled by its discharge, the contents passing close by my face and the leaf of my straw hat was cut by some grains of the shot. In carrying the gun through the bushes, wet with rain or heavy dew, the damp powder of the priming burnt slowly and I had no thought of its having ignited.

ADVENTURE WITH A HAWK.

I brought down one morning from the top of a very high tree, on Maryland Hill, a large "hen" hawk. It was only wounded so as to be unable to fly. Coming upon it in the thick undergrowth, where it had fallen, it attacked me fiercely with beak and talons. It was formidable from its size, and only after repeated and heavy blows from the muzzle of the gun did I succeed in giving it a quietus. But it was not dead; it held so tightly with its great yellow claws to the muzzle of the gun that its transport over my shoulder was thus safe and easy.

Arriving at the house I succeeded in shaking it off the gun and left it in the hall of the flat occupied by Mr. Gale. Returning home some two hours later to breakfast, I found the whole house in a state of uproar. The servant woman, when sweeping the hall, had attempted to move his "hawkship," when he developed himself fully, seizing a portion of her dress. The superstitious woman thinking, as she said, that it was "satan" himself, rushed from room to room, shrieking wildly, then down the stairs and through the yard, until all the people in the neighborhood had assembled and released her from an unknown enemy, minus such portions of her clothing as he had put under tribute.

A SECOND ADVENTURE WITH BRUIN.

Having become, as I thought, on friendly terms with a young bear chained in front of the officers' barracks between two of the old willows, I saw on one occasion a crowd of officers and civilians assembled at the shore for the purpose of giving bruin a swim. Unaware of the irritation caused by its removal to that place, I approached it as usual. Snuffing over my hands and pockets, and finding I had nothing for it, it seized me treacherously by the leg with its teeth, which he tore badly; and when escaping, pursued and struck me with its paw, stripping the flesh from the outside of my right leg at the knee. I managed to walk to the shop where the wounds were dressed by Dr. Fraser, and was from thence drawn in a wagon by the hands of Donald McLeod and other kind friends to my father's house. These injuries kept me at home under a mother's care for a month, and the scars are still plainly visible.

COMPANIONS AND WALKS.

A young Englishman, John Chalmers, a clerk in the Central Bank, having joined me in the purchase of a bark canoe, the hills on the opposite side of the river were occasionally visited, and I remember one morning when alone in the canoe making a bag of three heavy black ducks, near the mouth of the Nashwaak.

The physicians patronizing our establishment were Drs. Woodforde (late Rifle Brigade), Fraser (Scotch), Toldervy (English). The prescriptions were numerous, and the directions written in Latin kept alive my love for the study of that language.

My hours in the shop on Sabbath days were

from nine to eleven a. m. and eight to nine p. m. The companions in my walks on Sabbath afternoons were Charles Gregor, a clerk in the dry goods store of the late William Grosvenor, and Frederick Jewitt, clerk in the grocery of the late Spafford Barker. The former is yet alive and engaged in business in Kingston, Ontario. The latter is dead. These young men were of good moral character and much respected in Fredericton.

Our walks on Sabbath afternoons extended to the churches at " Maryland Settlement," "Springhill" and "Blake's Mills" (now Gibson's, at Marysville). The distance in each case was a round walk of about ten miles, and gave us pleasing and necessary open-air exercise.

At the time of my mother's death I was overcome with a sense of complete isolation and felt as if I could not be comforted. I slept in a small room adjoining the shop alone. I read my Bible and tried to pray. The Church ritual, by this time stereotyped on my memory, seemed cold and discomforting, affording me no consolation.

The pastor of the Methodist Church was the Rev. Enoch Wood, a faithful servant of God, but recently gone to his reward. I occupied my mother's seat under his preaching, and into my heart, tender with sorrow, he seemed to pour a healing balm and I felt as if he were preaching to me. The impressions of that time affected me long and seriously, and have, I believe, exerted a deterring influence against evil throughout the whole of my life.

Gale's shop was a place of resort to the officers of the garrison and the *elite* of Fredericton. I heard many rounds of wit and anecdote from officers, doctors, and the parish priest (Father McSweeney) assembled to imbibe pure soda and discuss the topics of the day.

A young officer, Lieutenant Herries, succeeded once in obtaining leave for me to go out on the river and skate. He was a young skater anxious to learn and I was anxious to instruct.

During the summer the music of the military band at the morning parade could be heard distinctly in the shop and had a charming effect. I could occasionally steal to the end of the platform to see the movements of the troops, which to me were very interesting.

The upper part of the building adjoining was the officers' mess, from the open windows of which were often heard music and hilarious mirth.

In the winter some of the officers took brisk walks with Indian guides in pursuit of deer, moose or caribou, and I have seen them coming in from the hunt on snowshoes, the Indian drawing on his toboggan as a trophy of the chase peltry or the remains of some monarch of the forest.

TRAMP OF OFFICERS IN HEAVY MARCHING ORDER.

A discussion having taken place at mess in one of the regiments as to the distance that might be accomplished in a given time in heavy marching order, a wager was made to be decided by two of the officers.

On a bright morning in summer two officers, named Cook and Barry, fully equipped, set out with a fair swing for a tramp to the Oromocto and back. Cook was tall, straight and lanky; Barry short, well-knit, but bow-legged.

Cook reached the stream first, sat down, put his feet in the water and lunched. Barry, arriving later, spattered some water from the stream in his face, wheeled about and continued the march, simply moistening his lips occasionally.

At four p. m. Queen street was lined with people; and later, cheers greeted Barry as friends met him with a hearty shake and a pull barrack-ward.

Cook was found sitting in a mud-puddle near the first bridge at the flats. The strap of his cartouche box, not being equal to the strain on a march of sixty rounds of ball cartridge, was tied up with his handkerchief. His appearance generally was dilapidated.

FRIGID WARFARE.

A snow fort, heavily walled and covering a large space in the officers' square, was erected by a regiment about this time. On a soft day, after the fort was solidly frozen, a portion of the regiment entered for its defence. The passage way to the interior was then hermetically sealed. The ammunition of defenders and assailants was balls of snow, hard and soft, large and small.

The advance to the assault was met with a well-aimed shower from the ramparts, and as vigorously returned. After several unsuccessful attempts had been made to scale the walls, the demolition of the fort was commenced. As the walls were broken down the harder portions were used by either party, which placed many a good soldier *hors de combat.*

After a fierce struggle, in which many were severely wounded, the defenders of the fort capitulated, but only at the instance of officers who then interfered.

CHEMISTRY AND CHEMICAL RECREATIONS.

While Mr. Gale was in England he attained a good knowledge of practical chemistry, which he found exceedingly useful in the preparation of medicines not always attainable. When chloroform was scarcely known in this country, he manufactured some, which Dr. Toldervy pronounced of fine quality.

Some persons who may have received benefit from this fine preparation, now in general use, may be interested in reading the formula, which is as follows :—

4 lbs. chloride of lime,
12 oz. rectified spirit,
12 lbs. of water.

During the winter a sand-bath covered the stove in the shop, from which the retort was scarcely ever absent. Many of the ordinary preparations now imported by druggists were manufactured in the shop, as also some of the finer preparations of mercury or iron from the metals.

The manufacture of one preparation, "fulminating silver," as I 'found to my cost, should only be undertaken by an expert. With Gale, its manufacture was a never-failing success, and I, fully aware of the nature of what I was handling, had an ambition to try the experiment. Into a Florence flask I poured the proper quantity of nitric acid, dropping into it silver coin of correct weight. The flask was then placed on the sand bath, and the dark poisonous fumes which soon arose were so controlled at the neck of the flask as to turn them back into the boiling liquid. When the silver was dissolved, a precipitate fell to the bottom and the first part of the experiment was completed.

The precipitate being washed and a filter prepared, I placed the funnel in an eight ounce measure glass and proceeded to pour from the flask into the filter. From an excessive weight of liquid or a defect in the paper, the contents went through to the bottom of the glass. A moment later there was a terrific explosion and I found myself lengthwise on the floor. The explosion was caused by the grinding of the shank of funnel on the wet fulminate.

The shop was soon filled with people, as the report was heard from a long distance, and I found that personally it was a miraculous escape. There was considerable breakage from fragments of glass and some of the beams in the ceiling may still bear the marks of larger pieces.

We put up large numbers of the detonating crackers in the winter season, and being used in various ways afforded much amusement. Some grave old men adorning pulpit or bench may have long since forgotten how they were placed on the stairs of King's College to give timely warning of the approach of a professor, old Cameron the janitor, or other curious ears to the doors of their dormitories. A half-grain of the greyish powder, a few grains of shot and a little sand tied up in tissue paper, would make a loud report, and the friction of dropping from the hand or treading upon would cause an explosion.

While returning to the shop one evening after tea, I saw a large number of men assembled, several of whom were engaged in a fight. As the crowd swayed back and forth over the road or sidewalk, having a few crackers in my pocket I

laid them on the hard ground near by. Presently,
as the din of the fight grew louder and some were
pushed over the crackers, they began to explode.
Some shrieked as if shot, and others, taking the
alarm, scampered with all their might to get clear
of the fray.

Chapter V

Early Navigation of the River St. John.

AN opinion is frequently expressed by tourists that the natural beauty of the St. John is not exceeded by any other river on the continent. The report made by its discoverer, DeMonts, to the King of France, was in these words: "The "great extent of the river, the fish with which it "is filled, the grapes growing upon its banks, and "the beauty of its scenery, are all objects of "wonder and admiration."

The distance from St. John to Fredericton, 85 miles, is made regularly in the summer season by steamboats; thence to Grand Falls, 125 miles, has been made by steamers at a high pitch of water, or during the spring freshets.

For a few months in the year, a steamer runs to Woodstock, and it is a great accommodation to the people living on or near the banks of the river with whom there is no railway communication.

The erection of several bridges across the river and the daily passage of trains to Grand Falls and Edmunston has almost effectually closed the navigation, above Woodstock, to any water craft.

My earliest recollection of vessels on the St.

John was the firing of a gun announcing the arrival at Fredericton of the "Governor's Yacht," used for the transportation of governors and their effects to and from Fredericton.

Before the introduction of steam as a propelling power on the river, a boat ran between St. John and Fredericton, driven by horse power. The first steamer was the "General Smith" in 1816. Following her was the "St. George" in 1825, commanded by Captain Segee, and later by Captain Wylie. The transport of freight and passengers was also done by "sloops."

A veteran commander, Captain Currier, is still living in Fredericton. The others of my time were Captains Parsons, Vail and Fradsham, residents of the same place.

A regular visitor from Grand Manan was "Drake's schooner," a tight little vessel, and her cargo sometimes exhibited an acquaintance with Yankee ports.

The "John Ward" and "St. John," substantial steam vessels, were followed by Whitney's fleet of high pressure steamers, "Water Witch," "Novelty," etc. The latter reached the highest rate of speed attained by any vessel plying on the St. John. She made the passage from St. John to Fredericton and returned in less than a day. In the year 1838 she visited Woodstock, and left her mark on Becaguimac Island, 10 miles higher up, where she was for a short time stranded.

The "Novelty" was a long, narrow vessel, very difficult to steer. I have seen her aground opposite Fredericton, with hundreds of red coats trying to lift her off the bar.

BENJAMIN TIBBETTS' STEAMER "REINDEER."

Among the young men of Fredericton with whom I was intimate, and whose life and conduct proved them benefactors to their country, was Benjamin Tibbetts. He was taciturn in manner, but possessed a rare genius. He was a musician; skilled as a portrait painter, and had acquired a wonderful knowledge of the mechanical arts.

He served his time to watchmaking with Benjamin Wolhaupter, Fredericton. When quite young, he made and finished a perfect key-bugle.

He was employed by Mrs. Shore and others of the *elite* to paint in oil their portraits; but his great work was the building of the steamer "Reindeer."

He showed me in figures on a slate in "Morgan's foundry" his first conception of that beautiful craft, his calculations of form, size and bearing, and they proved remarkably correct. She illustrated a discovery or invention entirely his own: the application of steam power under a high pressure and low pressure principle combined. The model of the "Reindeer" was beautiful. "She walked the waters like a thing of life," was of

4

light draft, and did excellent work on the river
for many years.

I enjoyed, with a large number of excursionists,
a trip to the Grand Falls on her. The Woodstock
band was with the party and contributed much to
a night's amusement at the Falls. Horatio Nelson Drake commanded the steamer and as we
returned received from the hand of Benjamin
Beveridge, Esquire, at Tobique, a pair of fine
antlers, which with music and becoming ceremony were made to deck the prow of our gallant
" Reindeer." A ready speech was made in ac-
knowledgement of the gift by the engineer,
Thomas Pickard, jr., whose father was the owner.

The ascent of this, the first steamer, made it a
gala day on the St. John River banks, and our
progress was greeted with shouts of welcome,
firing of guns, etc., etc. As we returned to
Woodstock a large number of persons were assembled at the landing. The band played and
the party on board joined in singing, to a then
popular air, some verses composed *en route* by one
of the band. A single verse will suffice :

> " Hurrah ! for the Restook River, oh !
> The Tobique stream that is not slow ;
> But the Saint John River is the stream,
> That we have now traversed with steam."
>   Then dance the boatman dance, etc.

Some years later, when standing with Tibbetts
on a wharf at Fredericton to which the " Rein-

deer" was secured, he expressed a wish that I would go through the old boat with him. Evidence of abuse, neglect and decay was everywhere present. In the running gear, pieces of rope, chains or wire were doing unsightly service. After viewing the wreck of what was once the pride and admiration of Tibbetts as a machinist and inventor, he raised his hands and said, "Strange that an harp of a thousand strings should stay in tune so long."

I have different versions of the following statement, therefore cannot vouch for its correctness. Several years having passed away, the "Reindeer" changed hands; she was plying on the Grand Lake. In a house on the shore of the lake poor Tibbetts was dying. It was his early home. A burning steamer, deserted by her crew, is seen drifting in the direction of that house; and simultaneously, the man and his work, things of life and beauty, become but as dust and ashes.

Mr. Tibbetts also built a steamer at Quebec on this principle, which as a ferryboat at that place worked successfully. He spent much valuable time in New York endeavoring to obtain a patent for his invention, but failed, as he told me, from want of money and a theft by some official to whom he had entrusted confidentially some knowledge of the secret.

A resident of the Grand Falls, in a letter to the *Telegraph*, wrote as follows: "Sir, I will

"thank you to communicate to the public through
"your paper that the steam boat 'Madawaska' is
"now in full operation. I have had the pleasure
"of being on board of her on her trip to Little
"Falls and back, and I am happy to state that
"she went through well and was warmly greeted
"by the young and the old of the inhabitants of
"Madawaska as she proudly passed them on. I
"congratulate Mr. Tibbetts on the high natural
"and acquired abilities which rendered him mas-
"ter of planning and forming the complicated
"machinery of the 'Madawaska' and 'Reindeer'
"boats.   As a native of New Brunswick you
"should all be proud of him, and I believe that
"there is no other person born in New Bruns-
"wick, Canada or Nova Scotia who could do the
"same. I would therefore suggest the justice and
"propriety of having some token of public appro-
"bation bestowed on him, whether medal or other-
"wise, to mark your esteem for a good man and a
"bright ornament to New Brunswick."

A stern wheel steamer, "The Carleton," was
built by the Craigs of St. John for George
Connell, Esquire, Barrister, of Woodstock, to ply
on the river between Fredericton and Woodstock.
She was well adapted for that service and for
many years passed safely through intricate passages in falls or rapids. Her light draught of
water (only fourteen inches) and an excellent
engine rendered her admirably adapted to glide

over the bars and shoals and through the rapid
waters of the St. John. The arrival at Woodstock of the steamer — the first one owned in that
place — caused much satisfaction to the people
there, who evinced their joy by firing a regular
salute from one of the artillery guns as she
rounded the island. In 1849 and '50 she proved
herself a great accommodation to the community
along the river and a success financially to her
owner.

Mr. Connell also built the "John Warren," a
side-wheel steamer of greater draught and requiring more power to drive her than "The Carleton."

Other stern-wheel steamers were placed upon
the river about the same time, which from their
lighter draught were enabled to make more regular trips and thus become the more popular boats,
making the "John Warren" not as profitable to
her owner as "The Carleton" had been.

The "Florenceville," chiefly owned by Woodstock men, now plies regularly between Woodstock and Fredericton when the water serves,
proving a great accommodation to residents along
the river where distant from the railway.

The "Andover," "Richmond" and "Bonny
Doon," all stern-wheel boats, did good service on
the upper St. John before the introduction of railways.

Many enterprises such as the building of steamboats, mills and factories of various kinds, en-

gaged in by spirited Provincialists in advance of their time, have failed to prove remunerative to their owners, often from prejudice or want of appreciation on the part of their fellow countrymen. All honor to those men whose persistence, loyalty, and faith in the future of this country has led them to invest their time, talents and capital in enterprises that have aided in giving the country the commanding position it now occupies. In every city and town of this Province, the lofty chimney, the puffing engine or the hum of revolving wheels tells of the genius of our people and of the rapidly developing resources of our Dominion.

Chapter vi.

Become a Soldier.

APART from the military spirit that I may
have inherited from my race, the very atmosphere that I breathed and that surrounded me
was military.   Many of the young men, clerks
and students, with whom I was acquainted were
members of volunteer companies, Cavalry, Artillery or Infantry.   Being tall for my age,
though slender, I was asked by Capt. William
McBeth, commanding the Fredericton Rifle Company, to join his corps, and in the summer of 1836
was enrolled and received a rifle and accoutrements.   The members of the company provided
uniforms at their own expense, the pattern of
which was decided by a vote of the company.
My first military suit was that of a private, dark
cloth, green facings, a heavy shako with cord and
tassels.   The rifle was short and heavy, a flint
lock.   The one that fell into my hands was the
only one in store, and the rear sight required
much adjustment and practice by firing to obtain
a true alignment.

The "upper part" in the work before me, as
a soldier, seemed to be to become a good shot and

obtain a thorough knowledge of drill. To this
end I commenced a systematic course of practice.
A square yard of cotton — my target — was
placed at a point on the shore opposite Peter
Fraser's. I fired from Gaynor's wharf (now
Temple's), one hundred yards distant. The bullets used were round, and cast by myself and went
out on the river in the direction of the mouth of
the Nashwaak. My practice was in the early
morning before many persons were astir.

The militia law at this time required a muster
and training for three days in each year. On one
of the days of the annual trainings was a sharp
competition in the Rifle Company for a gold
medal, the gift of the officers. Sergeant-Major
Philip Brannen, Sergeant Enoch Bradley and a
few others were excellent marksmen ; the breasts
of the above-named were covered with gold and
silver medals. The prize to be fired for the second
year of my being a member was a gold medal ;
distance, 100 yards ; object, a bull's eye the size
of a Mexican dollar, the centre of cross-belts on
the wooden figure of a man. My practice for
some time previous had been to perforate a business card, two by three inches in size, twice out of
three times at 100 yards. The object now before me was smaller ; I was a recruit at the
extreme left of the company ; more than one of
the veterans had twice pierced the bull's eye ; yet
I felt confident. The charges of powder had been

weighed to a grain; also the bullet, which was tightly covered with the kid of an old glove, to pass smoothly along the groove. Surrounded by our own officers and many of the regular officers stationed in Fredericton, I drew a sight on the mark and pulled. The report was quickly followed by the sound of the bugle from the target. Bull's eye! I loaded again and fired, with the same result; but it was too much for me, the third shot dropped a little below. The first shot drove a brass nail through the centre, the second almost cutting the edge of the first and securing to me the prize.

On one other occasion I experienced on that same flat, when in command of a company of " Woodstock Rifles," a sensation akin, and I cherish the occasions as affording some of the proudest moments of my life. This was to me another evidence that success, to be made sure, must be accompanied by long and persevering effort. *Palman qui meruit ferat.*

PROVINCIAL PARLIAMENT.

Our shop was frequently visited by members of the Government and House of Assembly during the sessions. I remember the long-time "Speaker" Charles Simonds; also Crane, Partelow, Colonel Allen, Colonels Weir, Boyd and many younger and lesser lights.

"Paddy" End, so-called, brought into the shop a newly fledged member from Westmorland, whom he initiated by giving to drink from separate tumblers the acid and salts of a seidlitz powder. The result may be imagined.

In those days of innocence and political honesty the best talent was concentrated in our Provincial Assembly and a sense of honor marked the treatment and bearing of antagonists in debate.

About this time political excitement began to run high. The appointments of Attorney-General, Surveyor-General, Commissioner of Crown Lands, Provincial Secretary, etc., were made by the Crown. Over these officers the people, through their representatives, had no control. They were not always approachable in their offices and their own conveniences, a dinner-party or a ball, would over-ride the necessity for an interview desired by the poor countryman. From this cause a feeling of dissatisfaction grew apace. A series of letters appeared in the *St. John Courier* over the signature of "John Gape," which caused intense excitement. Like the "Junius" letters, published in the reign of George the Third, no stone was left unturned to discover the author. Not only were the shortcomings in an official capacity exposed, but the gossip of the dinner-table and the ball-room, and even private whisperings, seemed to be uncovered to the gaze of the "great unwashed." I remember the names of

several persons supposed to have been concerned
in the publication of these letters, all clever men
and occupying good positions in society, but the
secret has been well kept.

Among the intelligent and educated young men
of this time and foremost among them were two
who had felt the smart, "not to the manor
born," but comparatively princes and giants in
moral and intellectual force. I heard what was
then said to be the first public addresses delivered
by L. A. Wilmot and Charles Fisher, in the old
Methodist meeting-house in Fredericton.

AFFAIRS OF HONOR.

The departure of the stage, driven by Larry
Stivers or "Green," every morning in the winter
at eight o'clock from Fredericton for St. John,
was a common event ; but a stage driven rapidly
down Queen street one morning in 1836 at an
earlier hour, attracted my attention. It contained
five persons : two principals, two seconds and a
surgeon. Words uttered in hot debate on the
preceding day by Thomas Gilbert (the honorable
member for Queens), insulting to Dr. Wilson (the
honorable member for Westmorland) were to be
atoned for in blood. A retired spot three miles
below the city was the place selected for a duel
with pistols. After two exchanges of shots, the
seconds considered the honor of the parties vindi-
cated, and they returned home scatheless.

Dr. Wilson was an Irishman, having an extensive medical practice at Dorchester, and but recently deceased. He was a kind hearted, benevolent gentleman, and many professional and social acts of kindness will linger in the hearts of recipients.

All such affairs of honor near Fredericton have not had as fortunate an ending. When a lad I visited with my father a place near John Segee's at the Maryland Settlement, back of town, and was shown by Mr. Segee the ground and the position of the principals where a fatal duel was fought while my father was in the 74th Regiment, an officer of the regiment being one of the seconds in the tragic event of that dark October morning. The following account, on undoubted authority, of the duel between George Frederick Street, Esquire, and George Ludlow Wetmore, Esquire, October 2nd, 1821, may be of more than passing interest and well worth preserving. The principals in this melancholy affair were members of the legal profession, living in Fredericton. The cause of the quarrel was the issuing of a bailable writ by Mr. Street, as the attorney, against a man named Jacob Smith, upon which he was arrested and imprisoned, though denying that he owed the plaintiff anything. It was soon afterward discovered that the wrong person had been arrested, that it should have been the son of the prisoner (also named Jacob), and the father was thereupon discharged from jail. He then brought an action against the sheriff for false imprisonment, Mr. Wetmore being his attorney. As the sheriff had made the arrest by direction of Mr. Street, he felt himself bound to indemnify the sheriff, but as the arrest was illegal and there could be no defence to the action, he did not plead to it, and judgment by default was signed and the damages were assessed by a sheriff's jury. It was during the proceedings to assess the damages that the parties quarreled. Abusive language was used by each of them to the other and Mr. Street struck at Mr. Wetmore. The consequence was he sent a challenge to Mr. Street. They met on the second of October, between seven and eight o'clock in the morning, about four miles from Fredericton, on the farm of Mr. John Segee in New Maryland, near to but not in sight of his house, being concealed by the woods. Mr. Street's second was Mr. Davies, an officer of the 74th Regiment, then stationed in Fredericton, and Mr. Wetmore's second was Mr. Winslow, the late Sheriff of Carleton County. The parties stood about fifteen paces apart. Two shots were exchanged. The first shot was harmless, the ball from Mr. Street's pistol striking the ground. The seconds then endeavored to effect a reconciliation, but, unhappily, did not succeed, and the parties fired again, and Mr. Wetmore fell. The ball struck his right arm, glanced and entered his right temple.   He never spoke afterwards, though he lived about two hours.   He was carried to Mr. Segee's house, where he died.   The principals and seconds had ridden on horseback to the place where the duel was fought, and had fastened their horses in the bushes.   As soon as Mr. Wetmore fell, Mr. Winslow went to the house and told Mr. Segee what had taken place, not mentioning any names, and asked him to go to Mr. Wetmore's assistance.   He also sent one of Mr. Segee's sons to Fredericton on one of the horses for a surgeon. Mr. Street and his second remained with Mr. Wetmore till they heard persons coming from the house, when they secreted themselves in the woods for a short time and then got their horses, joined Mr. Winslow on the road, and proceeded immedi· ately to St. Andrews and thence to Robbinston in the State of Maine.   They remained there until December, when Mr. Street and Mr. Davies returned to the Province and gave themselves up and were imprisoned.   Mr. Winslow did not return to the Province for a considerable time after that.

At the term of the Supreme Court in October, a bill of indictment for murder was found by the Grand Jury against Mr. Street and the two seconds.   Mr. Street and Mr. Davies were tried on this indictment at Fredericton in February, 1822. Judge Saunders (afterwards Chief Justice) was the presiding Judge, and Mr. Botsford, the Solici-

tor General (afterwards Judge Botsford), conducted the prosecution. The counsel for the
prisoners was Mr. Chipman (afterwards Chief
Justice) and Mr. Henry Bliss. At that time,
and for upwards of ten years afterwards, prisoners
on trial for criminal charges were not allowed to
be defended by counsel except to argue legal
points. The principal witnesses for the prosecution were Mr. Segee and his two sons, and two
surgeons, Dr. Woodforde, of Fredericton, and Dr.
Grant, the surgeon of the 74th Regiment, who
had gone out to Mr. Segee's on hearing of the
duel. Mr. Segee and his sons testified to having
heard four shots fired, and to Mr. Winslow's coming to the house for assistance, stating that a
gentleman had been killed in a duel. They had
also seen Mr. Winslow and two other gentlemen
ride quickly past their house soon after that, but,
as it was a thick and hazy morning, they were
unable to identify either of them clearly, except
Mr. Winslow. The evidence of the surgeons
proved that Mr. Wetmore's death was caused by
the ball which had entered his temple. Neither
of the prisoners addressed the jury, and their
counsel had no right to do so. The judge summed
up the evidence to the jury and explained the law
bearing upon the case, stating his opinion that
there was not sufficient evidence of the identity of
the prisoners as the persons who had committed
the offence to justify their conviction. The jury,

after a few minutes' deliberation, returned a verdict of not guilty.

LEMUEL ALLAN WILMOT

was born in Fredericton, January 31st, 1809. His father, William Wilmot, was one of the large lumbering firm of Peters & Wilmot, before referred to. He was a good man and a zealous Baptist. He was twice married. L. A. Wilmot's mother was a Miss Bliss.

L. A. Wilmot was remarkable as possessing a pleasing and genial disposition. He was ten years my senior, but when a student passing along the street, I have seen him lay down his bag of law books, ask for a marble, and, knocking the centre alley from the ring, move off laughing. He was a leader of the young men in athletic sports, and without any apparent effort excelled them all in running, leaping, shooting, singing, key-bugling and other exercises or amusements.

The leading jovial spirits of the time were clerks in the Crown land and other governmental offices. Fulton, Starrit, Scully, Gardner (organist), Beckwith and Vavasour were all good cricketers and racket players. Their favorite place of resort was the fashionable saloon of one Louis Goucheé, corner of Carleton (north) and Queen streets. Goucheé was a Frenchman, a keen sportsman, a taxidermist and a good fellow.

LEMUEL ALLAN WILMOT,

POLITICIAN, JUDGE, GOVERNOR, N. B.

Birds and pictures met the eye everywhere as you entered his rooms, which were kept in the neatest order. Liquors and choice wines were prepared and presented in Parisian manner to suit the palate. The salaries paid by the Crown to public servants were good and were freely spent. With these Wilmot for a time associated, but for him there was nobler work to do. The cloud that overshadowed the financial prospects of his father touched in him a spirit of pardonable pride, and brought into action the noble powers of mind which under other circumstances might have remained dormant.

He was a talented and popular speaker, and on him the public mind centred as the future champion of the people's rights. In this the people of New Brunswick were not disappointed. Having completed his studies and opened an office for the practice of law, he was one day escorted from thence by Harry Jones and Charles McPherson to the " hustings," where from a platform in front of the old market house he made his *debut* in a political speech of such power as to sweep down all opposition and return him, unopposed, a representative for the County of York. He was ably supported in his defence of the people's rights by his young friend and colleague, Charles Fisher, and their efforts were finally crowned with success, in the establishment of the principles of "*Responsible Government*" in the North American Colonies.

As a delegate from the New Brunswick Legislature, he represented at Downing street the interests of the lumber trade of the Province, threatened by the removal of the duty on Baltic timber. The burning in effigy of the mover of the bill, Sir Poulett Thompson, and the roasting of an ox on the occasion will never be forgotten by the Fredericton people of that day. Queen street resembled a forest of pine trees; and conspicuous in the procession was the figure of Sir Poulett on horseback.

The election contests in those days of open vote were sharp and bitter. The people were tasting, in a small degree, the sweets of liberty, while the aristocrats felt the power being wrested from their grasp. York County extended from the Oromocto to the Canadian boundary line. The candidates were present on nomination day at each polling place, and there were curious transpositions of the alphabet on some of these occasions. In several of Wilmot's elections I have seen tumults suppressed where sticks were freely used, and a passage-way for voters had to be kept open through the crowd by the military.

Railways at this time were comparatively in their infancy, and the inauguration of one between Maine and New Brunswick was a signal for the gathering at Portland of great minds, irrespective of nationality. Great and powerful speeches were made; but Wilmot's eloquence surpassed all the others, won the hearts of the multitude, and made his name in the New England States and Provinces as familiar as a household word.

His first wife was a Miss Balloch; his second a Miss Black, of Halifax.

Wilmot was a lover of military exercises, and active as an officer. When very young he commanded a rifle company, and was one of the best shots at the old battery on the race-course. He afterwards commanded a fine grenadier company, uniformed as in the line with scarlet coats and bear-skins; again a troop of cavalry; and finally a lieutenant-colonel in the active militia.

While most urbane and gentlemanly in his demeanor, he could not escape the shafts of aristocratic malice levelled at him. Knowing his long reach, his bitterest enemies had learned to keep well beyond, but persons less acquainted were pushed forward to suffer a scorching rebuke or political annihilation. Personal punishment was often threatened, but never attempted. When a cavalry officer, he was challenged by a young scion of nobility in one of the regiments stationed at Fredericton, but a few words in scathing reply cut deeper than a sword and ended the matter.

In the first military camp organized in the Province by the Governor, Hon. Arthur Gordon, composed of two battalions, ordered out for twenty-eight days' drill at Fredericton, Colonel Wilmot commanded the first.

He was appointed in 1857 one of the Judges of the Supreme Court of the Province. When practising as a barrister, like John Randolph, his forefinger swayed many verdicts, to the discomfiture of able opponents.

After the confederation of the Provinces, which he favored, the highest ambition was reached in the appointment of Governor of his native Province.

For many years previous to his death, notwithstanding the cares of state, he took a leading part in the affairs of the Methodist Church, and many now scattered over the earth have lived to bless his name as superintendent of the Fredericton Methodist Sabbath School. Being ten years my senior, I knew him all my life, and many times under different circumstances have I been honored with his confidence and associated with him in work. The ardour of his temperament sometimes led him to act impulsively, but those who knew him best ascribed the errors as of the head and not of the heart.

On the afternoon of the 20th of May, 1878, whilst out riding in his carriage, he was seized with a sharp pain in the heart, was at once driven home and a physician summoned; but all human aid was in vain and he shortly after breathed his last. "His end is with the just,"

Extract from the Boston "Journal."

"Hon. L. A. Wilmot, the newly appointed
"Lieutenant-Governor of New Brunswick, is a
"native of that Province, and is now in his 59th
"year. He is a lawyer by profession. Since
"1851 he has been Judge of the Supreme Court,
"and he has discharged the duties of the office in
"a manner highly creditable to himself and to the
"Court. Before his appointment to the Bench,
"he took an active part in the politics of the
"Province and had served in the House of Assem-
"bly and the Executive Council, and was also
"for a short time Attorney-General. He is one
"of the most eloquent speakers on this Continent.
"Those who attended the great railroad conven-
"tion in Portland in 1850, when the European
"and North American Railroad project was in-
"augurated, will recall the splendid address which
"he made, and by which he held the audience
"spell-bound by the brilliancy and fervor of his
"eloquence as he depicted the moral, social and
"intellectual influences which would result from
"the contemplated work. Governor Wilmot has
"always been a leading man in New Brunswick
"in every movement which had for its object the
"improvement and elevation of the people, and
"they are to be congratlated that a man of his
"experience and ability, his purity of life and
"nobility of character, has been chosen to fill the

"important position to which he has been ap-
"pointed."

SALAMANCA SHAM FIGHT.

The regiment of regular troops stationed in
Fredericton at this time was commanded by Col.
Maxwell. The 36th had seen much active service
and among other victories enrolled upon its ban-
ner was "Salamanca."

The anniversary of that day was to be com-
memorated by a sham fight, in which all the uniformed companies of the York militia were to be
engaged. The defence was composed of artillery,
one field battery; cavalry, one troop; rifle company, one company of grenadiers, and one light
company of militia. There was also attached to
us one company 36th Regiment; the whole under
the command of Major Cairns, 36th Regiment.

At four a. m. we were all on the *qui vive*, and
shortly after marched to take up our position.
The action was to commence at the flat below
Fredericton. On the first rise of ground the
rifles proceeded to throw up a barricade for cover,
behind which we were ordered to lie down. On
our right was the River St. John, on our left the
highway road, just beyond which in a ravine and
grove was concealed the cavalry. On the hill
(Nigger Hill) in our rear, covering the position,
was a battery of artillery masked by trees. The
main road bridge on our left rear was barricaded

with timber, and two heavy guns placed in position, to defend which the main body of our infantry was here massed. All this work was accomplished in a very short space of time, and to the eye of a casual observer our position would not be discovered.

About seven o'clock our bugler, far in advance, sounded the alarm, and shortly after the fixed bayonets of the 36th were seen glinting in the sunlight. Then the music of the band reached our ears, the enemy was in sight, and for the first time the nerves of the recruits tingled with the prospect of a battle.

When about 500 yards distant the regiment halted, wheeled into column, and the officers coming to the front were addressed by the gallant colonel. The doctor with his orderly (the latter carrying a large black box) took up a position to our right front, near the river. The regiment now deployed to its left and threw out a skirmish line, which at once proceeded to advance. The cavalry, dashing out suddenly from their concealment, caused the skirmish line to close rapidly in rallying squares, which on the retreat of the cavalry became good marks for our artillerymen from the heights in our rear.

These manœuvres, several times repeated, brought the skirmish line unpleasantly near to our position, which in the meantime we were defending by a rapid fire through the timber of

our breastwork. Every shot was well-aimed, and
had it been ball instead of blank cartridge, the
rifles on that day would have done good execution.

Presently a rush was made for the barricade.
I well remember the appearance of the soldiers as
they came up the rise : faces begrimed with powder from biting the cartridges, and white pants
soiled and wet with perspiration. The bugle call
" fire and retire " was quickly responded to, and
we retreated, continuing the fire in extended
order. We retreated to cover, and probably fearing an ambush were not pursued.

In the meantime the main body of the enemy
occupied the highway, advancing along which
their rear was harrassed by our cavalry. The
bridge reached, the grenadier company, led by
Captain Orange, assaulted the work. With
swords in hand, bayonets at the charge, they
crossed at the double. When half way over, the
guns were discharged from the battery, unlim-
bered, spiked and left to their fate. Notwithstanding a brave defence on the part of our
troops, the work was demolished and the rout
became general. Crossing the fences, the coat-
tails of some of our militiamen were pinned fast
with the bayonets on one side while they hung
helpless on the other. To avenge this, as they
ascended the hill in retreat, the wheels of unlim-
bered guns were hurled down upon the advancing
enemy.

Arriving at the crest of the hill, where we were ordered to make a stand, it was with great difficulty that the officers of the 36th could make the soldiers believe that it was now their turn to retreat. Returned to our original position, the prisoners — of which we had several — were exchanged under a flag of truce. Formed in one line, the rifles the advanced guard, we marched back to barracks about four p. m., hungry and tired ; but to me it was one of the jolliest days of my life.

The casualties were : W. Segee, cavalry, wounded, his own pistol ramrod shot through his hand, and some injuries to others which were slight.

A dinner was served in the barrack square, under booths formed from the green branches of trees, for the whole force, which was hugely enjoyed, and in the evening the officers' square was illuminated with colored lights suspended in the old willows. Music and dancing was enjoyed on the green sward until a late hour of the night.

A balloon manipulated by Benjamin Tibbetts floated gracefully away to astonish by its fall the good Welsh people of Cardigan. From a ferry-boat anchored in the river, a fine display of fire works was made, and from it a noble young fellow, Kerr Inches, an artilleryman, lost his life. He was a favorite with the volunteers, and his untimely fate tinged with sadness our commemoration of the anniversary of "Salamanca."

Chapter vii

Opposition in Business.

BESIDES Dr. Baldwin, who re-opened business on Regent street, William Simpson, a brother of the Queen's printer, 'also opened a large drug establishment on Carleton street, and another directly across the street from Gales' was opened by Amasa Coy, M. D., recently retured from Edinburgh.

Time flew apace, and at the end of three years of my apprenticeship, I began to look forward to grave responsibilities of my own. From a well-thumbed Dispensatory, to which reference was continually had in the preparation of medicines or compounding prescriptions, I had so stored my mind as to secure the confidence of the physicians and people generally in the manipulation of medicines. A young lad, Scott Wood, son of the Rev. Mr. Wood, a Church of England minister, having now entered to learn the business, I was no longer the shop boy, and began to feel the importance and dignity of my position.

With the patronage of the Government house, officers of the garrison, the principal M. D.'s and respectable families of the town, time never hung heavily on our hands. The doctors of the several regiments were also social in their visits, and the knowledge thus obtained, with the daily routine of shop work, gave me an insight extremely useful in the practice and conduct of my own business.

SOME ODD CHARACTERS.

There were several oddities whose names would be familiar to Frederictonians of that day. One of these, Archy McLean, before named, had given up his farm, "Vinegar Hill," and now lived on his pension in Fredericton. He had seen real service in a Highland regiment; was generous to a fault; and a wit.

When Sir Archibald Campbell, the hero of Burmah, was governor of New Brunswick, he frequently met and conversed with Archie. At times, when he received his pension money, he would promenade the streets dressed as a kilted Highlander, drinking many times a day, in dock-an-dorrish, "long life to the King and bonny Scotland." On one of these occasions, meeting Sir Archibald, he was offered a residence at the Government house, and his duty would be to herd the cattle. Standing erect and throwing out his plaided arm, he replied, "Na! a McLean will never be a coo boy for a Campbell!"

During the Peninsular war, while sacking a town, he entered with a portion of his regiment a doctor's shop. Every bottle that smelt like alcohol was soon emptied by the victorious and thirsty soldiers. Some castile soap, seized and devoured in mad haste, saved them from the bad effect of the strong doses they had taken.

Bryan Brady, alias Bryan Born, a butcher; Concave Smith, an architect; Peter Duff and "black Harry" were all oddities in their way and commanded their share of public attention. The last-named had been a soldier in the 104th Regiment. Under the influence of drink and irritated by a lad named Dalton he used his bayonet, stabbing him fatally at St. John. He was tried and acquitted. He lived in the farm houses above Fredericton and was a good cook. When visiting Fredericton he was harmless under the influence of drink, but his dress was made up of all the colors of the rainbow and a profuse sprinkling of tinsel, which in the bright sunlight made "Harry" an object of general attraction.

ELECTRICAL SOCIETY.

During the early period of my service with Mr. Gale, I induced a number of the young men to unite in forming what was called an "Electrical Society." L. P. Fisher, W. C. Tredwell, H. S. Estey and Charles Wolhaupter were of the number.

James Nesbit, an intelligent cabinet-maker, a

Scotchman, constructed for us a simple apparatus. Igniting powder or alcohol with an icicle held in the hand, while standing on the insulating stool, was thought wonderful, and to this day I remember the grimaces of men and animals as they bounded away from the influence and effects of the subtle motor.

We had frequent visitors at our room to witness the experiments, and when operated upon never complained of the leyden jars being too lightly charged. The spark that we felt on our knuckle a half century ago, that flashes across our vision, causing the heavens to reverberate with sounds, is to-day tamed to harness, to lead or to drive, and will, I believe, in the hand of science, become the great power of the earth.

MERCHANTS OF FREDERICTON, 1834.

The great staple of the country being lumber, the heaviest importations of goods were made by merchants engaged in that business. The firm of Robert Rankin & Co. dominated all others in that line, and the supplies furnished to operators in various parts of the Province was immense. The stock embraced almost everything that could be asked for of the best quality, and numerous cash accounts were kept with government officers or respectable residents of the town. Their place of business was at the upper end of the town, W. J.

Bedell, Esq., being manager, and Robert Gowan and Sherman Carman, bookkeepers.

North, with an alley dividing, was the business place and residence of J. A. & F. E. Beckwith. This firm also transacted a large lumber and cash business for many years in Fredericton. Of French descent, this firm controlled largely the trade of Madawaska.

Below, in the same block, was the firm of Langan & Robertson (T. R.), also in the lumber business.

Just above the Barker House was the store and dwelling of Jedediah Slason, who carried on an extensive lumbering business in many parts of the Province. He was long and favorably known as a merchant, and represented York County in the Provincial Parliament.

Merchants dealing heavily in those times, kept in stock a large supply of liquors of superior quality. At the decease of Mr. Slason, a large quantity of various kinds of liquors was remaining on hand. Joseph Gaynor, Esq., a conscientious Methodist, being the chief executor, determined to pay the cost rather than sell or distribute what he knew was then destroying some of his best friends. Casks of gin, rum, brandy and various kinds of wine were brought up from the cellar, rolled into the streets, and the heads knocked in. Mingling with the filth of the gutter, the fiery flood rolled on, and dippers, cups, kettles, etc.,

were speedily put in requisition. But there was
a draught being made unobservant, "a long pull
and a strong pull," by a quadruped. Minchin's
cow, knowing nothing of the effect, invested
largely. Presently in the thickest of the crowd
there was a stampede; right and left flew wildly
the excited people. Such gyrations of sound or
motion were never conceived by the maddest
buffalo on his native plain. With eyes rolling
like balls of fire and tail erect, the intoxicated
bovine cleared the way; but like bipeds under
similar circumstances she came at last to grief.
The cow ran into the wrong yard, where a well
was being dug, and surprised the delvers at the
bottom.

The largest grocery store was kept by the firm
of Pickard, Gaynor & Workman, above the new
market house and on the corner near the river.
This large establishment — store, dwelling and
out-buildings — was swept away by the fire of
1825. Mr. Gaynor opened on his own account in
Waterloo Row below the Cathedral grounds,
where a good country business was then being
done, and later in the brick building now Mr.
Temple's residence.

John and James Taylor also conducted a large
lumber-business store at Taylor's alley.

WATERLOO ROW.

Waterloo Row and vicinity embraced the residence of many of the aristocracy, viz., Attorney-General C. J. Peters, Colonel Shore, Judge Bliss, Archdeacon Best, Captain Hurd, Dr. Turner, etc.

A noted hostlery was kept here by Avery, sign of the golden ball; another, the Royal Oak, by Polly Vanhorne and her son Charles French, who was of the clever fast men of the time.

The principal settlements were Nashwaak, Sheffield and Maugerville, the trade of which centred largely in Waterloo Row.

Professional men and tradesmen of nearly every kind were represented, and but few persons visited the city without having occasion to call upon Clark, the baker, or Wolhaupter, the watchmaker, or Barker, the tanner and shoemaker. Kendall was also well known by the boys as making the best cricket bats.

There was but one street fronting on the River St. John. From the continuous row of houses there was, some forty-five years ago, a large sewer made to the river. It was partially enclosed.

One afternoon a noise was heard — loud, shrill, distinct. Everybody heard it, and everybody said such a noise had never been heard before. No two persons were agreed as to its cause or described it alike. Men, women and children were assembled upon the bank. Some said it came from above, some from below. A stalwart blue-nose, after weighing all the evidence, concluded that a hippopotamus or other huge denizen of the deep, must have, unobserved, crept into and taken possession of the newly made sewer. His first anxiety was for the safety of the females and children. With stentorian voice he shouted: "Women! this is no place for you!" While volunteers were being sought for to enter the drain, there came an explanation. The first steam-whistle ever heard in Fredericton made its appearance that day on the steamer "Madawaska," from the Grand Falls. She landed at the upper end of the town. This steamer had been built to ply on the river above the falls, but was taken to pieces and rebuilt below the falls, and this was her first trip to Fredericton.

The St. John people apparently at that time were not more familiar with steamboats than those of Fredericton. The first arrival of the steamer "Madawaska" at Indiantown, St. John, was in the night time. The people were sleeping soundly in their beds and suddenly were awakened by a loud and long-continued screech such as had never been heard there before. People rushed wildly from their beds into the streets, some shouting, others praying, and many believed the end of the world had come. One gentleman pitched headlong from his bed against the corner of a sharp old-fashioned high bedpost, dividing his forehead as with a sharp instrument. For a short time there was great excitement and confusion. Many incidents sufficiently ludicrous could be re-

lated to usher in a bit of history regarding the
first steam-whistle on the River St. John.

MY FAITHFUL DOG NUMBER TWO, "SAGO."

I had obtained as a great favor from Dr. Woodforde a young terrier puppy, a thoroughbred between the Irish and Scotch terrier.   He was wiry
haired, heavy chested, and white in color, with a
black mark over one eye.   I named him Sago !
I commenced his education young, and before he
was many months old would shut the door, take
soiled towels to the house and bring back clean
ones alone, jump through a hoop covered with
paper in flames, extinguish burning paper when
thrown down casually, etc., etc.   This latter feat
saved my place of business at Woodstock.   A
block of matches fell by accident on the floor behind the counter.   I was absent and the door was
locked.   I found on my return the place filled
with smoke, and a quantity of paper which had
been ignited, together with the singed appearance
of his face and paws, gave evidence of his battle
with the fire.

He was considered the most intelligent and
pluckiest little animal in Fredericton, and was a
favorite with all classes.   When suffering from
the distemper to which young dogs are subject,
beside sympathy expressed by Judge Carter, he
kindly used his skill in bleeding the little animal
and prescribed for his treatment.

He seemed to understand language. Although apparently giving no attention to a conversation, the slightest reference to him would bring him instantly to his feet. On Sabbath morning when the bells rang for church he would come in quietly and lie down on his bed, and occasionally when the bell rang on a week day, he would come to the door, if outside, looking askance as if in doubt whether he had a correct marking of time. He would. kill a rat or other vermin instantly, was a good hunter in the woods, and equally good in bringing game from the water. He was affec tionate and faithful to a fault, my companion in many rambles, and although many times roughly handled by large dogs, lived to the age of eleven years. He died in Woodstock, mourned by my two eldest children, whom he had often amused with his antics.

The following lines express but feebly my love, — aye, love! — for this faithful animal.

IMPROMPTU LINES ON THE DEATH OF A FAVORITE TERRIER DOG.

Alas! old dog, thy days are told,
Thy limbs now stiffening lie and cold,
  My tearful eyes doth see;
For true, thou wert a faithful friend
And ever through thy life did'st lend
  Thyself attached to me.

Though but a dog, doth mem'ry trace
When young and buoyant both did'st race
  O'er field or pebbled shore.

Thy name pronounced thou can'st not hear ;
With vig'rous leap or willing ear
   Thou answerest no more.

'Tis but a lesson : the same hand
Doth beckon mortals and command,—
   Its dicta is obeyed.
For animals and man at last,
When few more months or years are past,
   Will be in death arrayed.

Chapter viii

The Disputed Territory between New Bruns-wick and Maine.

THE rebellion under Papineau having now assumed serious proportions, troops were sent from England to be transported to Canada, overland via Fredericton. Sir John Harvey was then Governor of New Brunswick.

The Legislature of Maine, United States, began also at this time to exercise unwarranted jurisdiction over the land known as the "Disputed Territory," and by aggressive movement threatened an invasion of New Brunswick.

An area containing three million (3,000,000) acres of land of a superior quality and heavily timbered with large white pine, spruce and hard wood in variety, forming a part of New Brunswick and the north-east boundary of Maine, was claimed by that State as territory belonging to it. The claim was urged with such pertinacity by our American cousins as to cause honest John Bull to hesitate, and that hesitation proved fatal.

Had no concession been made, — had they been told to take the pound of flesh "but not one drop of blood," — the St. Andrews Railway would in all probability have long since been completed to Quebec, and that rich and fertile belt a flourishing district within the Province of New Brunswick. But the British Government dallied.

That astute lawyer, Daniel Webster, wound the subtle web of diplomacy and prevarication, which is said to be worse than lying, around his victims. The then Rothchilds of America, Baring Bros., succeeded in muffling the arguments of the British Commsssioner, Lord Ashburton, and there dropped into the lap of Uncle Sam one of his richest jewels.

Had an earnest protest been made by the Government and General Assembly of New Brnnswick against the cession of this vast and magnificent territory, the archives of Paris might have disgorged, as they did later, the only map in existence, excepting one secretly held by the United States Government, showing the true boundary-line to be the original one claimed by New Brunswick and the transaction unworthy of a great or honorable nation.

During the period of negotiations between the British and American Governments, a warden, Capt. J. A. McLauchlan, who had been an officer in the 104th Regiment, was appointed over the so-called disputed territory, whose duty it was to estimate the value of lumber cut thereon and floated down the St. John River.

These were the glorious days of irresponsible

government, when all the officers of public depart-
ments were appointed by the crown, the crown receiving from the Province certain revenues, called
" Casual and Territorial," to meet the expenses.

Some of us remember those gilded and happy
sunshine days of early life, as we gazed upon the
English horses and elegant coaches, breeched and
capped by liveried coach and footmen.

Whilst, so far as we know, but little remon-
strance was made by the Government of New
Brunswick against the cession of this territory,
the loyalty of its people was touched, and volunteers, representing the three arms of the service,
came nobly to the front. Nor was this spirit confined to New Brunswick. The Legislature of
Nova Scotia, in a true brotherly spirit of British
loyalty, voted a contingent of 10,000 men, and
money, to aid New Brunswick in repelling the
aggression of the State of Maine.

It was mid-winter in the year of 1837-38. The
regular troops in garrison at Fredericton being
the first to move, the Fredericton " Rifle Company " volunteered its services to perform garrison
duty, which was accepted. The 36th Regiment
went into quarters at Woodstock, supported by
the Fredericton Artillery and the Carleton County
Militia.

Reviewing a line of volunteers formed on the
ice above the Meduxnakic bridge at Woodstock,
the gallant old Colonel Maxwell addressed them

as "hardy and loyal sons of New Brunswick and as possessing bodies of adamant and souls of fire."

The Fredericton Troop of Cavalry acted as videttés, stationed on the road between Fredericton and Woodstock to carry despatches. A battalion of infantry was also organized in York County and occupied the Artillery Park Barracks, under the command of Lieutenant Colonel John Robinson.

Our captain, McBeth, being the first to volunteer, received the pass-word daily from the Governor; and our duty was to guard the garrison, Government House, and principal posts in the town.

A *posse* of United States officers, found in a lumber camp on the "Disputed Territory," were taken prisoners by Sheriff Winslow, of Carleton County, and conveyed, well guarded, on a sled to Fredericton.

The House was in session, and I well remember seeing the sled, with the prisoners, driven to the door of the Parliament Buildings, and the rush of members from their seats to view them.

Business requiring my attention during the day, except at the daily morning parade, my turn of duty came at night. As full private at "sentry go" I took my beat, and the colder the weather, the brighter did my military ardor seem to burn, carrying me over difficulties to which others during the campaign succumbed. For the three months' service in garrison we received no pay, and rations only for a portion of that time.

The several regiments were conveyed to Canada on sleds, a company arriving and occupying the stone barracks and leaving at sunrise the following morning.

The bloodless "Aroostook War" and the far-famed "Strickland's retreat" being now matter of historical and poetical record, I will not enlarge. Suffice it that the excitement brought out the best blood of our young men to enrol in the volunteer force and imparted a military spirit to the youth of that day, relighted to burn all the brighter in its recital to their children.

OWN RESPONSIBILITY.

My four years' term as apprentice having expired, Mr. Gale desiring that I should remain with him for a year, I consented. My salary was to be £30, with board and lodging. During my four years with Mr. Gale I had no vacations, and stipulated that before re-entering on work I should have a month's holidays.

I had been invited by two friends, young men studying French at Madawaska, to make them a visit, and this invitation I now gladly accepted.

Cook Hammond, of Kingsclear, a young man (since well established at "Violet Brook," where he now lives with his family), furnished a horse. I

hired a wagon and we set out on our journey.
Reaching the Grand Falls, we employed a Frenchman, whose *pirogue* we entered to complete our
journey. It was the month of July and the
weather being warm, I wore a white flannel jacket
slightly embroidered. Groups of French were
often seen on the banks of the river, the male
portions of whom, after a few words in French
spoken by Hammond, decamped instantly.

The excitement of Papineau's rebellion had not
yet subsided, and the announcement that I was a
Government agent taking the census, to the
French mind meant conscription and new
" Acadian horrors."

The simplicity and jollity of the people interested me very much. The ovens for baking were
formed of clay on elevated platforms outside their
dwellings, and of an oval or beehive shape. The
loaves resembled huge knots sliced from a tree
and the bread dark but sweet.

At the hospitable residence of Col. Coombes we
were made to feel quite at home, to which end the
young ladies performed their part charmingly.

Pushing on, we reached the house and beautiful
farm of Simonette Hebert, where my friend,
Charles Hartt (now a lawyer in New York) was
staying.

The settlement of the Boundary Question between England and the United States by arbitra-
tion gave to the latter, by a most unrighteous de-

cision, this and other superior farming lands on the western side of the St. John River to an extent of 3,000,000 of acres.

Simonette Hebert was one of the most respectable and well-to-do farmers in Madawaska. Before the division of the county, when jurors were brought from that place to Woodstock, the court was frequently amused by the crier calling, " Simon-eat-a-bear ! " three times, as is the custom.

The best way of obtaining a French education at that period was by residing for a time at Madawaska, where capable instructors were found from the Province of Quebec. The late Judge Wilmot and others thus obtained their knowledge of the French language. Hartt's tutor was an Englishman named Turner, a good scholar, but sadly demoralized by periodical sprees.

Making Simonette's for a time my head-quarters, Hartt and I sallied out daily with rod and gun to slay the innocent. A little above Hebert's, on the opposite side, the little Madawaska river entered the St. John. The only house then to be seen was a small log cabin on the lower side of the stream.

A half mile above, on the St. John, lived Squire Rice, a magistrate, and a good sample of a witty Irishman. John Emmerson, an Irish Protestant, lived there also. He was a very worthy man, and from good habits and close attention to business accumulated considerable property. The beautiful houses that embellish the rising village of Edmundston, erected by his sons, are evidence of a father's thrift.

The glorious sunshine, the deep meadows, and beautiful wild flowers, after a long and close confinement, seemed to me a very paradise, which passed all too swiftly away. At the close of two weeks thus pleasantly spent, Hartt accompanying me, we visited Joseph Hea, who resided at Paul Crocks, several miles below. His tutor was a Frenchman from Old France, named Joliette. The purity of the language as spoken by him was in marked contrast with the *patois* of the native.

Our new residence, *pro tem*, was also on the western side of the St. John. The settlement here was more populous, and the *Anglais* visitors the centre of attraction. We were frequently invited to evening parties.

I had taken with me an octave flute on which I had learned to play, but my pride oozed out from the ends of my fingers in the presence of twenty fiddlers all in a row. The voice and energetic motions of arms and legs, as time was beaten to the scraping of the bows, presented a phase in acoustics altogether novel.

Accepting on one occasion an invitation to Jerome Gonieau's, directly opposite to Crocks, we paddled over early in the evening, and found a merry young company assembled, male and female. Having enjoyed the French novelties of song and dance until a late hour, we started to return. Leaving the landing we paddled out from the shore. The night was intensely dark,— neither light nor star to guide our course.

When near the centre of the river we found the canoe lifted as by a fiendish hand, and turned upside down. We soon found ourselves scrambling for life among the branches of a floating tree. After many times sinking and rising among the smaller branches, we reached the trunk of the tree, which was a large one and sustained us nobly. We were also fortunate in finding our craft and a paddle entangled in the branches. Righting the canoe, she was soon bailed out, and we were once more afloat.

Through the jealousy of one "May Rose," the doors were fastened, and wet and weary we clambered through a window into the parlor.

As if in proof of the old adage that "misfortunes seldom come single," a step or two only had been taken by Hea when his foot encountered a treacherous rope, placed by cunning hands, causing his nose,— a good Roman one,— to be deprived of a considerable portion of its epidermis. The mirth of Hartt was soon checked, for leaping, as he thought, into a bed of down, he found a bed of thistles.

The period of my vacation having come to an end, with recruited health and bright visions of the future, I said, "adieu!" to friends old and new, and turned my back upon scenes Arcadian for others more prosaic.

The then central point of Madawaska was the chapel, around which clustered a few dwelling houses, with a single store. The village was on the eastern side of the river and was my first stopping place. I here saw P. C. Amireaux, a genial, intelligent Frenchman, well known in Fredericton.

Our prow again touched the shore at the landing of Col. Coombes, which proved to be the end of my canoe journey homeward. The colonel was in command of the militia of that section above the Grand Falls; a magistrate, therefore an authority in law among the French; spoke the language like a native, and was a fair sample of the solid yeoman of his day in New Brunswick. He well sustained the character of hospitality, for which our people are noted, and in its early settlement often tested their resources.

On arriving here I found that my seat in the wagon had been "spoken for" by a lady, the colonel's daughter, then living in Fredericton, and wife of Charles Beckwith. It was proposed that I should ride a beautiful and fast-pacing French pony, purchased for Major Magny, of the 36th Regiment. Accustomed to the saddle in my early morning rides to the shooting grounds, I gladly accepted, and any regrets or local rememberances of this one-hund-

red - and - fifty mile ride have long since been
obliterated.

RETURN TO FREDERICTON AND BUSINESS.

Re-entering the shop, I was now master of my
evenings. I joined a class of young men learning
to dance. The same teacher, John Reid, had an
afternoon class of the *elite* aristocratic youths of
the city. The "setting up" is a good deal like
drill, and some of the dances are pleasing and
teach graceful attitudes ; but the exposure to cold,
late hours, and the dissipation associated with
balls, leads one to suggest other channels affording
more real and lasting pleasure.

I soon returned to my old plan of retiring and
rising early, and continued it while I remained in
Fredericton.

In the spring of 1839 I visited Woodstock to
examine some druggist's stock, held by Dr.
Charles Rice, which he kept in connection with
his business as a physician. I arranged with him
for the purchase, and expected to be in possession
in August following.

Immediately after my return, Mr. Gale took
his departure for a tour through the United
States, leaving me in charge of the business.

During his absence an order was received for
the regiment to leave at three days' notice. On
the books were accounts against many of the
officers, which, by working late and early, I suc-

ceeded in making up and collecting, while the claims of many others went by default.

A thorough cleansing of the shop, re-labelling bottles, and the preparation of medicines in advance of requirements, had long since, in view of a final good-by, been completed.

I had now remained more than a month beyond the period of my engagement. Still Mr. Gale had not returned. The time was passing away in which I should have been making preparations for the payment of the stock purchased, and I remember feeling deeply mortified at the delay.

More than another month had passed away, when an arrival by the Woodstock stage, at four p. m., set me at liberty. Mr. Gale said he had stopped at Woodstock as he returned, thought it a poor place for me, and offered me employment for one or more years at an increased salary.

I thought it idle talk, considering every moment precious, received from him the amount due me, with a promise of a letter of credit to Dr. Walker & Sons, wholesale druggists, St. John, and at seven p. m. left in the steamer for that city.

Chapter ix.

Commence Business in Woodstock.

AFTER a restless night spent on the steamer, I found myself in the counting-room of Dr. Walker & Sons, St. John. Having stated the object of my visit, also Mr. Gale's promise to send me a letter of credit, and showing my list of sundries, the reply was : " We do not require a letter from Mr. Gale. If he had not found you trustworthy he would not have left you so long in charge of his business."

A staff was selected, which I joined in the loft, and by the following morning we had "coopered up" in thirty new fish-barrels my stock in trade. This precaution and expense I considered necessary as the sinking of a tow-boat between Fredericton and Woodstock was not of unfrequent occurrence.

On the evening of that day I arrived by steamer at Fredericton, made arrangements with Shaw & Brittain for the transportation of my goods to Woodstock at four shillings per barrel, and at seven p. m. was riding in a two-wheeled mail-cart *en route* for Woodstock.

Three nights having nearly passed without sleep I was easily lured by the gentle goddess whilst riding on a firm piece of road. But what an awakening! Suddenly I found myself going down a steep hill, buffeted by heavy leathern mail-bags, until brought to bay by granite boulders. The night, moreover, was dark and the rain fell in heavy showers. We were let down by the breaking of a wheel. There being no house near for shelter, I awaited under a projecting rock the return of the driver.

H—— (now postmaster at Edmundston), lost no time, and at ten a. m., in the midst of a terrific shower, we arrived at the Woodstock Hotel. This house was kept by Mrs. Grover, a kind-hearted lady, under whose care I completed my bachelor life.

After being refreshed, I examined the vacant stores of the village and rented one, formerly a bank office, owned by George F. Williams, an old acquaintance of my father. A carpenter was at once set to work, and on the fourth day after my arrival I stood behind the counter, not yet twenty-one years of age, and commenced the battle of life.

To obtain an outfit and pay incidental expenses, my father endorsed a note for £25, which I had cashed in the Bank of British North America at Fredericton, and which I paid at maturity.

My first customer was a good-hearted Irishman, Peter Gallagher, well known in Carleton County. He used to say, long after, that I owed my success to the lucky penny he gave me; and to this man I ver felt kindly inclined.

The physicians then at Woodstock were Dr. Wylie, a veteran who had seen service in the British navy; Drs. Rice, father and son, Americans; and Botsford, a young M. D. from Glasgow College and a native of New Brunswick, who afterwards removed to the city of St. John, where, as a successful practitioner and a useful member of society, he remained until the time of his decease.

At the end of a year, finding my business increasing, I removed to more roomy quarters, viz., the parlor of a house just vacated by Mr. Charles Connell, nearly opposite the corner now owned by myself and known as Apothecaries' Hall.

The morals of the young men of Woodstock, at this time, were very loose; and the tendency to improve was not increased by occasional visits of officers and other fast men from the garrison town of Houlton, United States.

In the winter of 1841 I visited St. John, and purchased from A. R. Truro a number of volumes of books with which to commence a "Circulating Library." The perusal of these—many of them standard works—employed more profitable the time of some of the young people of that day.

With increased facilties in space and position, I extended my business as rapidly as my abilities permitted. To medicines and a library were now added groceries, and I found an assistant necessary. I had now obtained the patronage of the officers and militia stationed at Woodstock, and

began to realize that I was really the proprietor of
an establishment.

Desiring to avoid much of the company with
which I was brought in contact at the hotel I
tried to amuse myself in morning and evening
walks, with "Sago" as my constant companion, or
in my room adjoining the shop, with books, music,
etc. I soon, however, arrived at the conclusion
"that it is not good for man to live alone."

On the bank of the River St. John, on the opposite side from Woodstock and on a beautiful flat
of rich and well-cultivated intervale land, stood a
comfortable farm-house, which, with a mile front-
age of land on the river and extending three miles
to the rear, was the property of an extensive
lumberman and farmer, also a popular and estimable man, John Shea. The first lot purchased at
the early settlement of the country, on which the
house referred to stands, was covered with valuable timber, pine and birch, from the sale of
which he made his payments; and by tact and
persevering industry added lot after lot on either
side to the extent before named. In carrying on
extensive lumber operations, he was a large purchaser of hay, grain, pork, and gave employment
to many men and horses. Added to this was a
genial disposition and an ever-open door to the
traveller, which made his name in the country a
household word. To my knowledge, for many
years strangers sat at his well furnished table al-

most daily, from whom no payment was taken, and the patience of the female portion of the household under such circumstances must have been remarkable.

My first formal visit to Mr. Shea's was in company with a Woodstock gentleman, by whom I was introduced, and was pleasantly received by members of the family. The eldest son, W. S., or familiarly "Sperry," I found to be a very pleasant and intelligent young man. He had just returned from school at St. John. To his energy and capital, at a later date, after his return from California, is largely due the establishing in Woodstock of the valuable and widely known nurseries of Sharp & Shea.

A bark canoe now became a necessary adjunct, as the ferry was not kept "at all hours." In old Mrs. Maloney's garden, a little flat near the water's edge (long since swept away), in her charge I felt my canoe, paddle and secret safe.

MARRIAGE.

Time went apace, and on the sixth day of January, one thousand eight hundred and forty-two I was married by the Reverend the Rector of Woodstock, S. D. Lee Street, to Sarah Ann Shea, eldest daughter of Mr. John Shea, of Northampton, in the County of Carleton, and Province of New Brunswick.

The upper flat of a large two-story building, recently erected and owned by Mr. Shea, on King Street, Woodstock, was comfortably furnished for us; and there, young and inexperienced, we entered upon the duties and responsibilities of mar ried life.

DEBATING CLUB.

A debating club, composed of the best-read and most intelligent men of the place, assembled weekly in the office of Louis Dibble, a lawyer, during the winter, of which by request I became a member. Amongst its members were Louis Dibble, W. T. Wilmot, G. W. Cleary, W. H. Needham, L. P. Fisher, lawyers; also, H. E. Dibble, customs; Richard English, merchant; W. Q. Ketchum and Frederick Dibble, the last named being president.

WOODSTOCK MECHANICS' INSTITUTE.

A public hall being sadly wanted in Woodstock, I wrote upon a sheet of paper a heading, and went out one day to test by subscription public opinion on the matter. Dr. C. D. Rice, L. P. Fisher, James Grover, J. R. Tupper, R. A. Hay, Stephen Parsons, James Robertson, with myself, subscribed ten pounds each, and smaller sums from others aggregating an amount which seemed to warrant our making a commencement.

From the early records of the institute interesting information is gathered as to the preliminary steps to the erection of the building, which for twelve years, or until the great fire of 1860, was a place of popular resort, and its platform honored -by the leading statesmen of the day, professors of universities, orators, etc.

Several public meetings were called, when, at a meeting held in Miss Drake's schoolroom (where Mrs. Chalmers' building now stands), on Thursday evening, the 11th of March, 1847, James Robertson Esq., in the chair, the following resolutions were submitted and adopted :

" *Whereas,* The increasing intelligence of the community requires the adoption of means for the more fully developing the mental energies of its members and the more general diffusion of useful information ; and

Whereas, The delivery of lectures upon literary, historical and scientific subjects will best effectuate these objects, it is deemed expedient to form an association for that purpose.

Therefore Resolved, That a society be formed in this place to be called the Woodstock Mechanics' Institute, and that the same shall be governed by a president, vice-president and three directors."

The annual subscription was fixed at five shillings, and the roll of members at the first meeting were twenty-six. The officers elected were John Bedell, President ; Jas. Robertson, Vice-President; Michael Keiley, Treasurer ; G. W. Cleary, Richard English, Lewis Smith, Directors.

Meetings and lectures were held in Miss Drake's school-room until the new institute building was ready for use. The first lecture was delivered by Dr. C. D. Rice, March 25th, 1847 ; subject, " The Atmosphere."

An act of incorporation was obtained March 30, 1848, and on the 8th day of the following June the corner stone of the new building was laid with Masonic honors by the Free Masons of Woodstock (Charles Perley, Master,) under the superintendence of Robert Gowan, Esq., Master of Solomon's Lodge, No. 764, Fredericton. The oration was delivered by Dr. C. D. Rice, followed by an address from Mr. Gowan.

The ceremony, from its entire novelty, did not fail to create the most intense interest, and the large assembly of ladies who graced the seene with their presence contributed much to the general effect. All things conspired to make it a joyous and gala day.

The site was given by Charles Connell, Esq. The architect and builder was Mr. William Stroup. The building committee, John Bedell, James Robertson, William T. Baird. Office bearers : John Bedell, President; Richard English, Vice-President; Charles H. Connell, Treasurer ; William T. Baird, Secretary; G. W. Cleary, Jas. Robertson, A. Hay, T. N. Baker, William Lindsay, E. R. Parsons, Directors.

The institute was erected on the lot next south

of that now occupied by Mrs. Chalmers, and was 50x40 in size and two storys high with tower.

The record of the secretary's report for 1857 shows the names of lecturers and the subjects delivered during the year as follows: Rev. J. Hunter, " Life and Times of Sir William Wallace"; Dr. Robb, Kings College, on " Geology "; Dr. Smith, "The Earth before Adam"; Dr. Woodforde, " History "; E. J. Jacob, Esq., "Language"; W. T. Baird, Esq., " India "; Dr. Dow, " Society and Its Prospects"; Rev. Mr. Seely, "The Opposition to Discoveries and Inventions"; Mr. H. Beardsley, "The North American Indians"; Rev. Thos. Connolly, " Fraternal Charity."

In the Lecture course of 1858 and '59 the Hon. Joseph Howe, of Nova Scotia, was one of the lecturers, and at the annual meeting of directors, dated February 6th, 1859, the following resolution was passed :—

" *Resolved*, That the thanks of this institute are due and are hereby tendered to the Honorable Joseph Howe for the very able lecture delivered by him before the institute of this place, and bearing upon questions of vital importance to the present and future of New Brunswick."

The honorable gentleman's theme was: " One Currency, One Customs, One Postal Arrangement"; in other words what has since become a fixed fact, " Confederation."

The following advertisement, from a Woodstock paper, published in 1848, showing the names of

some of the ladies who took an active part in the
erection of the institute is given asa fitting finale
to this short sketch of its history.

BAZAAR.

The following ladies have kindly consented to take
tables at a bazaar to aid in the erection of the Woodstock
Mechanics' Institute. The public are hereby informed
that the aforesaid ladies will receive all contributions
made for that purpose previous to the first day of September
next:— Mrs. Street, Mrs. C. Connell, Mrs. Cleary,
Mrs. Rice, Mrs. T. A. Perley, Mrs. C. Perley, Mrs. H. M.
G. Garden, Mrs. R. R. Ketchum, Miss Winslow, Miss E.
Dibble, Miss Perley, Miss C. Ketchum, Miss Wetmore,
Miss D. Dibble, Miss H. Connell, Miss English, Miss
Fisher.

(Signed)   A. K. S. WETMORE,
     CHAS. H. CONNELL,
     W. T. BAIRD,   Committee.
     E. R. PARSONS,
     JAMES GROVER,

As secretary of the institute and member of the
building committee, I cannot forget the valuable
assistance rendered by the ladies of Woodstock
and vicinity,— though often asked for yet never
refused until the building was completed.

Many were the devices of the building committee in procuring means for the erection and com-
pletion of the institute. Bazaars, lectures, tea-
meetings, concerts, etc., were put into requisition,
and were well patronized ; but the grandest suc-

cess was the gathering of a multitude of people to witness an

INDIAN CANOE RACE.

The inhabitants of the town went heartily into the work. A toll-bridge was built of floating timber from the foot of King Street to the Island, on which were erected booths for refreshments, and in the thick bushy undergrowth a platform for an Indian dance or pow-wow in the evening.

The value of the money prizes to be contended for by the Indians in their barks was sufficient to excite an interest, and an even number from the "Village" above Fredericton were pitted against their brother redskins from the "Tobique."

The larger number of the twenty-four men, stripped to their waists, the coarse black hair resting on their shoulders, seemed to be pure aboriginal stock, and the determination visible in their countenance as they waited, paddle blade in water, for the pistol-shot, gave evidence that every muscle would be exerted in the struggle. The distance to be paddled was from the head of Bull's Island upward and around a flat-boat anchored in the river where the passenger bridge now stands.

The race was fairly and severely contested, and the wild gesticulations of the Indians and the squaws during its progress exciting in the extreme. An old veteran, straight as an arrow, over six feet in height, and chief in his tribe, Joe Sebatis, managed the affair on behalf of the Indians.

In the evening all the available space around the platform was crowded with spectators to witness the Indian dance! The tall trees and bushes which completely surrounded the platform held numerous lamps, reflecting their light upon the band of swarthy warriors which now occupied its centre. Dressed in full costume with embroidered belts, each bearing a knife, and surrounding their chief, at a given signal the dance commenced. Facing inward, with a low guttural sound, they moved in a circle around their chief, keeping time with the motion of his hand, in which was held a powder-horn, carved and decorated, containing shot. Gradually their movements and utterances became quicker and louder, until they began to appear like very demons.

A panic in the crowd seemed imminent, when Joe, coming to me, said : "William, better stop! young Indian getin clazy !" (crazy). Their savage nature had really begun to assert itself, and this exhibition made quite evident to our senses the influence that may be brought to operate on untutored minds.

I had known Joe for many years at Fredericton. He was one of the leading spirits in the New Year's festivals at Government House, continued as late as Sir John Harvey's time, — and had won many prizes as an athlete and good shot.

Paddling his canoe on one occasion, as we passed up the river, he pointed to a grove of spruce trees just above the Government house, and said that his father, with the governor and other chiefs of the tribe, had, many years ago, made a treaty with the British Government, giving, for a consideration, all the land below that line. The grove referred to was on the bank of the River St. John and was an Indian burial-place. I have often seen in that grove, when a boy, rude crosses and marks of Indian graves.

The British officer in command of the detachment at Woodstock, Lieut. Thos. Wickham, entered fully into the spirit of the sports, and gave us the assistance of soldiers when help was required.

Chapter x

Early History of New Brunswick Indians.

IT may be a question whether the written or unwritten history of this country will be to its future historian of the greater value.

The red men have passed away, leaving no trace or record behind them. When stones were being worn by attrition to form the shingle we find deposited on Chapel Hill at Woodstock, the Indian may have called to his fellow on opposite mountain top, or witnessed in the sixteenth century the earthquake which formed, of a chain of lakes, the River Saint John. The subsidence of these lakes, now marked by stream or rivulet, form the islands and intervales so much admired for their beauty and fertility. The water line is easily traced on the mountain sides, and gives evidence of the physical geography of this section of the country in centuries past.

The Meduxnakic river occasionally pursues the course of its ancient channel around the head of Bull's Island, and through the lower end of this island is plainly seen the channel formed by Smith's Creek, when the island was a part of the mainland. Within our own recollection, a large piece of land has been severed from Major Raymond's intervale, forming an island.

The island opposite Woodstock has, until quite recently, been a favorite camping ground of the Indians. The bark canoe, a beautifully formed water craft, was the only means of transport for the Indian and his family, and with water at a stationary higher level, the portages were comparatively light and easy.

The Milicete Indians were very numerous along the St. John, whose waters afforded them abundance of fine salmon, and its tributaries provided them with beaver, otter, mink and other valuable fur.

The old Indian trail or line of communication with the United States touched the St. John River at the Meductic, and was by portages from the St. John via Eel River, thence by lake and stream to the waters of the Penobscot. An old man, George Tompkins, recently deceased, who lived near Woodstock, stated to me that in his younger days he, with other residents, had conveyed peltry by this route to the United States. The point of departure was about nine miles below Woodstock. Here a very strong palisade fort was erected by the Milicetes, and its remains are still visible. It was, at the time referred to, the headquarters of the tribe on the St. John. The governor and several hundred Indians occupied the fort. The whole country was then known as "Acadia," and the seat of government was at Halifax.

In a lecture delivered in the Woodstock Mechanics' Institute, by Judge John Bedell, the following circumstance, which occurred when the judge was a small boy, was related by him :

"With a view to extend the settlement of the
"country, two commissioners were sent from
"Halifax to make a treaty with the Indians.
"They were poled up the river by two men in a
"canoe from Fredericton. Approaching the Me-
"ductic at nightfall, they became alarmed at the
"huge fires burning near the fort, and the un-
"earthly yelling of the semi-nude Indians, dancing
"around them. Passing quietly by, on the oppo-
"site side of the river, they proceeded to the
"house of my father (J. Bedell, Esq.,) a few miles
"father on, where they were entertained for the
"night. On the following day I was permitted
"to accompany my father and the commissioners
"to the fort. Arriving at the entrance, the com-
"missioners made known the object of their visit.
"Presently a number of stalwart men presented
"themselves, dressed in gorgeous attire. After
"salutations, the commissioners asked : ' By what
"right or title do you hold these lands ?' A tall,
"powerful chief, standing erect, and, with the air
"of a plumed knight, pointing within the walls of
"the fort, replied : 'There are the graves of our
"grandfathers ! There are the graves of our
"fathers ! There are the graves of our children !'"

What language more eloquent ? Because the

simple language of the heart! What better title than that of possession? They had been able to defend that sacred dust for generations past.

Within my own time and recollection I have seen some of these children of the forest exhibit an ease and freedom of manner and a nobility of character becoming to true princes of the land.

A great blot on our national escutcheon was the introduction of that false type of civilization, *fire water*, which has swept, as with a besom of destruction, from a country once their own, a noble race.

THE DESTRUCTION OF THE MOHAWKS AT GRAND FALLS.

Written by request for *The Aboriginal*, published in St. John.

It is to be regretted that more has not been written by the early settlers of this Province descriptive of the habits, manners and customs of the aborigines whilst in a primitive condition, before being demoralized by a so-called civilization.

The writer, when a boy, took great delight in being paddled in a bark, deftly handled by Joe Sebatis. Joe was a tall, powerful Indian, straight as the arrow which he projected with deadly precision, and possessed that frankness and nobility of character which made him call and feel the white man "brother." Differing from many of the Melicite tribe. Joe was communicative, and although many years have passed, and the old Indian, we trust, safely moored in the happy hunting ground, his voice and manner are still with me, and, as you request, I will give you his version of "the first descent of the hated Mohawks" on the River St. John.

The Mohawks, *alias* "Iroquois," had their habitations along the banks of the Mohawk River. The Mohawk was a powerful tribe, and, by frequent extended incursions, became a terror to all other tribes. I have seen a Melicite Indian jump at the name being suddenly uttered. The battles between the Mohawks and Micmacs on the Atlantic Coast, or St. Lawrence, were frequent and fierce, but the Mohawks were always the victors. The St. John River and its tributaries had not as yet been paddled by these terrible warriors.

At the close of the season, the hunters of the Milicete tribe had returned, laden with rich furs, to their fort at the Meductic. In the midst of a scene of wild revelry, as they danced around the huge fires outside the fort, a strange, weird sound and form seemed to rise from the water of the river : "Mohawk ! Mohawk !" It was a woman's voice of the Milicete's tribe—faint, but distinct.

The blood of the braves seemed for an instant to be frozen ; but one, bolder than the rest, dashed to the river-side, and, aided by the light of the distant log fire, saw in a canoe the squaw of one of their braves, who, alas! was never more to return. "Mohawk!" was the only word she had strength to utter, but it had a talismanic effect, and she was rapidly borne in strong arms within the walls of the fort.

The gates were instantly closed and barricaded, and every preparation made for defence, before she had sufficiently recovered to make known her thrilling adventure.

A voyage in a bark canoe with a sober, intelligent Indian — and there are a few still remaining — up the Tobique River or Little Madawaska to the Lake is exceedingly enjoyable. The deep shades of the primitive wilderness, where it has not been desolated by fires, is awe-inspiring from its very loneliness, and a relief to those who can for a time escape the busy hum and anxious care of every-day life.

The Temiscouata Lake, still nearly surrounded by a dense wilderness of bold highland, bore on its surface 500 warriors in canoes, which, carried overland on their shoulders from the St. Lawrence, were now stealthily but vigorously pushed towards the *deigle* or outlet of the lake.

Arriving at early dawn, they surprised in a wigwam a Milicete hunter with his family. Saving the mother only, hunter and children were instantly killed. Placing the woman as a guide in a canoe between two chiefs, they entered the river and commenced its descent.

As they approached the Falls, on the Little Madawaska, near its confluence with the St. John, she signified that a portage must be made, as they were impassable by water.

Re-embarking on the St. John, exhausted by previous exertion, and learning from the guide that there were no more falls, they slept, and drifted with the tide. As they approached in the darkness the cataract (Grand Falls), the Milicete woman with her hand quietly paddled the canoe toward the shore, and gliding over its side, pushed it gently into the current. Hastening to a rock overlooking the "cauldron of waters," and just before the canoes descended the pitch, she gave the Milicete "war whoop." The snapping of the paddles and shouts of the stalwarts were drowned in the roar of the tumult of waters. One canoe alone remained from the wreck, to carry the maniac Indian woman to her home and tribe.

EARLY SETTLERS OF WOODSTOCK AND VICINITY.

The earliest settlers of Woodstock and vicinity were men true and loyal to their sovereign, choosing, rather than live under the American flag, to endure the hardships of pioneer life in the wilderness. They left "their foes their all for a home in a British land."

The land granted to and occupied by the first settlers is embraced in the district from Bull's

Creek to the farm of the late Col. Ketchum, inclusive, in the order as follows: Captain Bull, Parson Dibblee, Major Griffiths, John Bedell, Esq., William Dibblee and mother, John D. Beardsley, Michael Smith, Captain Smith, Captain Cunliffe, John Baker, Col. Ketchum. These properties, or portions of them, are still in possession of their descendants.

The church erected by those people was, for a long time, the only place of resort for religious services, and to that old churchyard now cling associations and memories dear to many.

Captain Smith's property extended from Wm. Smith's upper line to Hayden's mill. His residence was near the mouth of the Meduxnakic. He was a stern old warrior, and had many bouts with the Indians when they were under the influence of *buc-ta-witch*, or fire water.

On one occasion when overcome by them, and his family driven from their home, his daughter, a little girl, secreted herself on an island which covered the rocks now visible above Craig & Rankin's mill. This little girl was the first white child born in the Parish of Woodstock, and the respected and amiable wife of the late James Upham, Esq.

Later on, Captain Smith built a large two-story house on the lower side of the Meduxnakic, which has been but recently removed.

The Meduxnakic River abounded with salmon

and gaspereaux, and, as the stream at the site of
the present mill-dam was unnavigable for canoes,
they were dragged —- said the late Mr. James
Sharp — over windfalls and logs rolled down from
the clearing above, and filling to the shore the
space of the now King street and surroundings.

Highway roads are a comparatively modern institution in Carleton County. The River St.
John was the great thoroughfare. Many will remember Capt. Phillips' and other houses fronting
in that direction. A road being at length grubbed
out from Colonel Ketchum's to the church, the in-
genuity and skill of that gentleman was exhibited
on a fine Sunday morning to the good people
assembled for worship, and we venture to assert
that the most modern construction of wagon
does not command a more glowing or favorable
criticism.

Besides frequent intermarriages in the families
above named, a relationship has now extended to
embrace some of the most respectable families in
the Province. The effect of an early transplant-
ing of the little colony of intelligent and educated
men, who feared God and honored the king, could
not be otherwise than beneficial to a less favored
community, and the urbane and genial manner of
their sons in the conduct of public business is not
forgotten. I have heard the name of a Dr. Larlee
as among the earliest settlers, and possessing skill
and reputation as a physician.

On the opposite side of the river, too, were many early settlers and worthy men whose descendants have made their mark. The sons of Charles Connell, Esq., have occupied distinguished positions in the Executive Council and Legislature of this Province, and were the largest land owners in the county.

The large flat or intervale opposite Woodstock was a pine grove, a favorite resort of the Indians who camped there in great numbers. Two Scotchman, named Sharp, camped on the shore at the foot of the island which bears their name, and were often aroused from their sleep by shouting and nearly nude redskins, as with blazing torches they raced homeward from the spearing ground at Grand Bar.

It is a wise policy of the British Government to plant in its colonies loyal men who have fought its battles and become inured to the dangers of "flood and field." The names of several of the settlements in Carleton County imply the regiments to which the land was alloted, and the three nationalities have vied with each other in answering to the call as defenders of their Queen and country. When in the year 1832 York was divided and Carleton erected into a separate county, the nucleus of three villages had been formed, Lower and Upper Corners with Creek *inter.*

Through the liberality of Colonel Ketchum in

presenting to the county a site for the erection of the county buildings, the shiretown was established at the Upper Corner, by the then governor, Sir Archibald Campbell.

The first store or place of business was opened by the Messrs. Bedell at Bedell's Cove, about three miles below the present town of Woodstock. Next in order was Captain Philips' at the old Sisson place, Col. Ketchum at the Upper Corner, and Perley & English at the Lower Corner.

The first grist mill was erected by Captain Smith near the mouth of the Meduxnakic, and later on the opposite side of the stream a saw-mill by one Fletcher.

There being no bridge, the creek, so-called, was forded at low water near its mouth, and, when higher, near Elisha Baker's, and thence by the only highway road, by Doherty's farm, to strike the present main road, a mile above the town.

The public will feel grateful to W. F. Dibblee, Esq., for permission given to make extracts from a very valuable paper before me, viz., the manifest of a ship conveying the first settlers from the United States to this Province. The paper is in fair preservation and the writing and orthography of more than a century ago, excellent. Its heading reads : " Return of the families, etc., embarked "on board the 'Union Transport,' Consett Wil- "son, master. Began at Huntington Bay, April "11th, and completed April 16th, 1783." The lines are clearly drawn, showing the number of males, females, children and servants in each family, also the profession or trade.

The first name is Tyler Dibblee, Stamford, Connecticut, attorney-at-law ; wife ; children over ten years old, three ; number under ten years, one ; servants, two. The total number 209, as follows : sixty-five signers, thirty-five women, fifty-nine children over ten years old, forty-eight children under ten years old, two servants.

Business or calling : farmers, thirty-six ; blacksmiths, two ; shoemakers, eight ; seamen, two ; refiner of iron, one ; mason, one ; carpenters, six ; wheelwright, one ; joiner, one ; cooper, one ; weaver, one.

The greatest number coming by this vessel settled in Kingston ; only two are known to have come up the St. John River, viz., John Baker, grandfather of the late Elisha Baker, and the late Seth Squires. Many of the names written in the manifest are familiar at the present day : Perley, Raymond, Picket, Bates, Burden, Wade, Boon, Scribner, Ferris, Jostlin, Marvin, Seamen, etc., etc.

Reverting to the lecture delivered by Judge Bedell on the early settlement of this Province, I again quote : " Nearly thirty years had elapsed from the conquest of Canada (capture of Quebec) before any permanent settlement was made in this Province. Though as early as 1804, De-

Monts, a French navigator, discovered and explored the Bay of Fundy, sailed into the River St. John, and took possession of the country for the crown of France, which, however, remained unoccupied, except by the aborigines, for more than 100 years. The king of France, Louis XIV., gave to his subjects the country from the mouth of the river upwards to the Madawaska, granted in Signiories; and it is a little curious that the names of those old Signiories are retained, such as the Kennebeccasis, Oromocto, Nashwaak, Meductic and Madawaska. Coming down to a later period, we find that in April, 1764, three individuals located themselves near the mouth of the River St. John, where the populous and flourishing city of that name has long since taken the place of the dense and almost impervious swamp, which at that time covered the entire face of the surrounding country, and where, from the borders of Canada to the shores of the Bay of Fundy, one vast unbroken wilderness spread itself upon every side.

CHURCHES AND SCHOOLS.

The first church, previously referred to as erected by the Episcopalians below the town of Woodstock, was for many years the only place of worship, and the settlers of all denominations assembled there for religious worship:

In 1834 was erected a Methodist Church, adjoining a parsonage yet standing below the railway station. The building was of short duration. A lady saw in a dream, or a vision, the steeple of this church fall, its extreme end touching a small house on the hill side above Hayden's mill. The steeple was not really made to extend so far, but a connection may be found in the fact that the house was consumed with its owner, one Daly, and a little later the church was also destroyed by fire. The first ordained Methodist minister appointed to the Woodstock circuit was the Rev. Mr. Joll. In 1836 a new church was erected on the ruins of the one destroyed, and for many years served the convenience of residents of the Lower Corner and Creek Village.

In the graveyard about the church rested the remains of many worthy people who had done pioneer work in this new country. My first "firing party" in Carleton County was over the grave of Captain Thos. Cunliffe, of loyalist descent, here buried.

About this time, 1836, was also erected in Woodstock an Episcopal Church and a Catholic Chapel. The former was rebuilt and modernized on the site of the present church, and its clear-toned bell was for many years the herald of joy or sadness.

The first Catholic Chapel erected was an unpretentious building, and, being after many years much enlarged, served as it does still, the purpose of a school-house. The frame of the present fine structure was considered, when erected, too large for the population or ability of the Catholic people to complete, but its elevated position and finish gave it an early place as a landmark in the rising and beautiful town of Woodstock.

There were in Carleton County, a half century ago, itinerant preachers, who visited sparsely settled districts and cheered the hearts of former members of the different churches. Some house would be named for the gathering of these isolated families, hence the term of "meeting house." The names of Father Killan and Elders Hartt and McMullin and others are held in grateful remembrance.

The first school-house erected in the village of Woodstock was situated under the hill below the Roman Catholic Chapel.

In those days, to Solomon's persuader was added the fool's cap, as a stimulus to higher attainment. On one occasion the dominie, a worthy man, Mr. McCausland, ornamented the head of a bright youngster, now an oldster in the town of Woodstock, and placed him in an elevated position. Home having stronger attractions, the youth fled, and, reaching the Meduxnakic bridge, fearlessly passed out on one of the stringers, the covering having been removed. Close in pursuit was the dominie, birch in hand. Posed on opposite stringers, midstream, above the running water, and to the delight of an admiring crowd, stood master and pupil. The junior actor is well qualified, if he will, to embellish this fragment.

SOCIAL AND MILITARY ORGANIZATIONS.

Among the earliest social organizations was the Woodstock Musical Club in 1840-41, composed of a number of enterprising and spirited young men of Woodstock and vicinity. Music in this case, as in many others, moved the bolt that held in abeyance the most healthful aspirations of our nature, and there sprang almost immediately into existence public concerts, picnics, bazaars, and a Mechanics' Institute, in all of which the club rendered gratuitous and signal service. As another evidence of the effect of music, a worthy and intelligent Scot, living in Jacksontown, five miles distant, remarked: "Noo that we can hear the big drum, life's more tolerable in the woods." Foster, an American, was the musical instructor, and manipulated skilfully brass, reed and other instruments. His taste was of a high order and his lectures ever pleasing and instructive.

The spirit of loyalty, which had long slumbered in the hearts of our people, but rudely awakened by the threatened invasion by our Yankee neighbors, now acquired a tangible form in the organization of volunteer corps in Woodstock. A well-mounted and uniformed troop of cavalry, under

the command of Captain Frederick Morehouse ; a
battery of artillery, also uniformed and well up in
gun drill, was commanded by A. K. S. Wetmore ;
and a company of rifles, under the command of R.
S. DeMill, were annually assembled with the company of regulars for inspection and to fire on the
Queen's Birthday a *feu de joie.*

BUSINESS CENTRES.

The principal business centre for many years
was Bedell's Cove. A row of Lombardy willows,
silent sentinels of a century, still mark the site of
a once busy mart on the river bank. A tow-boat,
drawn by horses, was the only means of transport
in those days ; and the ice on the broad river in
winter time the only highway road.

As late as 1842, the Registrar's office, — G. A.
Bedell, registrar of deeds and wills, — was at
Bedell's Cove ; also a large hotel or tavern kept by
Pratt, an American. A large lumber business
was here conducted for many years by John and
Walter Bedell, which firm at a later date removed
their business to the Meduxnakic, erecting a large
saw-mill at its mouth.

The business firm of Perley & English was
established at the Lower Corner about the year
1830, and was soon followed by the custom house,
H. E. Dibble collector ; hotel by Stephen Tracy ;
store by R. S. DeMill ; blacksmith shop by R. A.

Hay ; tannery by Stephen Parsons ; carriage making by Deacon Grey.

In 1836 was incorporated the "Woodstock Stage Coach Company," one of the best lines in the Province. In 1841, the company having by this time sunk £1,000 in the operation, sold out to J. R. Tupper, under whose judicious management, as proprietor, the line was continued for more than twenty-five years.

Old residents will remember the handsome fours-in-hand, and some of the rollicking *whips* of those coaching days, — Thompson, Turner and others.

The river was twice crossed by ferry between Woodstock and Fredericton, at Burgoyne's and again at Rogers', five miles below Woodstock. At a later date the road was opened through on the western side of the river. It was not an uncommon thing to see fifteen or more passengers upon the coach who had enjoyed a full day's ride from Fredericton, and all for one pound currency.

Several places of business were now opened at the Creek, the principal of which was by Jeremiah M. Connell. There are persons now living who remember when there were but three houses at the Creek.

The land between Baird's corner and Vanwart's brick building, extending in parallel lines to Allan's corner, was purchased by J. M. Connell for £400 ($1,600). Persons seeking to purchase land in fee simple at the present day will be able to estimate the increase in value.

The land from the late post office (Leighton's building) to river, bounded by King Street and boundary of mill privilege, was purchased by Richard English. Captain Smith was the owner of all this land, and in a lease given to William Walton of land on King Street the lessee is required to keep a good and sufficient fence around it.

A large two story house was erected by Richard Smith and occupied by himself and wife ; later, Mrs. Morehouse. The house and field remained intact until 1860, and embraced the land from Cable House corner to Dr. Connell's dwelling and thence to Chapel street.

As the population of the county increased a struggle for precedence became bitter between the villages, — a triangular duel, to which every editor in the county and many correspondents added a ruff.

After the removal of Charles Perley, R. S. DeMill and others to the creek, the Lower Corner dropped out of the fight.

A correspondent addressing the Fredericton *Head Quarters'* in 1847, after a preamble, writes : I will show the existing disparity between the two named places, Hardscrabble, the shiretown, and Woodstock Village, and leave the decision to any person possessed of ordinary understanding as to where the public buildings ought to be placed. The distance between these places is one and three-quarter miles.

		Woodstock.	Hardscrable.
Banks		2	...
Insurance offices		2	...
Public offices {	Clerk's office	1	...
	Registrar's office..	1	...
	Post office	1	...
Printing office		1	...
Attorneys offices		6	1
Stores and shops		20	2
Mechanics		35	3
Hotels		3	...
Licensed taverns		7	3
Dwelling Houses		120	30
Population		609	150
Places of worship		4	...
Physicians		3	...
Schools		4	1
Flour mill		1	...
Carding mill		1	...
Fulling mill		1	...
Double saw mill		1	...

The war of words came, in at least one instance, to blows, and many clever things in prose or poetry were written or said by the champions of either party. We may judge that all shades of color entered into the strife, from the following poetical effusion, sung to the tune of a then popular air, "Nancy Paul":

> " Two darkies met the udder day
>   Who lived in the suburbs of the town.
> One gem'ens name was Sambo Clay,
>   De udder white folks called Jim Brown.
> Dar woolly heads dey put togedder,
>   And rolled up de corners ob dar eyes,
> Like coons in a hollow tree in stormy wedder,
>   In plantive notes dis chorus cry :
>   Oh ! Scrabblehard, dy glory's past,
>   And disoblutions come at last ;
>   In dis shiretown I nebber will stay
>   Cause dar gwine to move de court house away."

There being at this time no lock-up house at the Creek, the trouble and expense of conveying violators of tho peace to the county jail may be imagined.

Many of the settlers being disbanded soldiers, to whom the British Government had distributed axes, agricultural implements, a supply of food for two years, and an allowance in money for the erection of buildings, went earnestly to work, and many fine farms, the result of their labor, may now be seen on the St. John River in possession of their children.   Others less persevering and less prudent, visited too frequently the lumber stores, where bills were soon run up, for tea, tobacco, prints and rum, large enough to swing the farm. One hundred per cent was the profit charged in those days, and to this more than to their own extravagance is attributed the result of their failure.

It is true that in some instances merchants

dealt harshly, if not dishonestly, with the struggling settlers, and compelled them to surrender for a small amount of indebtedness their farms, and thus they accumulated property which in time became valuable.

This story has been told too often not to be believed, that on it is still based in election times the cry of country vs. town. There is one point, however, that cannot be lost sight of,— the merchant had also difficulties to contend with : he was compelled to buy on credit an eight months' stock, as the river was seldom traversed by tow-boats between the months of November and July. He received from the farmers oats and pork, and from the operator lumber delivered on the bank of the river. At his expense and risk the lumber was rafted and run to St. John, where it ran the gauntlet of surveyors or middlemen. All cash advanced was at a heavy rate of interest, and the price of lumber by combination or otherwise was fixed at St. John.

St. John was the toe of the stocking into which everything ran, and there remained until it suited the supplier or purchaser. In the meantime twelve months had passed away, and often for a much longer time was the helpless country merchant suspended on *tenter hooks.*

The large or *pumpkin pine,* as distinguished from the sapling or smaller pine of the present day, was for many years the staple of this

Province. Groves of this noble tree, towering
above all the other trees of the forest, were found
in the intervales or flatlands of the St. John and
its tributaries.

The lumbering firm of Peters & Wilmot, at the
Tobique Rocks, transacted for many years the
largest lumbering business on the St. John ; but
this firm, like all others engaged in the business
came finally to grief.

Among the causes already named as making it
uncertain was the large quantity of Jamaica rum
consumed from the boss to the cook. Every lumber store was well supplied, and it was not an uncommon thing for the crew of a camp to continue
on a spree for a week at a time.

The merchant made a big thing on the rum,
but a shortage on lumber, as other shortages at
the present day from the same cause bring people
out at the little end of the horn.

The employment in woods or stream has no
doubt produced a hardy and self-reliant race of
Bluenoses ; but much cannot be said for the
morality of people necessarily absent from the
restraining influence of home and fireside.

THE FIRST BANK IN WOODSTOCK.

The first bank established in Woodstock, 1836,
was an agency of the Commercial, — J. M. Connell president, George F. Williams cashier. In

those days of heavy lumbering transactions, the bank was a great convenience to the public.

In 1846 the offices of the bank were in the upper story of a building on the site of one now occupied by Mr. Estey, harness maker, from whence an attempt was made to rob the bank by carrying off the iron safe with its contents. A hitch in the arrangement caused the safe to plunge and fall with a loud noise, and fixed itself in the wall and stairway. The robbers were compelled to decamp without any spoil, but not without leaving the marks of an old offender's work.

After running a course of about thirty years, the agency succumbed to mismanagement.

Chapter xi.

Carleton County Militia.

THE threatened invasion of New Brunswick by the State of Maine having aroused the military spirit of our people, and under a proclamation made by His Excellency the Lieutenant-Governor, brought into existence a battalion for active service, a staff of officers was appointed thereto from the First Carleton Militia, as follows, viz. :

STAFF.

John Dibblee, Major; R. Woodward, Adjutant; J. R. Tupper, Paymaster; LeBaron Botsford, Surgeon; Patrick Murphy, Quarter-Master.

CAPTAINS.

T. G. Cunliffe, James Ketchum, William McKenzie, C. M. Lauchlan, M. Giberson.

LIEUTENANTS.

R. Ketchum, J. A. C. Phillips, R. D. Beardsley, William McDonald, Henry Baird.

ENSIGNS.

C Wolhaupter, G. McKenzie, A. C. Bull, Charles Upton, G. S Tompkins.

With the exception of the volunteer companies, in the cities and towns of New Brunswick the military force was merely nominal. Radiating from these centres the spirited and intelligent young men did good service in organizing corps in outlying districts, as circumstances or necessity required it, or acting as non-commissioned officers at the three days' annual muster of the militia. The musters afforded much amusement, and were viewed more as holidays than for the practical purposes of drill.

An enterprising and ingenious officer in a rural district was said to have applied hay and straw to the pedals of a worthy yeoman to quicken and correct his movements in the goose step.

The roll being called, an attempt was sometimes made to move from column to line ; but woe to that officer whose company marched by or through a pumpkin field.

After the manner of the times, he was the best and most popular officer who treated to bread and cheese and produced the best-filled bucket.

My first military duty in Carleton County was as a private in Captain R. Ketchum's company of militia, and my military experience in the capital and garrison town of New Brunswick suggested unfavorable comment — mental, of course.

Before me is a well-preserved book, entitled "Order Book of Captain Ketchum's Company Embodied Militia, Fredericton, January 2nd, 1813." The records in this book are interesting from a military or historical point of view, and

refer to the period of an exciting struggle for
British supremacy in Canada, and the march from
the garrison at Fredericton of the New Brunswick
contingent, the gallant 104th Regiment.   The
book has passed through the hands of Captain
(later Lieutenant-Colonel) Ketchum and Lieutenant-Colonel Dibblee into mine as commissioner of
the First Carleton Militia, and contains the
militia record of each, severally, until the year
1866.   From it I extract as follows:

FREDERICTON, July 25th, 1843.

The Commissioner-in-Chief has been pleased to make
the following promotions, etc.:   Rifle Company attached
to First Battalion, Carleton County Militia: W. T. Wilmot, Captain, *vice* Demill, resigned; Henry Halsell to be
1st Lieutenant, *vice* Ketchum, superseded; W. T. Baird
to be 2nd Lieutenant, *vice* Halsell, promoted

(Signed)   GEORGE SHORE, A. G. M.
Dated July 25th, 1843.

The senior officers of the rifle company knowing
but little of their duty, I was requested to act as
drill instructor.   In a short time the company
was recruited to the strength of thirty men.

The other volunteer companies then in Woodstock were a troop of cavalry and a battery of
artillery.

The above corps with the company of regulars
stationed at Woodstock, and the Woodstock band,
attracted, on the Queen's birthday and on other

public occasions, large numbers of people from the surrounding country and very often from the border town of Houlton.

Our parade ground was the elevated level below the Meduxnakeag, called Chapel Hill.

At this period, arms and accoutrements only were supplied to the volunteers. A distasteful dark green coat, swallow-tail, with pants, forage cap, and a stiff leather stock for the neck, were offered and respectfully declined. The officers furnished their own uniforms and equipment complete, with occasional contributions towards those of the rank and file, paid for the repair of arms, and supplied ammunition, medals and lunches on gala days.

To be an officer was no sinecure, but the attempt made to keep alive a military spirit in the country was not altogether unsuccessful. A few years later when the penny-wise policy of the legislature permitted all military duty to fall into desuetude, the effect became apparent. The young people of both sexes in Carleton County, deprived of the social gatherings at the annual trainings and Queen's birthday celebrations, hied annually to Houlton, to join in the sports, listen to the fourth of July spread-eagle orations, and return more or less tinctured with American proclivities. This thought of the display of our Yankee friends on the *fourth* may have been prominent in the minds of our Dominion statesmen when they selected as our natal day the *first* of July.

TOWN OF HOULTON, U. S.

The residents of Houlton and officers of the garrison were frequent visitors to Woodstock. Beside the courtesies extended from and between the garrisons, social parties and dances were of frequent occurrence, and a waltz composed by Major McGruder, — a lion of the Mexican war, — Commandant of the Houlton garrison, was popular on either side of the line.

I well remember a grand military display at Fredericton in honor of a visit made by the great American General Scott to Sir John Harvey. These general officers were old antagonists and opposed to each other at the battles of Stony Creek and Sundy Lane in 1813 and '14, and the true spirit of the soldier was exhibited in the giving and in the acceptance of Sir John's invitation to visit him at Fredericton.

Houlton is situated about twelve miles west of Woodstock on the Meduxnakeag River, which runs through both of these towns. My first visit to this smart Yankee village was in the company of Parr Phillips, a young man I had met in Fredericton, then a clerk for his brother-in-law, G. E. Ketchum. He was a peculiarly pleasing young man, retiring in his manner, and a good performer on several musical instruments. From Mount Desert, later Davis' Boulevard, on summer evenings the surrounding hills and valleys often echoed duets from our key bugles; or, for our own amusement, with flute and clarionette in more retired places.

The first object of attraction for us in Houlton was the garrison. It was the hour of morning parade, and my first inspiration was to pull down the flag floating nearly over my head. As young soldiers, during the Aroostook war, we were looking for an opportunity of that kind, hence the inspiration.

The young and handsome face of the French horn player was familiar to us. He was a deserter from the regimental band at Fredericton. He was of a good family in England where he had enlisted, and was by his friends placed in the special charge of the colonel of the regiment.

Desertions were frequent from either side of the line. On a cold winter evening, a stage, or closely boxed up double sleigh, was observed, with a pair of horses attached, standing for some time in front of our house on George street, Fredericton. A neighbor of ours, John Russell, was the owner, and in charge. It was growing dark, when three men hurriedly entered the stage and it was driven rapidly away. After passing the government house, a pistol was placed to his head and he was told their aim was to reach Houlton and that he

must drive for his life.   Russell now saw that he
was in the hands of deserters, and the game
a desperate one.   He appeared to comply,
and as he approached Wheeler's, about twelve
miles from Fredericton, he said his horses must
have water.   Driving to the door of the tavern
he called loudly for water, and, as he expected,
the night being very cold, his passengers, dis-
guised in colored clothes, entered for a drink
The moments were precious.   He dexterously
turned his horses' heads and stage homeward,
and, aided by the darkness of the night and the
potency of the liquor, delivered his charge to the
guard at the barrack gate, Fredericton.   Russell
doubtless received a good reward for his loyalty
and clever apprehension.

I have frequently seen American deserters coming. into Woodstock.   On one occasion three men
in uniform, carrying their rifles.

Of all the commanding officers of regiments in
Fredericton during my time, none was more noted
than Colonel Eels, Rifle Brigade.   He was a
brusque, daring officer, leading his men through
field or wood, and topping gayly, on a staunch
brown hunting horse, fences or windfalls that
came in his way.   On occasions of this kind he
was not choice in his epithets to delinquents, but
was admired as a brave and gallant soldier.

Accepting an invitation from the officers, Colonel
Eels visited the garrison at Houlton.   With a sol-

dier's eye, he noted from the road on the summit of Park's Hill the defenceless condition of the barracks. A good dinner had been discussed and the best feeling pervaded the company. Some of the American officers were already under the table, when one of them asked the Britisher, jokingly, what would be his method of attack on that position. Eels replied instantly that he would "blow them to hades with bladders of Scotch snuff from the hill beyond."

The garrison was situated on the high plateau of land to the right as you enter Houlton, and the barrack buildings were flimsy wooden affairs.

The Hotel Hasey's and principal business stands in 1840 and later were a mile nearer to the boundary line than the present site of the town.

The hotel and much land was owned by "Uncle Jimmy Houlton," the father of the place, a genial old gentleman, with whom I had many interesting conversations regarding the first settlement of the country. He had many peculiarities, one in never using a negative. His refusal therefore was in the blandest style.

The population was made up largely of people from New Brunswick, driven hither by misfortune or choice, and much of its trade was derived from British people residing on the border, or more distant, where the duties saved would be an object.

A good understanding has always existed between the people of these border towns, and to the frequent social intercourse may in some measure be attributed the smartness and business tact which has given to Woodstock and Carleton County ascendancy over many other portions of the Province.

The principal business of the place was done by Sheppard Carey, an extensive lumber merchant, controlling a large district of territory in Maine.

The witty, clever writer and brother-in-law of Carey's, Collins Whittaker, was also his bookkeeper, and later United States consul at St. John.

Holman Carey, a brother, was a clever original in many ways and a wit. He was well known in Woodstock and on the River St. John. Some strangers with swell titles booked their names at the Bangor House. Holman also booked his, with the appendage L. O. R. This new order of rank arrested the notice of one of the strangers, and was informed that it read "Lumbering - On-roostic." Being asked how cold it was, he said it was thirty below, but would have been colder if the thermometer in Houlton had been longer.

NEW STORE ON KING STREET.

The lower flat of the house occupied as my residence being designed for two stores, and the principal part of the cash trade being done on King street, I decided to finish one of these and occupy it. Having now ample room, I extended my business to garden and field seeds, agricultural implements, etc., and improved the appearance and convenience of the interior of the shop by adding cases of drawers, soda font, with machinery for manufacturing soda water, marble counter, etc. In this shop was first suspended in Woodstock a lamp for burning Albertine oil. Up to that time fish oil only was burned in the large lamps.

Prescriptions to which I had been so long accustomed, ceased with the departure of Dr. Botsford for St. John.

A slight opposition was offered in the sale of medicines by Dr. Wood.

Up to this period there was no resident dentist in Woodstock, and, having learned to extract teeth from Gale, the key and forceps were in almost daily requisition and proved a considerable item in receipts.

I invested £25 in a leasehold lot on Main street at a rental of £5 per annum. I also purchased from my father-in-law for £200, and easy terms of payment, the upper part of his farm in Northampton — my present home, " Willowell "—erected a house and barn and put a tenant on the farm.

I also purchased a pair of young horses, and to the older children of our family " Charley " and " Sal " were for many years familiar names. With this team, on a comfortable sled, I made annual journeys for a number of years in the winter time

to Bangor or some of the towns in Maine for a
load of clover and timothy seed.

WOODSTOCK TO BANGOR ON SNOW.

There being no railways, Houlton and all the surrounding country were supplied with freight hauled
by teams from Bangor. The roads were, therefore,
from much travel in the winter time, well-broken,
and no more hospitable place could be conceived
of than a tavern on the Houlton and Bangor road.

After a journey of fifty miles to Rollins', you
drive inside the spacious barn, where the reins are
taken from you by an active hostler, who grooms,
blankets and beds your horses thoroughly. I always found a *tip* at the outset on such occasions
to be money well invested.

On entering the house you are greeted by a
roaring wood fire, your buffaloes (robes) are hung
up, and you lose no time in stripping and washing,
ing, for you are likely one of a hungry crowd.
The bell rings and you are led by the landlord to
the supper room. Everything to satisfy a hungry
man is here: ham and eggs, fowl, venison of
moose or deer (found within a few hundred yards),
pies, doughnuts, and the inevitable apple-sauce.
Implements all bright and clean, and after a day's
drive through the keen frosty air, a relish is found
in food, to which you may have been a stranger.
Supper over, we adjourn to the spacious room with

the big fire-place,—bar-room so called. Here, in an atmosphere of tobacco-smoke from the pipes of a score or less of teamsters, lumberers, or others like myself, is a good chance to study Yankee character. Some interesting recital of facts may cause you to linger for a time ; but the profanity, for which the Yankee teamster is proverbial, soon becomes offensive, and, after a look in the stable to see that oats are fed to your horses and that they are not tied too short to lie down, retire to sleep soundly. At four in the morning the house is astir, you breakfast by candle light, don your big coat and muffler, the familiar sound of the bell announces that your team is ready, and well wrapped in warm buffaloes, with a cheery word to your horses, they shoot off in the darkness. The keen air gives a "fillip" to their speed, and ere "Aurora" shoots forth in golden rays the glory of her coming, Jack Frost's tonsorial hand has changed an ebony hirsuteness into grey.

Returning from Milo by the "Piscataquis" on one occasion, I was compelled to tie my horses on a cold night outside of a hovel, sleep in an un-plastered room, through the openings of which the stars were seen, and the only food offered was heavy buckwheat cakes, vernacular "plugs," and tea, without milk, sugar, molasses, butter, or any-thing else whatever. The people in the usual stop-ping place beyond were ill with fever, and I took my chance in a longer drive.

VISIT TO HALIFAX.

From many years close confinement to business my health began to fail. At the suggestion of Dr. Walker, a kind old gentleman, I took the steamer for Windsor, Nova Scotia. I found on board Robert Ray, also his son Charles, afterwards Mayor of St. John. Ray senior was a person well known for his peculiarities, in particular by the negroes. I found him an intelligent and genial old gentleman.

The sea was rough, the night dark, and I lay in the berth, back and knees well braced to prevent my rolling out. In a short time I felt a sickness indescribable and I clambered from the berth to the floor; four grains of Antim. Tart. could not have produced a better effect; the relief was immediate.

The following morning, while waiting for the tide to go up to Windsor, we anchored off Cape Blomidon, and I spent, with other passengers, a few hours visiting the farmhouses in Parrsboro.

The following morning I visited the "plaster mines," and the premises of Judge Haliburton, *alias* "Sam Slick."

Solicited by Mr. Ray, I took the coach at 10 a. m. for Halifax, of which city he had been a former resident. The naval yard, armory, and sail loft was visited (Ray was a sailmaker); also the house in the naval yard, occupied by the brave

Captain Brock of "Shannon" celebrity, and the lawn on which, whilst convalescing after the battle with the "Chesapeake" in Boston harbor, he was attacked by a savage bull and saved from severe injury or worse by the sentry.

I also crossed in the ferryboat to Dartmouth and examined some of the solid and extensive masonry in that great but mistaken enterprise, the "Shubenacadie Canal." A road skirting a large sheet of water called the "Basin" afforded a delightful drive to the Haligonians, and near the shore was pointed out to me a ruin — a few columns only — of Grecian architecture, called the "Prince's Lodge," at one time occupied by the father of Queen Victoria.

I had the pleasure of being present in the square at the morning parade of one or two British regiments stationed in Halifax, and purchased in the city a fine steel blade — a rifle sword — which has been much admired.

There being then no railway conveyance, I returned by coach to Windsor, thence across the country to Horton and Kentville. My travelling companions were a Mr. Binny, of Halifax, and his friend, a portly and jovial southern gentleman. Was visited here by two young men, W. A. Chipman and Charles Starrit, formerly clerks in Woodstock, and with whom I was well acquainted. They insisted on my accompanying them on the following day in a drive across and down the opposite side of the great marsh from Kentville, crossing again at the dyke near Horton. This section of Nova Scotia is called the garden of Nova Scotia, and is truly one of the most productive and beautiful places that I have ever seen. Pears and various kinds of fruit of fine quality are grown here, and in the old French orchards many of the trees resemble in size the trees of the forest.

On Monday morning at three o'clock we again entered the coach, our number increased by one lady passenger. We arrived safely at Annapolis in the afternoon. The only person I knew there was a professor of the college, an old friend, the Rev. George McCauley, but time would not permit my making him a visit. Embarking, we steamed away for Digby and St. John. Having had but little sleep the two previous nights, I was soon wrapped in the arms of Morpheus, and before reaching St. John discovered that we had taken a number of cattle on board at Digby, but of which I was happily ignorant.

Shortly after my return home I found my health very much improved, and was soon able to extend my walks to Upper Woodstock, a distance of two miles.

A DEER HUNT, 1846.

I often visited Lieutenant Wickham's quarters while stationed in Woodstock. He was a man of agreeable manner, temperate habits, good physique, and a lover of music, playing the cornet very well. Anxious to see something of the wild woods of America, and hearing of a place where deer might be found, we set off one bright morning, fully equipped, for the O'Donnell Settlement. Arriving at one of the most remote houses (Dougherty's), the horse hoveled, and ourselves regaled with Mrs. Dougherty's fresh eggs and hot barley cake, we mounted our snowshoes, and each carrying on our backs from forty to sixty pounds of food and camp equippage, entered the woods. Our guide and escort was a young lad, Dougherty's son, and his dog.

Descending from the high land to the Pocamonshine, a tributary of Eel River, the bound of the wolf on its snowy level surface, showed plainly where poor puss met her fate, and the fragments — hair only — the fierceness of the onslaught.

Pursuing our course down the stream until near nightfall, we prepared to camp for the night. Using our snowshoes for shovels, we dug a hole about six feet square and as many deep. As I chopped into logs the nearest birch tree, Wickham twitched with his comforter, and tumbled them into our nest for the night's fuel. Seated on our narrow couch of fir boughs and blanket, generous slices of bread and bacon having been disposed of, we sip from our tin cups a hot infusion of the fragrant herb, and discuss the merits of winter camp life in New Brunswick.

It was a clear, cold, windy night in March, the branches of a projecting tree our only covering. From our slumbers, not the soundest, we were frequently aroused by the howling of the wolves, whose curiosity, we thought, might give practice to our revolvers before the morning light.

While the stars were yet twinkling, our fire, which had penetrated the swamp a foot or more below our level, was re-kindled, another attack was made upon the edibles, and we were ready for the tramp. A little farther down the stream, we observed on a mountain side a growth of birch and other browse-supplying trees, and proceeded to ascend. Snowshoeing on a steep hillside while a hot sun is shining upon it, causing the snow to load and melt upon your snowshoes, is a test of both the patience and physical endurance of the hunter. This was our experience for a short time, when heart and load were lightened by a discovery: we had struck a deer-yard! The yard is a number of paths through the snow in a thick growth of hard wood, constantly traversed by animals, from which they can reach the lower branches and obtain food during the winter. Observing our course from the most recent marks of the animal, we throw off all encumbrance and start in pursuit. Following the yelp of our small terrier is the bound of a fine buck. After an exciting chase, the beautiful creature takes from a firm footing its final leap into the deep, soft snow, where it lies helpless and powerless. As we stood around the poor captive, its dark, lustrous eye spoke to me what I cannot forget, nor will I attempt to write.

The extra garments, *peeled* off during the chase, being collected, and a double load for myself, which now was lightly borne, we turned toward the clearing. Wickham led off, adopting a con‑venient method of carrying the buck : belly around his neck, with fore and hind legs extended in front and held by either hand. From its neck the blood dropped into his pocket, from which a handkerchief was occasionally taken to wipe his perspiring face.

Before night we arrived safely at the cabin. Wickham, who had been leading, entered first. As the door opened, a prolonged howl from Mrs. Dougherty startled us, the only distinguishable word being "murther !" On entering, I immedi‑ately discovered the cause of her alarm. Wick‑ham's face was smeared with blood ! The effect was heightened by the ragged appearance of his Kossuth, through which I had that morning fired two minnie bullets, before leaving the camp. A reviver, not of the ardent, but of good Congou, with solids, for which we had a relish, fortified us for the home stretch.

With Wickham and our trophy on the upper side of the sleigh, the roads being sideling, I, of less avoirdupois, took the lower and the reins, and after a merry ride, reached Woodstock without mishap.

Chapter xii

Smuggling.

THE word boundary in a national sense is usually a synonym for smuggling. Forty years ago, twenty-five cents on a pound of tea, twenty-five cents a yard on silk, or one dollar on a cooking stove might have been taken as the measure of the loyalty of the inhabitants on either side of the line in the vicinity of Woodstock or Houlton. Forty-five years ago the article of tea could not be imported into the Province from the United States. It was contraband. The profits of forty cents a pound was a temptation not to be resisted, hence the mettle of Harry Dibble's well-known roan horse was often tested in an exciting chase.

There were professional smugglers in those days, two Americans at Hardscrabble, and an old Hibernian on the Houlton road. No Russian system of espionage could be more perfect. The argus eye of the custom house officer failed many times to detect the concealed trophies of the bold smuggler, yet customs' sales were not unfrequent, and horses, wagons and contents were brought under the hammer.

ROWDYISM.

In the year 1837, and for many years later, the population of Woodstock was largely increased during the summer by idle, drunken and disorderly lumbermen. The civil force was often found inadequate to quell the riots of frequent occurrence on the streets ; hence a requisition was made by the magistracy of the county asking that a company of soldiers be stationed at Woodstock for the preservation of peace and the protection of its inhabitants.

An order having been issued to the commander-in-chief, a company of regular troops from the regiment then stationed at Fredericton proceeded to Woodstock. The officers were jolly, good fellows, and it cannot be said that Woodstock of that day was demoralized by the presence of troops. The officers were Captain Coate, Lieutenants Gore and Hazelen, and Doctor Irvine. Paddy Gore, familiarly, was an exceedingly clever fellow and a great favorite. As a wit and athlete, his peers were few in number, and, but for an enemy common to the British army, might have reached high distinction in the service. The officers were sociable and friendly with the people, and an interchange of civilities with the officers of the garrison of Houlton was of frequent occurrence. The moral effect of the presence of the little garrison stayed for a time the brutality and excess of the rougher element, but it had yet to be crushed.

These were the days of whiskey galore. Many sold it; nearly everybody drank it. But in the light of those days it was considered a harmless thing, and but few persons stopped to consider whether it might not be the cause of much of the riot and wretchedness it has since been found to produce. Among the vendors some fifty years ago was one Tom Gray. A person might almost step upon the roof of his shanty, situated at the west end of the now Vanwart brick building. From this place two soldiers were pitched, badly mangled, into the street. It was on some public occasion, and there were many people in town. Water (now King) street was thronged, the rowdy element in the ascendant. Strong, lusty men, in red shirts, brandished clubs and axe-handles. The air was filled with shouting and disorder. Presently a sub-division front of the soldiers, filling Water street from side to side, was seen advancing at the double with fixed bayonets. The crowd was not slow to discover that the red-coats meant business, and as leaves eddy and whirl before the thunder storm, so did the valiant (?) crowd disappear, rushing into front doors, cellar doors, and alley ways to escape the thrust of the bayonet. Pricking the building and front of stores occupied by Joshua Snow and Harrison & Jewitt (on the site of the Lynch building), the word "right about" was given by Sergeant Tracey, the non-commissioned officer in command of the sub-division, which marched quietly to its quarters. The majesty of the law was asserted, but the end was not yet. As gold excites the cupidity of men and attracts them to the opposite ends of the earth, so other minds, peculiarly constituted, are attracted by the "pomp and circumstance of a glorious war."

The concentration of troops at Woodstock, and the prospect of its being the headquarters of active military operations, should Maine insist upon her demand to advance her north-easterly boundary, brought to its principal hotel (Mrs. Grover's), among other newspaper correspondents, an officer of the British army, and late of the "Royal Irish." He was a man of good physique, had seen a good deal of the world, was a clever writer, and made no effort to conceal his Irish proclivities. He was intensely Irish, therefore a wit and a good judge of poteen, or mountain dew. The rank and social condition of many officers of high position in the British army he had at his finger ends, and he was an authority on all military matters. He joined with the young men in everything, and his rendering of the code of honor was sincerity itself. Words hastily spoken at the card table, or under other exciting influences, were no palliation. The word "gentleman" could to his mind bear no pollution by distinction, and,

as the fruit of this teaching, there occurred two
duels and other more disastrous results from the
use of his favorite weapon, the pistol.　The scene
of their "affairs of honor" was a small lake, now
visible as you approach the boundary line on the
Houlton road, but at that time concealed by a
dense forest.　The first of these was "taken off"
by an exceedingly clever writer in the Woodstock
Times.　I meet persons every day who can recall
the characters and principal actors in the scene, as
Count Bust-a-marki, Mustapha Mushface, Doctor
Wiggle-spoke and others.

The war ended, the gallant dragoon returned to
his now unincumbered estate, when married and
with a happy family about him, he may sing with
greater gusto the song of "Honest Jack Dwyer of
Stradbally Hall."

ORANGE RIOT OF 1847.

History is an account of facts, particularly
facts respecting nations or states : a narrative of
events in their choronological order, with their
causes and effects.　The events of life, grand or
simple, when recorded, are matters of historical
importance, as illustrating the life, character and
condition of a people at the period of their occurrence.　He who fails, from what cause soever, to
give a truthful narrative is unworthy the name
of an historian.

The population of Carleton County having been largely increased, and the Protestant element in the ascendant, watchful politicians were not slow to discover the necessity for a change of base.

Several merchants of Woodstock, — Irishmen, — formerly pedlars, who had made house to house visitations in the country, had considerable influence, which, up to this time, had been exerted in support of one political party. The boundary of the county, moreover, extended to the Province of Quebec, and embraced a large French population. The preponderance of Roman Catholics, therefore, from a political standpoint, made two things necessary, viz. : 1st. To separate the French from the English by dividing the county ; 2nd. To unite in one body the Protestants by organizing orange lodges. This latter bold stroke of policy was not an experiment in the Province ; the astute politicans of York had already proved it a success. That riots and animosities would be the result, or that former friends and supporters would be alienated, were points quite secondary and not to be considered with possible defeat by adherence to the old *regime.*

> " When self the wavering balance holds,
> 'Tis seldom well adjusted."

How to rule the Irish is up to this moment an enigma which no British Parliament has been able to solve. When Pitt said, "Let us divide the

Irish !" he splits in two parts a nation which, united, might have rent the Empire. The blow struck by a solid phalanx of expatriated Irishmen, breaking through Marlborough's line of battle at Blenheim, is but one example. In "field or forum" all down through the centuries, Irishmen have taken a first place in the affairs of Great Britain. From peculiar characteristics they are both loved and feared, and when the above sentence was uttered by the far-seeing Pitt, he may, as a statesman, have but chosen the least of two evils.

The worst use of power is its abuse, and this is an Irish failing. In Carleton County on election days respectable men, natives of the country, were beaten and abused. From this and similar causes, Protestants became exasperated, and the way paved for the introduction of a new political era.

One of the first to become an Orangeman was a well known resident of the town of Woodstock, by birth a Scotch Russian, a man of intelligence and good physique. A brother of the sitting member also joined the order and a charter having been obtained they proceeded to organize a lodge. The old country Orangemen rallied at the call, and with new recuits the number was increased to sixty or eighty.

An announcement that the Orangemen would walk as a body in Woodstock on the approaching 12th of July, put the Irish Catholics of the town and county on the *qui vive.* It soon became evident that a violent attempt would be made to crush this organization in the bud, and as the day approached, many rumors were afloat as to the strength and efficiency in drill of the opposing force.

A bright sun ushered in the morning of the 12th, presaging a day of intense heat. At an early hour the possession of Orangemen marched from their hall in Mallory Raymond's building direct to a Baptist Church in Jacksontown, about three miles distant.

While attending this service, and absent from the town, a body of men, numbering about three hundred, many of them strangers from the United States, marched through the principal streets in good form, armed with guns, swords, scythes, pikes. From this body a detachment was sent to remove from a raft floating down the river a yellow flag or handkerchief flying thereon, which was done.

They were then marched to the upper end of the town, where they were placed in position along the crest of the hill, where the Orange Hall now stands, parallel with and about fifty yards distant from the highway road. The commander was a Woodstock man, and in the ranks were several members of the Woodstock Rifle Company, among whom was a sergeant and the best shot in the company.

As the Orangemen were returning they were met on the road near Mr. Fisher's residence, halted by the magistrates and the Riot Act read. The Act had just previously been read to the opposing party. Three cheers being given for the Queen, they re-form and are ordered to advance.

The Catholics, lying flat upon the ground, with muzzles pointing to the road, waited.

In the meantime, the company of regulars stationed at Woodstock, under the command of Lieutenant Wickham, was ordered to take a position on the left front and at right angles with the line of the attacking party.

The long-looked for moment has at last arrived. The hated Orangemen are covered with deadly weapons, and the air is rent by a volley from the hills.

But the fire is not returned ; the party attacked is not permitted to carry arms. They appear to retreat, but are rushing to wagons in rear of the procession, where arms had been provided.

Now, armed with muskets and bayonets, they make no pause to fire, but dash with irresistible energy up the slope, bayonet some and capture many.

The flight and pursuit is continued through bush and field towards the Houlton road ; those not taken prisoners, crossing over the Meduxnakic on a jam of logs.

The Regulars received no orders from the magistrates to fire, therefore took no part in the fray; but the moral effect of fifty loaded rifles, while encouraging the attacked, must have made nervous and shaky the hands of the assailants.

The casualities were several severely wounded on both sides; none were found to have been killed.

A large man, active in the fight from No. 11 Township, United States, was shot through the lungs and carried to a lodging house, from which, in woman's garb, he was *stolen away* by his friends from over the lines.

An Orangeman shot through the thighs was immortalized in verse by a rustic bard, thus:

> "Brave Kerrigan charged up the hill,
> And cried out 'No Surrender!'
> But Jim McCabe fired off his gun
> And shot the legs off Camber."

These men, first and last named, were blacksmiths, having well known smithies in Woodstock. Kerrigan was Irish, Camber a New Brunswicker.

The remarks of the editor of a Woodstock paper on the occasion of the removal of the troops, in the October following the riot, read as follows: "It was with no small degree of regret that we witnessed the departure on Tuesday morning last of Lieutenant Wickham and the detachment of the 33rd Regiment under his command. A finer body of men and more orderly and correct in their deportment was never stationed in this garrison."

On October the 16th before the troops left, the magistrates and other inhabitants of the town presented the officer in charge of the detachment with a very appreciative address, expressive of the value of the services rendered by the regiment to the community during the riot and throughout their stay in Woodstock ; to which a very cordial reply on behalf of himself and regiment was made by Lieutenant Wickham.

PROHIBITORY LIQUOR LAW.

A prohibitory bill was passed by the Provincial Legislature of New Brunswick in 1855, for the suppression of the sale of intoxicating liquors. The legislation though wisely conceived was found to be in advance of public opinion. The immediate overthrow of S. L. Tilley and others then in power was the result.

To educate and prepare public opinion Divisions of Sons of Temperance were organized in many parts of the Province. The first organized in Woodstock was named " Carleton Division," No. 19, enrolling a large number of members. A little later, I united with others as charter members of " Melancthon Division," No. 34, in which I spent many pleasant hours, and to which many poor unfortunate inebriates were indebted for their delivery from the all pervading destroyer. A large number of men being employed at the iron foundry, Upper Woodstock, the Melancthon Division was removed to that place, and in a short time received from that source large accessions. Besides discharging its duty faithfully as a benefit society, its members were the principal motors in the erection of the spacious building at Upper Woodstock for a school and public hall.

The more important work for the members of the Division seemed to be the reformation of talented and influential men, whose example was producing a most damaging effect. To this end individual members and deputations exerted themselves, and the result was a most valuable addition of intelligent and useful members, the balance of whose lives were devoted to the cause, and who died honored and respected in the community in which they lived.

No great moral reform can be effected without exciting the ire of the vile and vicious. Temperance men supporting the authorities in the enforcement of the law, were met and overcome by ruffians, excited by drink, and individual property damaged or destroyed by fire to an extent that may never be known. In revenge and to punish an energetic marshal of the town, his workshop on Main Street was fired by a drunken tramp, and nearly all the business part of the town laid in ashes.

At a later date, a fine block of brick buildings on King Street, including the " Renfrew House," a large hotel, in which was invested the value of all I possessed, was destroyed by fire. A drunken vagrant was charged with firing a barn, which caused the destruction of the hotel and other valuable property.

Thus, although not directly in contact with these unfortunate miscreants, I was made to feel the terrible power and influence that has so long cursed the earth.

At this distant day, I recall with pleasant memory evenings spent in the Division. Of the well-read and thinking members were A. K. S. Wetmore, A. N. Garden and L. P. Fisher, lawyers; Judge Bedell, Richard Dibble, Joseph Harvey, sr., Samuel Watts and others; and of intelligent mechanics and farmers, D. J. Day, Hugh Cowperthwaite, H. Emery, A. Broderick, Buxton, Black and others. There were also, connected with the iron foundry, David Munro and others.

Many of the above named were clever debaters, and beside being an excellent training school for young speakers, the duties of the various offices in the Division, based on parliamentary practice, imparted a confidence and manner useful in after life. Perhaps there is no society in which is presented more varied phases of humanity than this.

The tavern-keeper, drinker, and some time Bible-reader, was portrayed by the inimitable Black, with Irish pleasantry; and Buxton, with Welsh accent, related his terrible periodical

struggle with Satan, *alias* Appetite, before a surrender.

Some one has said, "let me write the ballads of
a people and I care not who makes their laws."

THE RUMSELLERS' MARCH

was written by request, and embraced licensed
and surreptitious sellers of the ardent in 1853.
The shaft of ridicule often pierces more deeply than
law or logic ; and the song, having become popular,
had in this case the effect of closing up four of the
illicit dens in Woodstock.

Air, "*Blue Bonnets.*"

March, march, Urbin and Stave-in-son !
  Why my lads don't you march forward in order?
March, march, regiments of ragged boys,
  Rummies galore from the Creek to the Corner.

There's Pat at the alley, and further up Sally ;
  Then Michael, the Autocrat; Johnny, the daisy ;
Mrs McGee sure will say "tisn't me, sur"
  Then Tom, by the Town Pump, and Martin, the lazy.
March, march, Urbin and Stave-in-son !
  Why my lads don't you march forward in order ?
March, march, regiments of ragged boys,
  Rummies galore from the Creek to the Corner.

Sir Oliver Crum-well, to water his rum-well,
  A lesson may learn at the "Royal Arcade."
To give it the rale hue, the post-boy, when mail's due,
  Will look in the glass and it never can fade.
March, march, Urbin and Stave-in-son !

March along gaily over the border.
Hould up your head, Tim, be aisy there fightin' Jim!
   Mind the step, Murphy; you're all in disorder!

There's Henry More-cottage and Bills Ham-and pottage—
   The heroes of Maine law would form a battalion.
But one more in rhymin' can be made to chime in,
   The boy with the short neck that rides the big stallion.
March, march, Urbin and Stave-in-son!
   Why my lads don't you march forward in order?
March up, you gummies, your doe-heads and dummies
   To the time of the blue-devils over the border.

Chapter xiii.

Children and Amusements.

YOUNG horse from the farm that we called "Teddy" was now able to pull a sleigh, and with the two eldest children, George and Helen, a favorite route for a ride often taken in winter was over the river to the farm, thence to the foundry at the Upper Corner, and home. We enjoyed toboggan slides from the high bluff near the Methodist Cemetery towards the Catholic Chapel, there being then neither house nor fence to obstruct the passage.

For open-air exercise in the summer, a paddle in a bark canoe around Bull's Island, with an occasional stop to fish, was often indulged in.

Our children being musical, I purchased a piano, and with other musical instruments in the house and an ample supply of books and papers the evenings were very pleasantly spent, and I found home and with my family the happiest place in which to spend the little leisure time I enjoyed.

As the younger boys became strong enough to carry a stick of wood, they joined the elder, and on Saturday evenings received their quota of pay. I well remember the little group of four, waiting until I was disengaged, to give them their pay, and the satisfaction they evinced on receiving it, and I am still inclined to think this a correct course to pursue with children. It establishes early in life a principle of independence, that what they receive is the reward of industry, possession forbids the desire to obtain dishonestly, and for the time dissociated with vile urchins of the streets.

I thank God that my children, now grown up to men and women's estate, possess habits of industry, and have escaped the demoralizing influence of a street education such as Woodstock afforded in their young days.

As the boys grew older they enjoyed themselves in playing on musical instruments, which occasionally led them to provide amusement for others. On the occasion of a Catholic picnic on Bull's Island, the large crowd assembled were surprised and delighted to see the band of juveniles with flutes, drum and triangle marching down the flat. The pleasure to me was the greater, as the priest then in Woodstock and the general manager of the affair, the Rev. Thomas Connolly, now vicar-general in St. John, was a former Fredericton boy and an old schoolmate, and for whom I have always entertained the highest regard. From this little effort the boys ever found a place in the warm hearts of their Irish friends, and when George and Willie, the two eldest, passed away, although many years later, the circumstance was kindly remembered.

A few years later, the boys' "fife and drum band," by the addition of a few others, became quite effective, was attached to my rifle company, and with it visited St. Andrews and was highly complimented by the large crowd assembled to hear their performance in the square, and under the " curfew bell " of that ancient town.

SCHOOLS OF WOODSTOCK AND RICHMOND.

As a trustee of schools it was my duty to visit semi-annually the schools in Woodstock and Richmond parishes. Associated with me in the work were Church of England ministers for the time stationed in the former place.

A school-house at the mill (where now is Debec Junction) was reached by a circuitous route *via* Richmond Corner. Another at the Watson Settlement, and again at "Strong's" on the Meduxnakic. I name these distant points as traversing a large district of country, then mostly wilderness, some portions of the road being only grubbed out and impassable with a wagon.

Of late years in travelling through Richmond, which now presents, in the district named, but few intervening blocks of woodland, are many fine houses and broad acres of cleared fields, and a tribute of respect, mentally at least, is called forth for those brave pioneers whose energy and perseverance have in reality made the wilderness to blossom as the rose.

A pleasant companion in this work was Charles H. Connell, son of the Hon. J. M. Connell, who through his father's political influence, was well and favorably known. He was the eldest of the family and was the first to fall, as did all of his brothers and sisters, with that dread disease — consumption.

Among the early teachers in Woodstock were James McLaughlan and McCormack. Our elder children received their first instruction from Miss McIndoe, thence transferred to Miss Drake and Miss Jacob.

The Latin school in which George first became a pupil was taught by Michael Keiley, a companionable, well-read man, intensely Irish in manner and expression. Following him came James McCoy, whose first location was among his connections at Bairdsville. He was almost a self-educated man, but his high attainments as a mathematical scholar brought him under the notice of the professor of King's College, Fredericton, and he was induced by Sheriff Winslow and others to establish himself at Upper Woodstock. Being also a hard student of the classics, he was, after a few years, offered the Grammar school at Woodstock, which he accepted and continued to teach for more than twenty years. All of our boys are indebted to Mr. McCoy for the education they have received. He was ever a painstaking and devoted teacher, and in many competitive provincial examinations his pupils won scholarships or high honors. As a trustee of the Grammar school and from many years personal acquaintance, I found him an estimable man. *Requiescat in pace.*

MILL AND CONCRETE HOUSE, BRIGHTON.

It is a fiction that because men are called by professional or mechanical names they are fully entitled to such, but we often learn by sad experience the contrary. The old world plan (a diploma or indenture of apprenticeship) is the best test of efficiency or service. The people of this country are often imposed upon by unscrupulous persons, whose knowledge is obtained at the expense of life or capital. An enterprise in the line of a mechanic, who is willing to invest his own money and labor therein, should be an earnest of its success.

A stream about five miles above Woodstock, called Ackerson's Creek, was selected by two millwrights for the purpose of erecting a grist mill thereon. They presented to me the advantages that would accrue from a mill thus situated, and offered to take some machinery I had received from Dr. Wylie as my quota of expense in the erection, and return to me one-third of the profits.

Unable to sell the material, I entered into an agreement with them, dated April 29th, 1851, on conditions aforesaid. The work having proceeded for a time, these partners in succession became involved, and in order to secure what I had invested I was compelled to purchase their interest in the concern. I had now on hand a serious undertaking, involving a large expenditure. Had there been a sufficient supply of water, it would have proved, I have no doubt, a paying investment. From it I have learned the lesson that it is by far the safest for a man to confine himself to his own legitimate business, leaving that of which he knows but little to others.

After much weariness of mind and body, the Brighton mill became a fixed fact, was in reality the best mill in the county, attracting people from long distances ; but the failure of a supply of water in the winter season, when most needed, prevented its proving a profitable investment.

An efficient oat kiln and grinding apparatus were in operation in connection with the mill.

From Tobique, and long distances, farmers brought their grain to the mill, and the Scotch and Irish from Richmond and elsewhere boasted of the oaten bannocks they enjoyed, so long looked for.

For a store and dwelling house I erected at the mill a concrete building forty by twenty-two, one and a half story, with a stone cellar of the same dimensions. The cement of which the walls was built was made of one part lime to eight of sand and eight of large and small gravel stones. The mortar was mixed the day previous and when used was of a consistency to pour from a pail. Studding the height of the wall was used, to which the planks were screwed. These planks resting upon each other were screwed to the studding to receive the cement, the lowest being brought to the top each successive day. The studding remained in the wall. The width of door and window frames was twelves inches— the thickness of the wall. The wall was raised one foot daily in fine weather. Part of the chimney was built in the same manner. A round log of wood, eight inches or the size of flue, was placed in an erect position, and around it a box sixteen by sixteen, to receive the cement. A stick through the top of the log was used to turn it around occasionally, also to raise it higher as the building of the chimney proceeded.

On a good foundation a house of this description should stand for ages. It bleaches to a good stone color and is in reality a thorough stone house on which the weather makes no impression. I am surprised that the success of this experiment has not induced others to adopt it. The failure of an attempt made in Woodstock by W. Ganong, who used St. John, while I used Becaguimac lime, may, however, explain. The latter is more like a cement, as the walls, so far as the composition is concerned, are intact after a service of thirty-five years.

NARROW ESCAPE FROM INSTANT DEATH.

I have now to record a serious accident which nearly cost me my life, the recollection of which is almost invariably accompanied with a shudder. I drove a pair of colts to the mill; my third son, John, then a lad, was with me. I had on my feet a pair of Indian moccasins, and I attempted, as I had often before done, to walk from the platform of the mill to the dam on a single plank. The plank was covered with snow and was twenty-seven feet above the bottom of the dam. The ice of the winter in an oval form, with a light, recent snow, covered it. While walking on this, my attention was arrested by the colts starting, and in an instant I found myself passing through the air. I well knew the character of the ground beneath me, — ice and rocks. I closed my teeth tightly, and compressed my muscles to the greatest possible tension, then waited for the shock ; it seemed a long time. I felt the blow, and, having my senses, thanked God for His wonderful preservation. A hole but a few feet square, from which stones and gravel had been forced by the water from above, but now covered with ice, was the place into which I had fallen. All around it were boulders of rock. The day previous an attempt had been made to break this ice with a handspike, which failed. I fell directly on my head, on the front of which the scalp was raised from the skull. I inserted my fingers and finding no fracture and not feeling sick, I thought it a miraculous deliverance from instant death. The break through the ice seemed just large enough to permit the passage of my body, as the flesh from my arms, which were pressed closely against my body, was stripped from the outside in places. I have no recollection of coming out of the water through the opening. The ice and snow on which I stood was soon covered with blood and water. I heard Aaron McLeod, the miller, coming towards me through the basement of the mill, exclaiming, "Oh! my God! he's killed!"

TRAPPING A HORSE THIEF.

On leaving Woodstock early one morning for a drive to the mill, I observed the deputy sheriff sending off in different directions *posses* of men to intercept and capture a man who had stolen a horse and carriage and escaped from Calais, Me. He had been taken prisoner at the Grand Falls, but escaped by a daring leap from the high bank above the Falls, and evaded his pursuers. A reward of $20 was offered by Sheriff Winslow for his apprehension.

When less than a mile from the mill and des-

cending a hollow in the old road, I observed a
man, apparently a stranger, approaching in the
distance. As I arose from the hollow, I just
caught a glimpse of him as he disappeared behind
Kimball's barn, which stood alone in a field and
just beyond which was the steep river bank. He
was a tall, smart looking fellow, well dressed, and
carried a stout cane in his hand. His conduct
excited my suspicion ! Was he the horse thief?

A few minutes later, I met on the road a well-
set, round shouldered and good-natured man, and
a constable, Lyman Shaw. I told him what I
had seen, that I believed him to be the horse thief,
and that he would get $20 for his apprehension,
and advised him to go to the mouth of Cogswell
Creek, the next stream below, hide in the alders,
and catch him as he jumped the stream. He as-
sented and I drove rapidly to the mouth of the
next stream above, that he might not escape in
that direction. Seeing nothing of him, I hurried
through my business at the mill, and as I returned
homeward, reflected on what might be the result
of a magistrate even suggesting the seizure of a
person, against whom no charge had been laid.

Reaching Fred Phillips' place, I found, under a
willow tree by the road-side, the constable with
his man. Addressing the latter sharply, I said,
" You are a man of too respectable an appearance
to be guilty of what you are charged with." He
replied, " it wan't me took the hoss and buggy;

'twas another fella told me to drive it a-ways for him." I felt relieved, and directed Shaw to take the man over the river and deliver him safely to the sheriff, which he did.

Shaw subsequently related to me the incidents of the capture as follows : " I hid in the bushes close by the path where it crosses the creek. I saw him coming down the shore, and laid low. Just as he jumped over the creek I sprang and grabbed him by the legs. He whacked me so hard on the back with a stick that I thought I would have to let him go ; but I jerked his legs out and got on top of him. He was pretty stiff to handle, but I kept him there till he promised to go along all right. I took a good hold of his collar and we walked down the road about a mile, where they were selling the mending of the roads. He said I'd be sorry for this, but I told him I'd risk it. When we got quite close to the crowd he said, ' Let go of my collar.' I let go and just stepped up to one of the men, when he took back tracks like a shot. I sung out, ' Horse-thief ! $20 reward !' and in a second the men were all strung out in chase. Grey, a tall, slim man, led off, and the race continued over level ground for about a mile. The stranger did not turn with the road near the bridge, but seemed to pitch down the steep hill towards the river. The men were close upon him, when he went out of sight. We searched the woods in all directions, and at last gave up the hunt.   We all sat down on a wind-fall on the hill side, and I was telling them about it, when one of the men stooped down and stuck the point of his jack-knife into a stick to whittle, when he saw a piece of cloth, which proved to be a part of his coat.   There he was, right under the old log we were sitting on!"

Chapter xiv

Tramp on the Old Indian Trail, New Brunswick and Maine.

THE drug business is said to be an unhealthy one. If so, I must attribute, under Providence, to early morning and occasional longer excursions in the pure open-air, the good measure of health I have generally enjoyed.

From my own experience there are many places I could point to in New Brunswick as an answer to the interrogative of the poet :

> " O solitude ! where are the charms
> That sages have seen in thy face ? "

Toward the last of September, 1852, J. S. McBeth, deputy sheriff, myself and two Indians, Pete Loler and Loler Newell, embarked for the Eel River lakes. Passing the site of the historic " Indian fort," we landed, and the Indians carrying the canoes, and a team we had employed our camp equippage, we tramped about seven miles to the navigable waters of Eel River. Where we touched the stream, at that time a wilderness, a few logs were held in position by stakes, — the commencement of a dam and mill, now surrounded by the flourishing village of Benton.

Proceeding up the river to a point where a small tributary, the "Pokamonshine," enters it, we camped for the night. While the tents were being pitched, I cast my line and lured to its fate a beautiful river trout, weighing about two and a half pounds.

In the early morning we were again in our canoes. The quiet beauty of the passing scenery was only interrupted by the darting of a salmon beneath, the wake of an unsuspecting muskrat, or the castinet-like sound of the king-fisher. As we approach Denning's mill the stream becomes rocky and unnavigable for our canoes and a portage across the ox-bow, which is here formed, necessary.

Again floating on merrily, by the more vigorous push of our guides, we approach the long-reach or outlet of the lake. On the left bank is here noticeable an extensive and peculiar formation of land, called in New Brunswick "horse-back." The reach entered, we have a long, unobstructed view, which widens as we advance. In the distance numerous wild fowl were seen disporting in the placid water.

With Mac's consent, I land and push my way up the stream, concealed by the thick growth of bushes on its right bank, called by the natives "Labrador." Judging the distance, I approached the brink, and was rewarded with a scene of natural beauty such as I had never beheld : ducks of all sizes and names disporting themselves, many of them entirely new to me. I was for a time fascinated with the graceful motions and beautiful plumage of the birds. The waving motion of the tall rushes, the water-grass and pond lillies disturbed in sportive play, heightened the effect.

More than once I looked over the barrels of my "Mantou," and lowered it again to gaze. Two reports in rapid succession brought up the canoes; and a little later another course was added to the viands of our evening meal. After paddling some distance, we enter the lake, pass a rocky point and select our camping ground.

Supper over, Pete and I set off for a paddle up "Dead Creek," so called, from its sluggish flow. The objective point, a fording place where wild animals crossed the stream; and, it being the mating season, to call and perchance shoot a moose or caribou. The night was clear, starlight, and cool for September. The stream is tortuous, and for a continuous width of fifty yards or more on either side covered with a thick growth of "Labrador." Forest trees then form lines in solid mass, and the open space appears as if the Titans of the wood had been removed by the hands of mighty mowers.

Having reached the ford or shallow place in this deep stream, Pete places to his mouth a straight, trumpet-shaped horn made of birch bark, the echoes of his call through which was heard in the far distance. Our canoe was placed touching

the shore, that the body of the animal against the
sky-light might present a fair mark. Then followed patient waiting ; not a whisper and breathing almost inaudible. An hour passes ; Indian
gives no sign. Another hour ! Is Indian dead ?
A sensation of numbness from cold and inaction
is creeping over me. A sound in my ears, — the
evidence of intense stillness, — has become a roaring noise ; and yet no sign from moose or Indian.
I had reached the point beyond which forbearance
ceases to be a virtue, and dared to move. A
sharp paddle warmed our blood, and we reached
camp about midnight.

I awoke about daylight, and aroused the camp
by shooting from the tent door a brace of ducks.
Breakfast over, we again visit "Dead Creek." I
never tire in learning from these red brothers.
The lesson of the previous evening was one in
moral philosophy or patience exemplified.

Approaching a sharp turn in the stream, a jerk
of the canoe, caused by a quick motion of the
body, puts you on the alert to cover and shoot
before startling the game, — a disturbance of the
water, which a practised eye only could discover,
giving evidence of its presence. Approaching, for
a second time, the ford, five miles distant from our
camp, Pete exclaimed, with unusual vehemence,
"Moose ! sartin, moose !" I looked ; could see
nothing unusual, and asked his meaning. He saw
from a distance that a large moose had crossed

during our absence. The soft mud in the stream, through which the animal passed, coated its body well up the sides, a portion of which was detached by the bushes through which after crossing it forced its way. Relieved of the weight, the branches would spring back to their original position. This the sharp eye of the Indian detected ; and from the height of the bushes, thus plainly marked, the animal was a large one.

Before striking our tents, we explored the fine sheets of water called the " Eel River Lakes," beyond which, by a portage road, the old Indian trail led to other lakes and streams, tributaries of the Penobscot River in Maine, United States. The weird-like screech of the loon, that came over the water during the night, and now heard in many directions, indicated an approaching storm and hastened our departure.

All aboard ! and our prows homeward turned, with feathers not a few. Our paddle blades spring to the work, our programme being for that day " Pokamonshine and a basket of fish." The portage reached, our Indians vie with each other in a race from water to water.

The trail is a crooked pathway through the woods, and windfalls or other obstructions are avoided or skipped over with wonderful dexterity. The bark canoe, in which is secured the pole and paddles, is turned by a graceful motion over the head, one of the centre bars resting on the shoulders.   With the hands it is kept in position, front slightly elevated.   The movement is an easy trot, but much faster than a walk.   The weight of the canoe is about eighty pounds, and its length eighteen feet.   To save the time of another trip by the Indians, Mac and I carried the tent and balance of supplies.

We soon found ourselves far behind in the race; the greater the speed, the greater the buoyancy of the inverted canoe, from increased atmospheric pressure ; hence *quid nuncs* are often left to wander, and —— wonder !

Being the younger of the two, I reached the water first, and pulled away with Pete for the fishing ground, where, alone in the bark, I managed to pull in some fine trout.   Pete, meantime, had prepared supper, pitched the tent, and made all snug for the night.   The ground on which we then camped, with a large section of country in that district, has since been covered with water, by the erection of the dam at Benton.

On the following day we reached Woodstock without mishap, adding another to the many pleasing reminiscences of "rod and gun" on the lakes and rivers of New Brunswick.

OPPOSITION IN BUSINESS.

From the healthy condition, as a rule, and small population of the county, a living could not be obtained from the sales of medicines only.   I therefore varied my stock as my ability to do so increased, to the full occupation of my time. My success, however, was attributed to the sale and profit on drugs; and the following persons, for a period more or less brief, were my competitors. A young Irishman, O'Flaherty, opened a shop in McCann's building, King street. A love of the ardent soon upset him, and his stay was short.

Following O'Flaherty came Morton, supplied by W. O. Smith, St. John; he also collapsed after a short stay. His shop was in Lindsay's building over the bridge.

Dr. H. Bridges was the next in order. Like those who preceded him, he knew but little of the preparation of medicines. He followed the mistaken plan of many beginners, — underselling to gain customers. His professional and drug business was also short-lived, and he, too, disappeared.

Again, W. H. Ferguson, of Fredericton. He learned the business from J. W. Brayley, who opened a shop in Woodstock and put him in charge. He was a prudent young man, of steady habits, and married shortly after coming to Woodstock. His shop was on the front street, near Paxton Baird's present stand, and several things conspired to give him a share of my business. Firstly,—Being for several years the only druggist in the place, I never refused medicine because people had not the money to pay; many of these would avoid entering where they might be asked to pay. Secondly,—I had on more than one occasion, taken an active part in elections for representatives to the Provincial Legislature, which was made a personal matter, and the patronage transferred to a new comer. Thirdly,—The policy of the leading politicians of Woodstock at that time was to dwarf or destroy the energies or ambition of any young man who might from education or popularity possibly become a rival for political honors.

From these and other causes, Ferguson succeeded moderately well. His ambition, however, led him to the practice of medicine. The business, originally Brayley's, had now become his own; and he sold out to Dr. Stephen Smith, with a view of studying medicine in Scotland, whither he went.

Returning home a few years later, he received an accidental blow on ship board, which affected his brain, and he became partially deranged. He was staying at Greenbank, five miles below Woodstock; wandered into the woods and could not be found. The people of Woodstock were asked to join in the search. The steamer "Carleton" was lying at the wharf, and early on a Sabbath morning a number of men, among whom were many of my volunteers, embarked. Having reached the place where he was supposed to have entered the dense forest, I organized, as previously requested, the line of advance. The men were placed

twelve paces apart, and the movements regulated
by buglers on either flank. Having penetrated
through brush or water for nearly a half mile,
Ferguson was found under a tree, prostrate and
helpless. He survived but a short time. He was
a steady and inoffensive young man, and possessed
a fair share of natural ability.

A Dr. Brown having commenced the practice of
medicine in Woodstock, he also opened a drug
shop. My brother Henry, who had learned the
business with me, was employed to conduct it.

The population of both town and county had
now largely increased, and although the drug
stores on the front street were more central and
convenient for the public, I had the continued
custom of many old and true friends through all
the changes.

FINANCIAL DISASTERS, 1854.

The year 1854 proved most disastrous to the
commercial interests of New Brunswick. A panic
in the lumber business — the staple of the country
— brought to bankruptcy many of the oldest and
best established houses in New Brunswick. Business of all kinds was most seriously affected, and
in many cases suspended.

Many of the farmers in Carleton County were
also engaged in the lumbering business, and when
pressed for payment on account of supplies were

compelled to mortgage their farms, or surrender them to creditors, which in many cases was done. Add to this the invasion of Asiatic cholera, its prostrating effects upon the general health and trade of the country, and the year 1854 will be one long remembered by the people of New Brunswick.

CHOLERA IN WOODSTOCK.

About fifteen persons fell victims to cholera in the town of Woodstock, and eleven of this number on King street, where we resided. People were dying all around us, and their cries were heard at all hours of the day or night. Those addicted to the excessive use of intoxicants were the first to fall. Several families in our immediate neighborhood removed from the town. I was aroused many times during the night to supply medicine for the sufferers. Nearly everyone attacked succumed to the disease.

We lost a lovely child, about two years of age; and were all more or less affected with the disease.

One of the first victims was a tailor, Peter Melody, a man of dissipated habits. Dying suddenly he was coffined, but not buried. On the same upper flat lived an old man, McElroy, who had not been seen for some days.

At a meeting of the Board of Health, held in the "Carleton House," two of the members, Michael McGuirk and myself, were appointed a

committee for the burial of Melody. We proceeded at once to the house, near the corner of
King and Main streets, north. Mac fortified himself with brandy and water, and I placed in my
mouth a piece of camphor.

Ascending the stairs, we found the body and
coffin on a table, which had been his work-board.
Passing along the hall a few steps, I opened a
door to the right, where, partially covered with
some tangled clothing and lying on the floor, was
the old man McElroy, bearing evidence of a dying
struggle. His knees were drawn up to his chin,
and his hands clenched in the clothing. I stepped
over the body and opened a door looking into the
yard below to let in some fresh air, but the unhealthy odours arising therefrom compelled me to
retreat as rapidly as possible.

These bodies buried, a blacksmith and his wife,
living at Thomas Collins', employed by the friends
of the deceased to wash the bedding, were the
next victims, and others rapidly followed.

At that time the streets were very filthy, King
street receiving the drainage of streets from the
hill side north. The water was also very low in
the Meduxnakic, and deposits therein were poisoning the atmosphere.

Westward and adjoining our residence lived
James Phillips, a tailor, and his wife. The house
was two story, his own property, and he was very
comfortably situated. Leaving one morning for a

drive to the mill, I observed him sitting on his door-step playing with a dog, and in apparent good health. Returning in the evening, I heard his piteous cries,—- he was in the grip of the monster.

A journeyman saddler, Doherty, nobly risked his own life in his attendance upon the sufferers; and many times in the night in answer to a loud knocking I met him at the door to learn of some new victim, and supply the needed wants. The last duties performed by Doherty were connected with the coffin containing Phillip's body, which was left at the bottom of the stairs for burial. No one could be found to convey it to the grave-yard, and it remained there until evening, when Parson Street and John Balloch, the latter with a horse and wagon, came for the burial in the evening.

The people of the town were becoming reckless. King street in particular was avoided. Brandy was thought by many to be a preventative; hence it was used freely by those who never used it before.

A ball-alley on Connell's wharf was a place of popular resort by the young men. To this place I sent Obder Foster for assistance. He was met by men, hitherto sober and sensible, with ribald jest and unseemly reply. He returned without help, and by an effort of the few persons present the coffin was placed on the wagon.

As the small procession moved away, lighted by a torch, I saw, peering through the blind of an upper window, the now lonely widow ; but, within twenty-four hours, her body was conveyed in the same manner to be laid by the side of her husband.

Eastward, adjoining the Carleton House, lived J. S. McBeth and his wife. They were good neighbors, friendly people, and old-time acquaintances of my wife's family. Auntie Mac was a frequent visitor, and a great favorite with the children. In sickness, unremitting in attention ; and a covered dish, with Ann Huff the bearer, was sure to meet the capricious taste of the invalid. Mrs. McBeth was a large, fleshy woman, and in dread of the cholera. Many had died and among the rest their nearest neighbor, Mrs. Truesdell, whose death impressed her deeply. When attacked, my wife visited her, and as the virulence of the epidemic had in some measure subsided, her suffering was protracted.

After her death, McBeth returned to Bridgewater, Me., at which place he was a book-keeper for my brother, J. D. Baird. A few days later a messenger informed me that Mr. McBeth was dead, with a request to meet the funeral, which I did. The last sad rites were performed, too, at night ; and time has not effaced the gloom and anxiety which overshadowed reflecting minds during the existence of the terrible scourge in Woodstock.

Duty seemed to demand our presence in the town ; so we remained and made the best of it. Our food was of the simplest kind ; rice and nutritious vegetables, easily digested. Our windows were raised a little, and in each a saucer containing chloride of lime, renewed daily, was placed.

A young man named Carman, while removing a shutter from the window of John Leary's store, opposite to our residence, fell backward into the street; and one of a flock of geese crossing the street was seen to fall dead.

I crossed the river one day, during the worst stage of the disease, to visit the farm and for change of air. Walking up the other side, I was overtaken by William Hale, who invited me to ride on a two-wheeled cart, which I did, standing with him as we rode. I alighted at the gate leading up to my house. In an instant I had lost my sight, speech, and the partial use of my limbs. The pressure upon my heart and a sense of suffocation were very distressing. I was conscious of my condition, and crept, feeling my way, towards the house. After a time relief came in a profuse perspiration ; my sight returned ; and I found myself prostrated, with scarcely sufficient strength to rise.

AN OTTER HUNT.

On a cold winter's day in the year 1855, whilst riding with a friend along the bank of the St. John

River on the front of my own farm in Northampton, the curious movements of a dark object out upon the river and some distance above us, arrested our attention. At times in an erect posture, about the height of a small child; again lying down and gliding swiftly over the smooth surface of the snow.

This several times repeated led us to conclude that it was an otter. Tying the horse to a fence by the road-side, and each of us seizing a short stick or stake from the sled on which we had been riding, started in pursuit. It was our intention to intercept the animal before it reached the opposite side of the river, in which direction it was moving; but the snow being deep we only arrived in time to see it disappear over the summit of an almost perpendicular wall of drifted snow.

By a round-about-way I came upon the trail, which I followed to a hole in the snow, where I heard the sound of running water. It was a brook running down the hill-side to the river. Following it in that direction there darted out, a short distance below, a large and beautiful otter. Seeing S—— approach, it returned to the brook. All my efforts to baffle its ascent proved unavailing, the deep snow and brush affording it a complete protection. We continued the search for some time when I suggested getting his dog, which was a good hunter, to ferret it out.

As we moved down the river in the direction

of his home, we saw what appeared in the distance like two dogs engaged in play, but on nearer approach it proved to our great surprise to be the dog we were seeking and the otter, engaged in a fierce fight. Its long, sharp teeth and powerful jaws kept the dog at bay, while it instinctively drew nearer to an air-hole or open space in the river near by.

S—— had to deal several heavy blows with his cudgel before life in the animal was extinct. We found later that the otter had been hunted by an Indian from a lake on the eastern side of the river, but on reaching descending land it had left its pursuer far behind.

Chapter XV.

The Calm Before the Storm.

AFTER several years of continued and persevering effort, I was at last released from the strain on my business through the erection of the mill at Brighton, the purchase and improvement of property in Woodstock, including house, store, etc. To the main house I added by purchase the Wiley property adjoining, and improved the buildings and freed them from all indebtedness. With ample accommodations for store and business and dwelling for myself, with buildings rented as stores bringing me in three hundred dollars a year, and with a good paying business, we supposed, at the end of eighteen years, the hardest struggle of our lives to be over and past.

DESTRUCTION OF WOODSTOCK BY FIRE.

On the evening of the 16th of April, 1860, a meeting of the Bible Society was held in the Mechanics' Institute. I had returned at a late hour from the meeting and was not yet asleep, when we heard the alarm of fire, and saw the reflected light on the opposite buildings. We had

a fire department in the town, but had not had
much drill upon a " Perry" hand-engine, recently
purchased. Being at the time chief fire-warden, I
hastened to the fire. Under the direction of the
captain, the suction-pipe of the engine was passed
through the bridge, and, some twelve feet below,
an opening in the ice for the purpose of reaching
the water. It was found, when too late, that the
water in the stream had fallen, and that the
mouth of the suction-pipe had not been immersed.
It was evident in a few moments that the fire was
beyond control. It originated in a large three-
story building on the corner of King and Main
streets, owned by J. M. Connell. The lower flat
was occupied by Charles Connell as a store, and
upper flats as printing and other offices. The entrance from the street to the stairs above was
never closed, and at the first landing were broken
gaps in the plastering, into which paper or rubbish
was swept or had fallen. Here the fire was first
discovered, and whether caused by accident or design may never be known. The building was soon
enveloped in flames, which spread rapidly along
King and Main streets.

Having lost very precious time at my post of
public service, I hastened home, and removed
my family to a place of safety. Charles Beardsley, Henry Dow and others rendered valuable
service in removing the piano and some furniture ;
but from kitchen, pantries, or attic — where was

most of our clothing and many articles of value —
nothing was saved. By this time volumes of
flame and sparks were sweeping over and around
the building. A few trips only of a single wagon,
drawn by hand, laden with light goods from shelves
or cases, were made to Connell's wharf.

A valuable library of books, as also books and
accounts, fixtures in shop and dwelling, furniture,
pictures, soda machine, marble counters, etc., a
stock of paint, value £100 sterling (just received
from England and not opened), the spring supply
of field and garden seeds, a ton or more of oat-
meal from the mill for farmers in Richmond, together with a large stock of agricultural implements, drugs, medicines, dye-stuffs and sundries,
all were destroyed. To one of the marble slabs in
the counter I attached more than an intrinsic
value, as it had formed a part of the counter at
which I had stood when a boy in Fredericton.
Above the roar and din of the fire was heard at
intervals the explosions of barrels of oil and burning fluid, and these in the rear part of the building in which we were working.

Under a carpet spread over some articles of
furniture on Connell's wharf the family found
shelter till daylight.

Johnny, twelve years of age, guarded, stiletto
in hand, from miserable thieves, the articles saved,
but many things we knew to have been carried
from house or shop were never found.

Passing the Institute in search of our youngest child, — conveyed to the house of a friend at an early stage of the fire, — I observed a flaming cinder strike the cupola. In an instant it was ablaze. I rallied a few men to remove the rifles, etc., of my company from the armory within ; and in a short time our " Mechanics' Institute," around which clustered so many pleasing associations, was a thing of the past.

The morning of the 17th of April broke cold, clear and windy. The ice in the river was firm and smooth ; and, with her father's help, my wife and children passed over it to temporary quarters at her brother's.

From the Meduxnakic to the top of the hill near the English Church, including both sides of Main street and thence to the River Saint John, the fire had devoured everything combustible. This area embraced every business place in Woodstock, and from its fortunate escape up to this time, the amounts insured were comparatively trifling.

Part of a shoe-shop owned and occupied by Daniel Day — on the site of the new post office — was kindly offered me, whither, without delay, I removed my entire stock in trade, now, alas ! contained in a few small boxes. I ordered a stock of medicines and sundries ; and, being the first to reopen, George and I were busily employed, and a good business was done during the summer.

A dwelling house, owned by the Rev. Thomas Todd, was rented, to which we removed our effects.

A change of position so thorough and sweeping; heavy bills to pay for stock, without the stock to realize from; and the bald fact before you that the labor of eighteen years is lost and your fondest hopes dashed in a minute, produce on the mind demoralizing effects which extraordinary efforts only can overcome.

THE RENFREW HOUSE.

Encouraged by an offer from T. W. Smith to rent for three years an hotel at $320, $360 and $400 from the 1st May, 1861, and after weighing the matter, I determined to embark in the enterprise, and, if possible, carry it through and build an hotel and two stores. I had land affording ample room for all the buildings; available lumber on the farm; an income from the mill; an almost unlimited credit; but, above all, I *felt* that I could accomplish the work.

The expected visit of the young Prince of Wales to New Brunswick under the cognomen of Baron Renfrew, suggested to me a popular name for the hotel.

With an old and well-tried mechanic, Hezekiah Stoddard, I bargained to put up the frame of the main building, 52x40 feet, three stories; also an ell, 40x22, three stories. With James Morse, I agreed for the erection of a barn, 50 x 30 feet, two stories.

The stone for the cellar walls — much of it slate in large slabs — I had quarried in Jacksontown. An important item in the structure was the stone columns and pavement for entrance, base for building, also sills and caps for windows. Saint John was supposed to be the only place where these could be procured, and for that place I embarked on the steamer. Whilst passing through the falls below Woodstock, a thought struck me that the great granite boulders in view would supply, and much nearer home, the stone required. Acting upon this, I selected, a few days later, a granite rock, 18 x 25 feet and about ten feet in height, on the highway road above the falls. The rock proved to be a good quality of coarse, grey granite, supplying not only what I required, but the wants of a majority of other builders, who adopted my plan. The columns of this stone, supporting the entrance to the hall of the "Renfrew House," were each twelve feet in length, by fourteen inches square. All that now remains to me of that fine building, is the stone on which these columns rested, now at the entrance to my dwelling house in Northampton.

The first day of May, 1861, Mr. Smith was put in possession of the hotel, and "The Renfrew" was pronounced one of the most spacious, convenient and comfortable hotels in the Province. In the short enjoyment of this property I felt what may be considered a pardonable pride. The whole block, with adjoining blocks, was destroyed by fire in 1867. The fire originated in a stable on an adjoining property owned by a man named Johnson.

THE COLD FRIDAY.

The "cold Friday" occurred on the 8th of February, 1861. The shop was the only part of the building finished, and the weather being intensely cold and scarcely a person to be seen in the street, it was closed about four in the afternoon.

The drift above Hayden's mill proved too deep for the mare, and I left her in Smith's stables for the night. Going home on foot, I faced a strong wind and stinging frost. Willie and Johnny had reached home from school, assisted by my brother Henry; the former was badly frozen, a mask of ice falling from his face when placed in cold water.

DIPHTHERIA.

While living at Mr. Todd's place after the fire this virulent and often fatal disease made its first appearance in Woodstock. The disease was treated for ulcerated sore throat, and the two persons first attacked succumbed at once. The second of these was a fine young man, Robert Campbell, a cabinet maker, and one of my riflemen. I was with him at intervals during his suffering, and witnessed the closing struggle. He was buried by the company with military honors. Contagion was not at this time suspected.

George, leader of the boys' band at the funeral, was the next attacked. He complained of a violent headache, and I gave him some aperient medicine, a bowl of hot sage tea, and sent him to bed. He spent a most restless night and the fever increased until morning, when great beads of sweat appeared on his forehead, and his agony was relieved. I discovered ulcerated patches about the uvula, which were cauterized by Dr. Smith, and he recovered.

Other members of the family were also attacked, and under similar treatment restored.

"TRENT AFFAIR."

When the rebellion in the United States broke out the sympathies of the Province people were with the North, and some of our own brave volunteers, who joined the Nothern Army, were wished God speed. One of my Prince of Wales' men, Sergeant Watson Honeywell, was killed in battle at Antietam, in 1862, while bravely carrying the colors at the front of his regiment.

The sympathies of many were changed instantly on reading a letter over the signature of Cassius M. Clay, American Minister at Paris, to the effect that England *dare not* identify herself with the

Southern cause. And the heroic zeal and spirit of
self abnegation, evinced by officers and men alike
of the Southern army, together with their isolated
condition and the overwhelming force they had to
contend against, gave a bent to many minds that
even the horrors of slavery could not overcome.

An overt act was now perpetrated which gave
England no choice of action. Two Southern
gentleman were seized and taken in November,
1861, by force from an English vessel, the
"Trent," sailing under British colors, by United
States officers of the "San Jacinto," a United
States man-of-war, and conveyed to Boston, where
they were incarcerated in a prison. A demand
made by the British Government for the surrender
of these men, was replied to by the press and by
the people of the United States that "Mason and
Slidell will never be given up."

The "Trent" affair soon became the leading
topic, and a powerful naval armament was ordered
to sail to Halifax. Troops were under orders for
America: and with the news of these preparations
in England came also the sad news of the death of
Prince Albert the Good. A regiment of the line
having been ordered to Woodstock from Halifax,
and other regiments to pass through on their way
to the Upper Provinces, with the high bounties
offered for men to enlist in the American service
by emissaries at Woodstock, led me to suspect that
attempts would be made to tamper with the

military *en route*. With the view of defeating such object, I prepared a chart or map showing all the roads and by-roads leading to the American boundary between Eel River and the Grand Falls ; also the points at which pickets might be placed to intercept deserters and their abettors. This chart, with an explanatory letter, I addressed to the Governor of the Province, Hon. Arthur Gordon.

Some little time elapsed, during which a regiment of the guards arrived, and, as I anticipated, a cute Yankee, with a fleet horse and a sleigh, ran one of these stalwart defenders over the line. Another was abducted at Florenceville.

Very shortly after a gentleman entered my office and handed me a note from Governor Gordon, introducing the bearer, Colonel Crealock, who produced my letter, with the chart, and proceeded to say that the suggestions therein would be carried out under my supervision, if I were prepared to act.

The next morning I drove the colonel to Richmond Corner, where the roads from Woodstock, *via* the Red Bridge, and the Maine Houlton road converge. Here the main road was established, and an armed patrol traversed night and day all roads leading to the United States. The guard was composed of my well disciplined and trusty Prince of Wales men, and some who attempted to run the blockade found behind the rifle and bayonet a stiff New Brunswick soldier.

I was also authorized to appoint officers and establish out-posts at other places named in my letter, viz., Florenceville, Tobique and Grand Falls, and so well and faithfully was this post-duty discharged that not another man of the soldiers that passed through escaped, though many attempts were made.

Captain Percy, who had a general supervision of the military as they passed through Woodstock, reported to me at nine o'clock every night the state of the garrison present and absent. If any were absent at roll call a description of his person was given, and a search made until found.

The troops, *en passant*, occupied Connell's Block, a large brick building, west of Main Street, near the bridge, which was well guarded. The contractor, J. R. Tupper, always had a relay of comfortable sheds and good horses, owned and driven by New Brunswick men, to carry forward in the morning the arrivals of the previous evening. The soldiers were warmly clad with good fur caps and sheepskin coats, and were picked corps of the British army, — Grenadier Guards, Scots Fusiliers, London Rifles, Artillery and Transport Corps, etc. Lord Russell, a nobleman of high rank, commanded these corps ; and the rank and file were of more than ordinary intelligence.

The streets were occasionally enlivened with the music of a regimental band, and on one occasion by the bag-pipes and drums of the Highlanders.

The cheery note of the key-bugle from an officer's sled could be heard in the distance, as, early on frosty mornings, they filed off through the drifted snow.

A daily inspection of the main guard and outlying pickets in Richmond, with reports from outstations, and a summary of all to headquarters, gave me anxious waking hours, and at times but few for sleep.

Colonel Crealock was a special agent sent by the British Government with the first body of troops to America in the "Trent affair." His authority was but little, if any, inferior to the Governor's in certain lines. I met him several times while in command of out-post service on the American boundary; found him an exceedingly straightforward and able officer, and was on more than one occasion honored with his confidence.

Before Colonel Crealock left for England, I received a few lines from him in which was written, "I have reccommended you for a Lieutenant Colonelcy." I received a letter from him also when he was at Gibraltar, enclosing his photo. He was the General Crealock recently in command during the Zulu war in Africa.

The trouble between the two countries was settled without actual warfare by the unconditional surrender of Mason and Slidell on 2nd of January, 1862. The United States government having previously declared they had not authorized or sanctioned the act of Captain Wilkes in capturing them.

For all the work in connection with the "post service," I received nothing; while the name of every other officer employed was on the roll receiving pay, mine was not. The omission was my own, and for this reason: I suggested the establishing of these posts; felt the responsibility; and assumed that if acted upon and the issue proved successful, I would be rewarded.

General Doyle was at that time Commander-in-Chief of the Lower Provinces, and at a dinner at Government House, I was introduced to him by the local Governor, Hon. Mr. Gordon. The general said, "Your name seems familiar." Mr. Gordon replied, "Captain Baird had command of the out-posts on the frontier during the Trent affair." The general addressing me said, "I hope that you were well paid for that service." I replied, "I received a very nice letter from your Excellency." He said, "Is that all? I'm very sorry. The expenses of the Trent affair are now closed; but you should have sent in a good bill for that service."

The sincerity of these officers is shown, as expressed in letters supporting my application for staff appointment in the militia service of the Dominion at the Confederation of the Provinces.

Returning from my first drive to Richmond, with Colonel Crealock, I gave George the lines to

drive home, and that was the last I ever saw of
my beautiful mare, "Nancy." Full of life, and
moving homeward, she shied at a flash of light
passing McDonald's store ; a hook or eye, to which
the cross-bar was attached, snapped suddenly, let-
ting one end fall to the ground. Presently the
other broke, and dragging George from the sleigh,
she went off at high speed with the shafts. One
of these broke off just behind her shoulders, and
the continued blows from its sharp edge, as she
galloped, broke the bone, and she fell never again
to rise. The news was immediately brought to me,
when I directed Mr. Jacques to make an examination, and if the case was hopeless, to put her immediately out of pain, which he did. She was
nearly a thorough-bred "John O'Gaunt," raised by
me ; a great favorite with the children, and beautiful and gentle as a fawn.

REMOVE TO FARM AT NORTHAMPTON.

Having paid rent for two years, we decided to
remove to the farm at Northampton. The necessary repairs upon the house having been made, a
garden enclosed and cultivated, fruit and other
trees having been planted, and a fountain supplied
with water from highland behind the house, and a
flower garden laid out, — we had all the surround
ings for a pleasant home.

Some Jersey stock, the first introduced into

Carleton County, was purchased from the York Agricultural Society and from Chandler's herd, Houlton, and placed on the farm.

The farm was about a mile from the store and while the river was a serious obstacle, the exercise in the open air was more healthful than otherwise. Crossing through and over the ice at certain seasons was often sufficiently exciting, and not unattended with danger.

Chapter xvi

The Prince of Wales' Visit to Fredericton.

AVING received in 1849 my commission as Captain of the Woodstock Rifle Company, I reorganized the same, and although the Militia Law of New Brunswick had been for some years in abeyance our efforts were not relaxed, and at the celebration of the Fall of Sebastopol, in 1855, it was found to be the only efficient company in the Province.

On the reorganization of the militia of the Province, about the year 1858, I received my quota of the new breach-loading rifles and a drill sergeant as instructor of the company. It was composed of the most active and intelligent young men of the place, and the opportunity was embraced to obtain the same degree of thoroughness in foundation drill and training as in the regular service.

An invitation,—General Orders in those times were rare, as we had to pay all our own bills for clothing, rations, transport, etc.,—received in the summer of 1860, from the then A. G., Lieutenant-Colonel Hayne, to visit Fredericton as part of a Guard of Honor at the reception of the Prince of

Wales, was accepted by the company and gave renewed zest to our efforts.

In bayonet exercise, or light infantry or bugle drill, I considered the company as near perfect as possible; also, in company movements and the manual platoon exercises. Our uniform was a tunic and pants of Oxford grey cloth, with bead facing of scarlet (officers, silver), caps of same material and neat pattern. All were fresh and new. Thus equipped, and with the confidence that thorough preparation imparts, two officers and fifty men embarked in a tow-boat for headquarters.

The day previous I had left Woodstock for Fredericton in my own wagon, and arranged for a camping ground within the barrack enclosure. Arriving at the Capital, I found that Major Carter, in command of the regiment, whom I had previously met, had gone to St. John to return with the Prince and party. The camp was formed just within the barrack gate and near the shore, which gave us easy access to the boat, and rations therein prepared. The men had slept but little during the night of the journey, and the morning until noon was occupied in pitching the tents.

The Fredericton volunteers, under the new *regime*, having been organized a little earlier than the Woodstock, were clamoring for the right of the line, a position seniority would assign to me.

The officers of the corps presented the matter,

asking my opinion. I replied that if they could produce a company of better drilled men from among the volunteers, I would waive my right to the position. Shortly after Captain (Judge) Wilmot, then in command of a troop of Fredericton Volunteer Cavalry, accompanied by an old rifleman acquaintance, Duncan McPherson, entered our camp and invited us to an afternoon parade on the Flats. He urged this strongly as the easiest solution of the point above mooted, and after consultation with my officers, Evans and Strickland, I consented.

We marched from the barrack yard about 4 p. m., with fife and drum, and halted at the lower end of the Flat, at the first bridge—the old-time ground for target practice.

With a few encouraging words I left them, retiring with my bugler, Holland Snow, about a quarter of a mile up the Flat.

The cavalry were manœuvring near, and the rise of land verging the road was, for the whole distance along the Flat, covered with spectators. My pivot-men were cornet blowers who knew every note and sound of the bugle, and the movements were performed with promptness and precision. No movement in light infantry drill was omitted, and finally, as the company marched up the Flat in company line, it was greeted with cheers from red-coats and civilians alike.

When within a few yards, I spoke the words:

"Halt!" "Stand at Ease!" and at this distant
period, I can find no words to express my feelings
on that occasion. I have not lost sight of one of
the fifty men then before me, and have stood at
the bedside of some in sickness, and others as they
bade adieu to all that is earthly.

We were soon surrounded by officers of the
army and other friends receiving their congratula-
tions, among them my old friend Captain Marsh,
of the Fredericton volunteers, who added, "Your
men will take the right to-morrow."

The following morning at 9 o'clock, the volunteers assembled in the Barrack Square, viz. :—

Fredericton Rifles—2 Com , Capts. Brannen and Marsh.
St. Mary's Rifles—1 Company, Capt. McGibbon.
Queen's County Rifles—1 Company, Capt. Gilbert.
Portland Battery, St. John—Capt. Rankine.
And the Woodstock Rifle Company.

Our fellows astonished them with their precision
in the bayonet exercise, which was new to the
country corps.

Re-assembled at 2 p. m., it being as yet unknown
who should be in command, an officer of the regulars approached me on the parade, and, touching
his hat, read from a telegram in his hand, received
from Major Carter, that I was to take command
of the "Guard of Honor" on that day for the
reception of the Prince of Wales. At my request
he made the announcement to the other officers in
command of corps, after which I proceeded to form

a line and practice the movements we would be required to execute.

At 3 p. m., headed by the Woodstock band, we marched to our position on the wharf at the old Gaynor Landing. The crowd assembled was immense. After waiting for some time the steamer was sighted, and shortly after the music of the Fredericton band reached our ears. The beautiful " Forest Queen," in her new dress of white, gay with colors and a gayer throng of living beings, glided gracefully to our front.

Major Carter was the first to land ; came quietly forward, and, in a few kind words *sotto voce*, complimented our line. This was also done by the correspondent of the *Illustrated London News*, who was one of the suite.   (See issue of August, 1860.)

The Prince and party now landed under a salvo of artillery and salute from our line, and passing slowly along our front, the colors sweeping the ground at a royal salute, they proceeded to the carriage, which, having entered, moved off under an escort of cavalry to Government House.

The following day a *levee* at Government House gave the officers a nearer view of the Prince. There was also a military display, at the opening of a fountain, on grounds fronting Government House, a pleasing feature of which was the singing of the National Anthem by the Sabbath School children of the city.

By special request of the Adjutant General,

Colonel Hayne, the Woodstock Rifles formed the Guard of Honor at a ball given by the citizens of Fredericton in honor of His Royal Highness, in the halls of the Legislative Assembly, where were present a good representation of the *elite* of New Brunswick.

VISIT OF THE DUKE OF EDINBURGH TO WOODSTOCK.

The announcement, in 1861, that the second son of our beloved Queen, Prince Alfred, would pass through Woodstock, *en route* for the Upper Provinces, was received with great satisfaction by our people. Accompanied by Lieutenant-Governor Manners-Sutton, and the commander-in-chief, General Trollope, he arrived by steamer at 4 p. m., and was received by my rifle company and the Woodstock band at the wharf with a royal salute — His Royal Highness was supposed to be travelling *incog.* The Prince, being the first member of the Royal Family that had visited Woodstock, there was much curiosity to see him, particularly among the ladies, and a large number of people from town and country, far and near, were assembled and occupied every available point near English's landing. As he walked along an old lady, scrutinizing him closely, remarked : " He don't look any better than some of our own boys."

After being driven around the principal streets, the Prince and party returned to the steamer, which was at once moved to the Northampton side of the river, when I was summoned to visit His Royal Highness on board. Before leaving the steamer, the Governor informed me that he would telegraph the date of his return from the Grand Falls, as he wished the General to see my company.

Woodstock, during the evening of the Prince's visit, was brilliantly illuminated, and the effect heightened by transparencies, torch-light processions, etc., etc. The Prince was discovered, during the evening, moving quietly through the crowd. The steamer, with party on board, remained at the Northampton shore during the night, and sailed for the Grand Falls at an early hour on the following morning.

Late one evening, a few days after, I received a message from His Excellency, who had just arrived in Woodstock (the telegraph line not working), that they would see the company at eight o'clock the following morning.

At 7.30 a. m., every man was in his place. Shortly after the Governor and General approached ; were saluted, and the drill commenced. Every movement was executed with rapidity and precision ; there was no failure. The General could scarcely be convinced that they were not discharged soldiers from the regular army, and said they were far in advance of any of the Nova Scotia volunteers.

After a friendly good-bye, they at once embarked

on the steamer for Fredericton, and the company was marched to a position, where it was formed in line, and a photograph, standing at the "Present," taken by one of its members, Ed. Estabrook. Some copies of which, enlarged and framed, I still have, and in which the features of officers and men are easily distinguished.

ST. ANDREWS RAILWAY SEIZED BY NAVVIES.

In 1861, while the St. Andrews and Woodstock Railway was being built, and when completed as far as Richmond, several hundred navvies, in consequence of their not being paid by the company, seized all the rolling stock and plant at that place, and threatened violence to any persons attempting to take possession.

The facts were represented by the company to the Governor, the Hon. Mr. Gordon.

I received a telegram from him to hold my rifle company in readiness for active service at a moment's notice. The company was mustered in full strength ; sixty rounds of ball cartridge served to each man, and further orders awaited.

His Excellency arrived by steamer on the following day, and with him several companies of soldiers. He proceeded at once to Richmond, leaving the troops and volunteers at Woodstock, where he was able to make a satisfactory arrangement with the men, resulting in personal loss financially,

but infinitely more to his credit than the exercise
of an authority causing bloodshed.

This railway was the first built in this Province,
and the line was surveyed over the New Brunswick territory to the Canadian boundary, and
thence to Quebec. The original projectors of this
line were St. Andrews men, Wilson and Hatch. I
had heard their hopeful speeches at Woodstock
during its inception, and was present at St.
Andrews at the opening, but these worthy men
had gone to their rest.

THE GOVERNOR'S VISIT.

(From the Woodstock *Journal*, Sept. 4th, 1862.)

On Tuesday, at 7 p. m., His Excellency Lieutenant-Governor Gordon arrived in this place in his
own carriage, and took rooms at the Blanchard
House. His Excellency was accompanied by
Lieutenant-Colonel Crowder, inspecting officer of
militia for the western district, and by Captain
Moody, aide-de-camp.

A review of Captain Baird's rifle company took
place at eleven o'clock, and occupied more than an
hour. On His Excellency's arrival on the ground,
accompanied by Colonel Crowder and Captain
Moody, the company presented arms. This was
followed by an inspection of the men, the company
marched past in slow and quick time to music
from the drums and fifes of the juvenile musicians,

The Hon. ARTHUR HAMILTON GORDON.

LIEUTENANT GOVERNOR OF NEW BRUNSWICK, 1861–67.

was a preparation for duties of the most trying kind which might be required of them. He had recently inspected volunteer companies in other parts of the Province—some of them a long way from here on the Northern shore—but he had not regarded them with the same interest that he regarded volunteers in this district, for he felt that their services might never be required. But with respect to the men before him, and others in this district, should any difficulty arise, as they might well fancy, they would have to bear the first brunt of the battle. And, should such an event unfortunately occur, each man would feel that upon his steadiness and knowledge might depend the fate of all that was dear to him. In such an event, he felt sure, from what he had seen to-day, that they would so acquit themselves as to recommend them to the warmest approbation of their Sovereign, and to the heartiest gratitude of the country which they loved."

His Excellency's manner, during the delivery of these remarks, was marked by much feeling and earnestness. The review was followed by a *levee* at the Court House, after which His Excellency lunched, in company with a number of gentlemen, at the residence of the Hon. Charles Connell.

After the lunch he visited the grammar school, also Miss Jacobs' school, and at four o'clock proceeded to the iron foundry at Upper Woodstock, to observe the process of drawing off the molten iron.

A considerable number of gentlemen, with a sprinkling of the other sex, were present. His Excellency appeared to regard the operation with great interest and pleasure. After its conclusion he made a visit to the iron mines at Jacksontown.

PROMOTION.

(See Book Militia Correspondence, 1861-1863; page 4.)

In the fall of 1862 the Hon. Mr. Gordon visited Woodstock. He sent for me from the Cable House and I reported immediately. After some flattering remarks as to my services in the past, His Excellency said, " I would like to give you the command of the 1st Battalion, Carleton County Militia ; but I fear it would be the means of breaking up the fine volunteer company you command."

Having served nearly fifteen years as captain, I felt at the moment stung by the remark, and, rising from the chair, said, " If merit is not the passport to promotion, may I ask your Excellency what is ? "

During the winter I received my commission as Lieutenant Colonel 1st Battalion Carleton County Militia, January 1st, 1863, and as Deputy Quarter Master General for New Brunswick, June 8th, 1863.

The officers who preceded me in the command of the 1st Carleton County militia were Lieutenant Colonels Richard Ketchum and John Dibblee.

They were good types of the old New Brunswick gentlemen : kind and courteous in their manner, and slow to mark or punish breaches of discipline.

An Order Book before me, dated Fredericton, January 2nd, 1813, shews the officers above named as captain and lieutenant in a company of embodied militia, performing garrison duty in Fredericton at the same time with the gallant 104th Regiment. I might say that this order book is a poem in itself, and may, at some future time, be valued as containing interesting and important historic data, and the names of men whose heroic deeds will ensure to them a warm place in the heart of every loyal Briton. Thus brigaded for a short time with regular troops, the quota of officers and men, from a district later known as Carleton County, brought back with them such knowledge of military duty as enabled them to instruct in the simpler field movements of column and line.

Immediately after my appointment I proceeded to reorganize the battalion. The greater number of the officers in command of companies were past the middle age, and a new rifle and drill having been adopted I considered it important that intelligent young men should be trained to take their places.

At the close of my first inspection of the battalion, in 1864, I invited young men of education and position to assemble at Connell's hall, also the officers of the battalion. After stating the case, the resignations of all the officers of the battalion excepting one were immediately handed in.

The following winter about sixty young men attended regularly once a week from all parts of the district. The drill, under Sergeant Hewetson, was thorough, commencing with balance step, extension motions, etc. From this large number I was enabled to make a good selection of company officers; and it is somewhat remarkable that although seventeen years have passed away the officers then appointed are at this writing (1883) in command of companies in the 67th Carleton Light Infantry.

Chapter xvii.

Military Commission and Camp of Instruction.

THE Camp of Instruction at Fredericton was one of the results of the peculiar political position of the British North American Provinces during the rebellion in the United States. The immense resources of that nation; the masses of men, unexampled in modern history, that were assembled to meet the emergency; the ironclads and improved methods of destruction that were brought into action, if not existence, during the rebellion, led the statesmen of the British Empire seriously to consider the sentiments of the people and the defensive condition of the Provinces. Canada, one of the brightest jewels in the British Crown, sounded on this test question the first note of alarm. Her refusal to make an appropriation for the defence of the country, in the support of a militia force, staggered the belief of many Englishmen, who had hitherto considered the loyalty of the Canadians as unimpeachable, and excited everywhere a feeling of anxiety as to the cause of this alienation.

The political parties, governing the Provinces of Upper and Lower Canada, were found to be so equally divided that legislation on any important question was brought to a dead-lock; and questions affecting the most vital interests of the country made subservient to the destruction of the opposite party.

As a cure for the ills which were thus distracting this fine country and cramping the progressive energies of the people, a bold scheme was suggested, viz.: The Confederation of all the British North American Provinces.

This scheme had the approval of the Home Government; was heartily endorsed by the leading statesmen of the Provinces, and as its leading features embraced a system of defences and the erection of an Intercolonial Railway, the idea of its rejection at the polls was scarcely entertained. New Brunswick was the first to express an opinion and rejected Confederation.

The Governments of the remaining Lower Provinces declined endangering their position by a similar test ; but all seemed desirous of palliating the circumstances, and endeavor to prove by some action on their part that annexation was not the other and only alternative.

To establish this and appease the Home Government two things were necessary. Firstly, a liberal appropriation toward the defence of the Provinces ; secondly, the organizing and maintaining a militia force.

To this end the Government of New Brunswick

pledged itself to an appropriation of $20,000 for militia purposes for 1865—increased by their successors to $30,000 ; and the Commander-in-Chief assembled a commission to assist in devising some plan of operation, as follows :—

MILITIA COMMISSION.

(See Militia Report New Brunswick Militia, 1864, page 53.)

At a meeting summoned by direction of His Excellency the Commander-in-Chief, and held at Government House, Fredericton, on the 3rd Jan., 1865, and continued on the 4th and 5th January, the following officers of the New Brunswick militia were present :—

His Excellency the Commander-in-Chief—Hon. Arthur Gordon.
Lt.-Col. Thurgar—St. John City Rifles.
   "   John H Gray—Queen's New Brunswick Rangers.
   "   Hon. John Robertson—St. John City Lt. Infantry.
   "   Hon. L. A. Wilmot—1st Battalion York Co. Militia.
   "   Foster—New Brunswick Regiment of Artillery.
   "   Baird, D. Q. G.—1st Battalion Carleton Co. Militia.
   "   Otty—3rd Battalion Kings Co. Militia.
   "   D. Wetmore—2nd Battalion Charlotte Co. Militia.
   "   R. W. Crookshank—St. John Volunteer Battalion.
Captain Simonds—1st Battalion York Co. Militia.
   "   Saunders—New Brunswick Yeomanry Cavalry.
Lt.-Col. T. Anderson, Adjutant General of Militia.

Honorables Tilley, Watters, and other members of the Provincial Government were present at the sessions of the commission, and the legislature contributed liberally for an appropriation for the special military service.

The amount of information elicited in the discussion from officers of intelligence and long experience in the militia service, together with the long military service of the A. G. M. in the regular army, contributed much to the establishment and success of military camps in this Province, and later in the Dominion.

The commission, as one part of their conclusions, recommended a "Camp of Instruction." The conception of a camp of instruction "is due in a great measure," says His Excellency Governor Gordon, "to Lieutenant Colonel Thomas Anderson, adjutant general of militia." It was a source of regret to many of that officer's friends that he was not able to participate in its success. A thorough soldier, a capital drill instructor, and an admirable organizer, Colonel Anderson did splendid service in New Brunswick. The militia law of New Brunswick, adopted as the result of the deliberations of the commission, was largely the work of Colonel Anderson, and after Confederation it elicited from the late Sir George Cartier, minister of militia of Canada, the remark, "that it was the best militia law in any of the Provinces." He had seen service in India in the 78th Highlanders, rendering very important service for a time in Russia and India; he acted as interpretor to the 64th Regiment for a time during the Indian mutiny, and when retired from that duty returned again to the 78th. He succeeded Colonel Crowder as adjutant general of this Province in August, 1864. He was in command of the force sent to the frontier, in 1866, to repel the threatened Fenian invasion, and by his admirable soldierly qualities did much to inspire the force with confidence of success. He was a good officer, thoroughly understood his duty, and, whilst very pleasant and agreeable to those under his command and whilst exercising a strict discipline in camp, commanded the respect of all. The nearest approach, however, to actual warfare was on the night of the supposed attack by Fenians at about eleven o'clock, when Her Majesty's ship "Cordelia" beat to quarters, the sergeant-major (McKenzie) of the St. John Volunteer Battalion sounded the assembly call, and the whole force met at the place appointed, fully armed and ready for defence or attack. After waiting two hours for the approach of the enemy, it was found that the alarm was through the ship beating to quarters only. More of an alarm, possibly, to the force generally than to the officers commanding.

After leaving New Brunswick Colonel Anderson returned to England, and lived in retirement in Devon until his death. The announcement of his death caused much regret among his many friends in this Province, and time has not obliterated the many kindly recollections entertained for

COL. THOMAS ANDERSON,

ADJT. GEN'L MILITIA, N. B.

him by those who were privileged to be associated with him during his term of service in N. B.

CAMP OF INSTRUCTION.

Following out the recommendations of the commission, the military camp of instruction was held in Fredericton, July, 1865. The quotas, from the battalions that furnished volunteers, were marched into barracks on the 5th and 6th July, 1865, and numbered nine hundred men. The force was divided into two battalions, called "The First and Second Battalion, Service Militia," commanded respectively by Lieutenant-Colonel Wilmot and Lieutenant-Colonel Baird. Each battalion was divided into seven companies, with a captain, lieutenant and ensign to each company. The commandant of the two battalions forming a brigade, was Lieutenant-Colonel Hallowes, captain in the 15th Regiment, then in Fredericton; Major Willis, late of the 15th Regiment, discharged the duties of Brigade Major, and Captain Moody, A. D. C. to His Excellency, acted as Quarter-Master General. The officers comprising the Staff of Battalions were as follows:

First Battalion.

Lieut.-Col. Wilmot, Commander.
    "   Otty, (acting) Senior Major.
Major Simonds, Junior Major.

Second Battalion.

Lieut.-Col. Baird, Commander.
    "   Wetmore, (acting) Senior Major.
    "   Hurd Peters, (acting) Junior Major.
Captain C. W. Raymond, Adjutant.

The law contained a provision for a draft should men not be found to volunteer to the number required, but for this there was no necessity as volunteers were found in sufficient numbers, and generally a good class of men. Kings, Charlotte, and the river counties were well represented. Westmorland, Northumberland, and the more distant counties had no representation. The barracks were well chosen. The exhibition building furnished a convenient place for camping and drilling the volunteers. Its vast area afforded ample space for drilling a whole battalion, thereby preventing any lost time in wet weather. Its extensive galleries, and lofty, well-ventilated dome supplied comfortable berths for the repose of the men, and circulation of pure and healthy air. In short, the men pronounced it a gay place—its airy appearance and decorations lending a cheerfulness and buoyancy such as barracks never lent before. The ground floor, also, furnished space for the orderly room, quarter-master's store and reading room. The duties of the orderly room commenced at early dawn, and twelve o'clock at night often found the patient, orderly clerk with pen in hand. These apartments will not soon be forgotten by officers whose duty it was to sign papers, try prisoners, etc. The reading room was evidently the institution of the building—books, magazines and papers were seized upon, and the contents devoured with an avidity that marked well the intel-

lectuality of our embryo soldiers; but the drill-
book appeared to be even more popular than these,
and in the camp bore the sobriquet of the soldier's
bible. The parade ground was a fine level piece of
ground, extending from the exhibition building to
the base of the high lands in the rear of the city,
nearly a mile in circuit, and with space for
manœuvring an army of five thousand men. In
the distance, looking from the exhibition building,
are some noble elms and other shade trees, and the
camps of the commandant, officers, hospital tents,
etc., etc., give the ground a military appearance,
heightened by the shrill bugle note, or roll of
drums from the wood beyond. At the lower end
of the enclosure proper, was the brigade office;
nearer still the gymnasium.

The uniform furnished by the government to
the volunteers was a tunic of red flannel and blue
cap of the same material; the first battalion was
distinguished by a blue facing, and the second by
a yellow. The order of drill was from six to eight
and from ten to twelve in the morning; and
from three to five in the afternoon; and no volunteer was permitted to leave the enclosure, except
upon special business, until after five o'clock.
From that hour until tattoo, nine in the evening,
they could go where they pleased; provided always that they presented in passing the guard a
respectable appearance—boots blackened and uniform orderly. At half-past five in the morning

the dress bugle sounded, and before six o'clock the companies were assembled in quarter distance column, each man answering to his name as called by the respective orderly sergeant. The companies were then proved by their captains, and at the command of a superior officer each battallion moved in fours into the park, where they were initiated into the mysteries of modern warfare. During the first week a marvellous change was observable in the appearance of the men; and having attained to some proficiency in the foundation drill, the rifle is placed in his hands and he begins to feel himself a soldier. Having passed the ordeal of the goose step and manual, he feels that without the platoon he is yet at the mercy of an enemy. The explanation of the thirty motions in loading and firing appear to him interminable; but he goes in to win, and in a very few days, counting their time, at four the hammer comes down with remarkable precision. After two days' drilling in companies by the instructors of the 15th Regiment, or the most competent among the officers and non-commissioned officers of the volunteers, the companies were formed into battalions under the immediate command of their colonels, and the upper and more interesting part of the duty commenced.

INSPECTION BY GENERAL DOYLE.

On the 18th of July the brigade was inspected by General Doyle. With him were also distinguished visitors, the Marquis and Marchioness of Drogheda. The brigade was formed in line with open ranks, and received His Excellency with a salute. Afterward, marched past in quick time and being formed in close column, facing outward, His Excellency proceeded to address the officers and men in language most complimentary on the astonishing progress made in drill, and the conduct and bearing of officers and men under review.

TROOPING THE COLORS.

On the 22nd of July was a grand review of the Volunteers and 15th Regiment, His Excellency the commander being received with a salue. The brigade formed two sides of a square, and with ordered arms looked anxiously to their front on the gallant 15th, who were now to show them what a well-officered and disciplined regiment can do, and what they themselves had yet to learn before claiming in full the honorable title of soldiers in the service of Her Majesty.

Trooping the colors is a military spectacle which one never tires in viewing, and on this occasion the slightest fault or defect was wanting to make the performance in any way imperfect. Next in order came the bayonet exercise by the 15th, Major Simonds commanding. No weapon has obtained for old England more brilliant victories than the bayonet. Armed with the Enfield rifle and bayonet, a body of well-disciplined and plucky troops may successfully resist every impediment, as the *high, low, right, left* and *about* of the 15th on this occasion clearly demonstrated.

The regiment and the 1st and 2nd battalion now marched past in quick time, the commander-in-chief receiving a salute from mounted officers.

Programme of Manœuvres.

The programme of manœuvres for the review by Colonel Cole was proceeded with in order as follows, viz. :

1. Quarter distance on leading companies.
2. Mass columns on the 15th.
3. Wheel to left into line of contiguous columns.
4. Advance in echelon of battalion at wheeling distance.
5. Wheel to left and form line of contiguous columns on left battalion.
6. Form mass on centre battalion, left in front.
7. Wheel to right into contiguous columns.
8. Deploy on left company 15th Regiment.
9. Change position to right quarter circle on right company 2nd Battalion.
10. Advance in direct echelon of companies from right.
11. Wheel eighth of circle to right and at the "alarm" form square on leading companies.

COLONEL COLE,

15TH REGIMENT.

These movements were performed under the command of the gallant colonel of the 15th with but few and trifling mistakes, and be it remembered that this was the first time the volunteers were brigaded with regular troops, or had attempted movements so intricate and complicated. The address of Colonel Cole after the review was highly gratifying to officers and men, and the march home in close column to the soul-inspiring music of the band closed the proceedings of the grand volunteer review.

THE MARCH OUT.

A camp rumor on the morning of the 24th bespoke that a gala day for the volunteers. The splendid band of the 15th was kindly offered in a march out, and, as this was the first appearance of the volunteers through the town under arms, every man seemed determined to put his best foot foremost. The now familiar sound of the dress bugle, at 2.45, startled officers and men from the dull reverie excessive heat imposes, and in a few moments the square was swarming with red jackets and glittering arms.

The call of "orderly sergeants" from the indefatigable Hewitson soon brought the incongruous mass into shape, presentable to the military eye, and in a few moments "fours right," "left wheel," "quick march," put in motion the long line of volunteers. Good music is the real secret of marching made easy, but some do not seem to understand why the cadence is lost in a body of men marching to the same music. The longer the line the more perceptible the wave in it, as the sound of the drum is longer in reaching the ears of those at the greater distance, the troops marching nearest to the music will, as a rule, keep better time. The marching of the men on this occasion was closely criticised, and, as the opposite extremes of the line was nearest the band going out and returning, each battalion received its quota of praise. The march was continued to the Flats, where greater space afforded a " Front form company "; presently " Close to quarter distance on the leading company," " Halt," " Pile arms," "Stand easy." The reverse of this last order followed the command, and in a few moments a raft at the shore was covered with recumbent red jackets, and the noses of the proprietors immersed in the waters of the St. John. Some bayonets on this occasion obeyed the law of gravitation, astonishing in their descent the finny tribe, and leaving a blank which Sergeant Somebody would have to inquire into.

Again, descending along the river bank in fours under a scorching sun, the command " March at ease " was instantly and literally obeyed, every conceivable position in which a rifle could be carried was adopted. The break from Sherman's ranks, in his celebrated march through Virginia, on the hen roosts and piggeries, were cast in the shade by the raid of our fellows on the wells and springs in the line of march. The paper shirt collars that strewed the road, marked also the telling effect of the heat, and when at two and a half miles below Fredericton the command "Halt, front" was given, the idea to officers of the straggling of an army was fairly understood.

"Fours left." "Band to the front." In reversed order we now retraced our steps. The roar of the steam-whistles in passing the mills, added to the music of the relief band, tried the metal of the horses, and laborers and cottagers turned out to view the passing pageant.

LECTURES.

In the evening of the day of the march out, a lecture was delivered to the volunteers by Lieutenant-Colonel Gray; subject, "The Hero of Kars." The position of the besieged was illustrated by diagrams. The point of the lecture — what a comparatively small number of well-disciplined troops, under a gallant and determined commander, may accomplish under the most desperate and trying circumstances, — told well upon the audience. At the close of the lecture Governor Gordon, after thanking Colonel Grey, referred to an important point he had omitted, viz., that the hero of Kars, and the commander of the garrison of Lucknow, were officers from these lower Provinces — Williams and Inglis — blue-noses of whom the people might well feel proud. The energy with which this omission was supplied by His Excellency touched the hearts of the volunteers, who responded in loud and continued cheering.

A lecture was also delivered by Lieutenant Farquarson, drill instructor of the 15th Regiment, showing the improvement made within the past few years in the manufacture of rifles, and the destructive power of this arm as compared with the "old brown Bess" of former days.

On Wednesday evening, the 26th July, Lieutenant-Colonel Wilmot delivered his lecture on the "Relief of Lucknow." The lecturer seemed to feel the force of his subject, and held his audience at the point of enthusiasm for an hour and a half.

The morning following, the men were assembled on the parade for the last time under arms. By companies they were marched into the exhibition building and surrendered with some degree of regret, to the quarter-master, their rifles — a weapon they had only begun to know the value of. At 12 a. m. the volunteers were formed in hollow square. Colonel Cole, staff, and other officers of the battalions, mounted and on foot, assembled within. The commander-in-chief and

staff having arrived, the general order, as follows,
was read by Brigade-Major Willis :

[Extract.]

MILITIA GENERAL ORDER.

Head Quarters, Fredericton,
27th July, 1865.

No. 43.

His Excellency the Commander-in-Chief has been
pleased to direct that the camp of instruction should be
broken up on Friday, the 28th inst., and has much pleasure in expressing his entire satisfaction at the conduct of
the force therein assembled during the whole period of
its continuance. His Excellency desires to express his
sense of the highly efficient manner in which the duties
of commandant of the camp has been discharged by
Lieutenant-Colonel Hallowes; to his temper, tact and
judgment no small portion of the success which has
throughout attended this experiment is greatly attribu-
table. With the field officers of the brigade His Excellency has ample reason to be more than satisfied. Lieutenant-Colonel Gray has evinced an assiduous attention to
the important charge committed to him, which His Excellency cannot omit to notice. Lieut.-Colonel Wilmot has
shown himself, as on all previous occasions, zealous and
indefatigable, and the example afforded by the conduct
of one holding his high position and influence cannot
fail to be productive of the best results. In Lieutenant-
Colonel Baird, and Lieutenant-Colonel Otty, His Excellency is happy to know that he possesses officers on whose
knowledge, zeal, and discretion he can rely, and from
whom he might look for efficient aid in the hour of need.
The officers of the different companies have discharged
their duties in a manner satisfactory to His Excellency.

Finally, and in the most emphatic manner, His Excellency thanks the non-commissioned officers and men of the brigade for their admirable conduct during their period of service. Their willingness to learn their duties and aptitude for learning; their readiness to submit to the necessary discipline of a camp; their constant cheerfulness; their habitual sobriety and good order have surpassed his expectations. His Excellency earnestly trusts that they will strive to maintain the high character they have gained, and that the habits of regularity, promptitude and order, which have distinguished them, will ever be characteristic of the militia of New Brunswick.

The following morning, July 28th, the contingent from Carleton and Charlotte counties, under my command, embarked on the steamer at an early hour from Pickard's wharf for Woodstock. His Excellency, Colonel Cole, and a large number of the officers of the 15th Regiment, with many of the citizens of Fredericton were present to see us off. The many courtesies extended by His Excellency Governor Gordon, and his constant attention to all the details contributing to its success, aided in no small degree in ensuring to both officers and men very pleasant memories of the first military camp in New Brunswick.

To the 15th Regiment much was due for the spirit of the camp. The number of drill instructors furnished by that regiment; the fraternal feeling that marked the intercourse between the volunteers and the soldiers; the reviews and marches in which the band and regiment joined with the volunteers, all went to prove the hearty good-will of Colonel Cole and his officers, and contributed much towards making light and pleasant the duties of the volunteer.

A pleasant journey by steamer to Woodstock, the officers and men were dismissed to their homes, carrying with them many pleasing reminiscences of their twenty-six days of military camp-life.

Chapter xviii.

Fenians.

IN the fall of 1865 rumors were rife that a
large number of Irish in the United States
were organizing for a raid on the British Provinces. Information having been received that a
descent was about being made from Eastport,
Robinstown or Calais, Lieutenant-Governor Gordon visited Woodstock and gave authority to
organize in Carleton county a body of men to be
called the " Home Guards." Orders were at once
issued to the officers of the Carleton County
Militia to enrol men under conditions of service as
follows : " We, the undersigned, do hereby agree
to serve as a Home Guard for the protection of
iife and property against raiders and incendiaries
crossing the frontier during the present winter."

An excellent class of men, the real yeomanry of
the country, came to the front ; and weekly drill
under their own officers, assisted by Drill Inspector
Sergeant Hewitson, was at once established.

It was my duty to inspect these companies in
their several localities weekly during the winter,
and to make a report of progress monthly to the
commander-in-chief. The companies were organized in localities and under officers as follows :

No. 1—Captain George Strickland, Woodstock.

    2—   "   J. Kilburn, Richmond North.

    3—   "   J. Y. Hoyt, Richmond South.

    4—   "   Richard Ketchum, Upper Woodstock.

    5—   "   Chas. Burpee, Waterville.

    6—   "   A. Lindsay, Williamstown.

    7—   "   H. Emery, Jacksonville.

    8—   "   G. E. Boyer, Victoria Corner.

    9—   "   G. E. Shea, Upper Northampton.

  10—   "   G. S. Baird, Lower Northampton.

Some of these visits meant long rides over badly drifted roads, and in the coldest weather.

Sitting quietly in my house in Northampton one evening about the last of April, we were aroused by a loud knocking at the door and the almost breathless utterance of a messenger, "that the Fenians were coming." The river was running full of ice and the night very dark. I donned my uniform with the least possible delay, and arriving at the ferry landing found it impossible to cross the river.

The roaring of the running ice prevented my hearing anything distinctly from the opposite side. I awaited with much anxiety until near daylight, when we succeeded in forcing a canoe over. I found every man of the Woodstock company in the Institute, fully equipped ; also a telegram from Lieutenant-Colonel Anderson, chief officer in command at St. Andrews, "to hold the train and be ready to embark all the available force at a moment's notice." Orders were immediately sent to the outlying companies to march in with the least possible delay ; and further orders from the front awaited.

The presence of a ship of war in the harbor of St. Andrews, and the land bristling with bayonets of regulars and volunteers, proved too much for the nerves of the patriots, and the invasion was abandoned.

The 62nd Battallion sailed from St. John for St. Andrews in Her Majesty's troopship "Simoon," May 10th, 1866. The contingent from Fredericton under command of Major Simonds, were Lieutenants McCausland and Carter, Sergeant-Major White, Color-Sergeant Fowler, Sergeants Skeene and Simmons, Corporals Lockhart, McLaughlan, Fowler, and Lance-Corporals Street and Fowler, with twenty-seven privates. The journey was made in wagons from Fredericton to St. Andrews.

The last of May the St. John companies left St. Andrews for home in Her Majesty's troopships "Cordelia" and "Fawn." The Fredericton contingent returned to headquarters, *via* Woodstock. As deputy quarter-master general it was my duty to .make provision for the transport of the company, which was done. Before embarking on the steamer for Fredericton I read, under instructions received, an order issued by Colonel Anderson, the officer commanding the force on the frontier, then in Woodstock, relieving the corps from duty, and expressing his entire satisfaction with the conduct and soldierly bearing of officers and men during the period of their services on the frontier.

His Excellency having announced his intention of inspecting the "Home Guards" at Woodstock, on the 26th of June, 1866, the whole force assembled on the flat in rear of the Catholic chapel. Previous to the inspection every effort had been made to obtain from the Governor authority for the purchase of a uniform—a cap and tunic of cheap material. Failing this an *esprit de corp* was aroused, which resulted in the purchase by the several companies of a serge scarlet tunic and military cap. When formed in line,—the first time of the company's being formed in battallion,—many were astonished at the precision of movement in the manual and platoon and field exercises. Before the arrival of the steamer conveying the Governor and his staff, a double line was formed by ranks facing inward, extending from the steamboat landing at English's to Main street. On landing His Excellency was received with a salute and "God save the Queen" from the band. As he walked through the lines he was not a little surprised to see the uniformed and soldierly appearance of the men, and of which he several times expressed his approval.

After dinner,—provided by the Governor at the various hotels, and which the officers and men enjoyed heartily,—the battalion was assembled for review. The towns-people and friends of the soldiers from all parts of the country were present in large numbers.

The movements in line and column were executed in such a manner as to elicit from His Excellency the highest praise for steadiness and soldierly conduct in the ranks, also for the spirit of loyalty manifested in a prompt response to the call to repel invaders from our land.

By request I proceeded on the following day by coach with His Excellency and the deputy adjutant general, Lieutenant-Colonel Maunsell, to Florenceville, for the inspection of the Home Guards of the 2nd Battallion Carleton Militia, under the command of Lieutenant-Colonel J. R. Tupper. This, the last speech delivered by His Excellency in New Brunswick, did credit to his head and heart. He referred in glowing terms to the brightness, clear-headedness, versatility and hospitality of the New Brunswickers; to the beautiful scenery and the many happy hours he had spent in the forests, or on the lakes or rivers of New Brunswick.

Returning immediately to Woodstock and the Cable House, I was honored by His Excellency with an introduction to his wife, the newly married Hon. Mrs. Gordon, who presented me with a photograph of His Excellency. A few minutes later he was on board the steamer for Fredericton, where I bade adieu to a gentleman whom, whatever his political opponents might say, I found to be a friend and an honorable man.

(From Militia Report, New Brunswick, 1866)

The Lieutenant Governor to the Secretary of State for the Colonies.

CAMP OF INSTRUCTION,
Torryburn, near St. John, 2nd July, 1866.

Sir,—

1. I have the honor to enclose for your information the copy of a General Order by which I have relieved from active service that portion of the militia force which had been under pay and performing permanent duty for the past three months.

2. The strength of this force has from time to time varied, but has generally been about 1,000,—a large number to be withdrawn for so long a time from agricultural and industrial pursuits in so small a community, and whose absence was in many places seriously felt.

3. I have every reason to be entirely satisfied with the conduct of this force, and have to express my strong sense of their cheerful endurance under somewhat trying circumstances. The utmost readiness to come forward in defence of the Province from attack was on all occasions evinced, and had I deemed it requisite I should have had no difficulty (however great the inconvenience such a step would have caused), in calling out a much larger force under the pressure of any temporary emergency.

4. In addition to the militia forces permanently embodied companies of militia, under the name of "Home Guards," have been formed, who, though not under pay nor abandoning their usual avocations, have devoted a certain portion of every week to drill and military exercises, and who would have largely added to the number of trained men in time of need. I was present at a muster of a body of this description in connection with the 1st Battalion, Carleton County Militia, held a few days ago at Woodstock. At a very trifling expense a body of four

hundred men had been drilled, at least as well as an
ordinary volunteer company, and taught to perform battalion movements with considerable steadiness and precision. The men of the force had, at their own cost,
provided themselves with rough uniforms of scarlet
flannel and caps, and presented in all respects an appearance most creditable to themselves and to Lieutenant-
Colonel Baird, the commanding officer of the battalion.

I have, etc.,

(Signed)   ARTHUR H. GORDON.

*The Secretary of State for the Colonies to the Lieutenant-
Governor.*

DOWNING STREET, 18th July, 1868.

Sir,—I have the honor to acknowledge the receipt of
your despatch of the 2nd July, enclosing a copy of a
General Order relieving from active service that portion
of the militia force which was recently enrolled for the
defence of the Province.

I have perused with great satisfaction your report of
the local force of New Brunswick, and shall not fail to
bring under the notice of the Secretary of State for War a
statement so creditable in all respects to the loyalty and
patriotism of those who have devoted their time and
energy to this service.

I have, etc..

(Signed)   CARNARVON.

VISIT OF PRINCE ARTHUR TO WOODSTOCK.

Prince Arthur, Duke of Connaught, visited
Woodstock *en route* to the upper Provinces. A
guard of honor,—the third I had the honor to
command to the sons of our beloved Queen,—

composed of several companies of volunteers in
uniform, extended from the Cable House to the
bridge which crosses Meduxnakic River. The
bridge presented a very pleasing appearance, several arches erected thereon being covered with
evergreens, flags and flowers.

Arriving in front of the hotel the Prince was
received with a royal salute, the band playing
"God save the Queen." After entering the hotel
I was requested to present myself, and was met at
the door of his room, in which also was his staff,
by the Prince, who shook my hand in a very cordial manner.

A few hours later he held a *levee* at the Mechanics' Institute, at which I had the honor of presenting the people of Woodstock. The platform
was gaily dressed with vases of flowers, to which
as he approached bouquets of flowers from the
hands of fair New Brunswickers strewed his path.
The Prince occupied a chair kindly furnished by
Mrs. Charles Perley, which had been the property
of his grandfather, the Duke of Kent, in Nova
Scotia.

The Prince is a genial, soldierly-looking man ;
and, as I walked by his side to the Institute, he
seemed to enjoy the hustling of the crowd that
pressed around us and the humorous remarks that
occasionally reached his ears. A good natured
Irishman in front and crowding rather closely
upon him, was requested to move out of the way,

replied, with a comical shake of his head, "Indeed, I'll have a good look at him! Didn't I see his mother many a time!"

This young Prince, being the last of the royal family with whom I was brought in close proximity, it has been my experience that many' occupying inferior positions in life might learn from these lessons of cordiality in manner and gentlemanly bearing far more becoming their position.

RENFREW HOUSE AND GUESTS — FIRE.

During the period of three years occupation of the hotel by Mr. T. W. Smith it was honored with many distinguished visitors. The almost complete blockade of the southern ports during the rebellion compelled an overland journey through the British Provinces, and thence south, to avoid detection and arrest.

The proprietor of the Cable House, Blanchard, being an American, the Renfrew was the headquarters of many distinguished Southern gentlemen, bearers of important despatches to Europe and *vice versa*. During the winter they arrived by specials with fleet horses at all hours, and Smith's suavity of manner and despatch in providing for their wants was often most generously rewarded by the spirited Southerners. For physique many of them were a fine type of men and of noble bearing. Slavery, in a true history of the rebellion, may be proved to have been the one spot that tarnished the Southern escutcheon.

During stormy weather, or a press of business, I took an occasional meal or lodged at the hotel, and thus had the pleasure of meeting and talking with some of the brave men whose country was passing through a terrible but unequal struggle for independence.

At the end of three years, the terms of Mr. Smith's lease having expired, and having made considerable money, he retired from the hotel business and invested in a woolen factory in the Harvey Settlement. A good business was done by his successors until October 12th, 1867, when the Renfrew House, with other buildings in the block, was destroyed by fire. I had that evening returned from St. John, where I had successfully arranged for stock usually purchased at that place. I had scarcely closed my eyes in rest when the ominous sound of the church bell came over the water, and with it the glare of burning buildings in Woodstock. It was but too evident from the direction that our property was at least in jeopardy. With George, our boat was soon forced over the river. We found a barn in rear of the hotel in flames. A hand-engine was our only reliance, but this was monopolized by Colwell & Sons for the protection of their property, and liquor was dealt out unsparingly to the half-drunken crowd in possession. A fine block of brick buildings was thus left to the mercy of the flames, with a considerable quantity of druggist's stock in the basement.

For the second time in seven years George and I stood in the street over a remnant of our stock-in-trade, damaged and broken. It was now three o'clock in the morning. The rain was falling. Dejected and for the moment almost broken-hearted, we commenced putting under care the remnants saved. George's first remark, after all was over, was, "Well, pa, I suppose this will prevent my going back to Montreal!" His time for resuming his medical studies was then near—the first of November.

Before daybreak I had secured a shop in Connell's brick building, and during the day, with a new experience and surroundings, our door was again opened to the public.

Chapter xix

Confederation of the North American Provinces.

THE subject of a union of the Provinces of New Brunswick, Nova Scotia and Prince Edward Island having been for some time freely discussed in the papers and several public meetings held, in which politicians advocated strongly the principles of union, the subject of a union of all the North American Provinces was broached, and finally, on this larger ground, the best talent of both political parties was arrayed for battle. As matters then stood the legislation of one Province was as hostile to another as to a foreign country.

The Hon. S. L. Tilley, then Provincial Secretary of New Brunswick, visited Woodstock. Charles Connell, C. Perley, and others were consulted, and a campaign organized to carry Carleton County for the larger scheme. Mass meetings were held at Florenceville, Richmond, and other places, at which, by request, I was one of the speakers.

One of the strongest arguments against a general confederation, and which has since proved to have had some weight, was the overpowering influence of the Upper Provinces of Ontario and Quebec, which would make us subject to their will, or in the language used, " Hewers of wood and drawers of water."

The Conservative party was then in power ; and the best evidence of statesmanship, in the framing of a constitution without a precedent to guide, is the little friction which over twenty years of operation has produced.

The first effect of confederation was to remove some of the best and most talented men from our Provincial Legislature to Ottawa, and with a true desire to establish on a sound basis the new order of things the appointment of such men only to places of trust under the government as had given evidence of their fitness or ability to discharge the duties of the office.

Up to the time of confederation, our military organizations were entirely voluntary. Neither officers or men received pay, and few if any drones were found in the ranks. Thirty years continued service should, I felt, give me a good claim to a staff appointment under the new *regime*.

General Hastings Doyle was the commander-in-chief, with headquarters at Halifax. I met him at the Government House, Fredericton, and to him was submitted for review my reports on frontier post-service during the Trent affair.

To the general I wrote, and received in reply a

kind letter; also an official letter that I might use at Ottawa. He furthermore gave me the address of the Hon. Arthur Gordon, our late governor, then in London, and advised me to address him on the subject of a staff appointment. I did so, and the promptness and matter of the reply were to me a great and pleasant surprise.

LETTER FROM GENERAL DOYLE.

My Dear Sir:

I have only lately returned to Halifax, and hasten to explain to you why you have not received an earlier reply to your letter.

The fact is I had left Paris, to which city it was forwarded, and the people of my hotel having unfortunately lost my address, my letters, and yours amongst their number, all remained at my hotel, until by chance a friend of mine went there and claimed and forwarded them to me, or they would have been there now.

With regard to the request you make of me, all I can do (if that will be satisfactory to you), is to speak of you by hearsay, Mr. Gordon having, when I visited the camp near Fredericton, mentioned your name favorably to me. More I cannot do, as from your not having served under my immediate command I have had no opportunity of judging of your merits.

I told you, when I had the pleasure of seeing you at Fredericton, that I was prepared to see that justice was done to you, and, if I had any patronage to distribute, must of course have been guided by reports of others which had reached me from other official quarters, but the militia having now passed from under my command, I can only report what I have actually seen; and if you

would allow me to recommend as the best thing you can
do to attain your end, it would be that you should write
to Mr. Gordon, under whose immediate observation I
believe you served, and get him to speak to your capa-
bilities for staff employment. If not, I will of course
state that when I visited the camp your name was mentioned to me with others as a zealous and good officer.

I remain, dear sir,

Yours truly,

HASTINGS DOYLE

P. S. — I send an official letter in case you prefer making use of it instead of communicating with Mr. Gordon,
who is at present in London, and any letter addressed to
him at Sir John Shaw LeFevre, 8 Spring Gardens. London, will be sure to find him.

H. D.

GOVERNMENT HOUSE,
Halifax, Nova Scotia,
5th September, 1868.

Sir :

I have much pleasure in stating that when I visited
the camp at Fredericton with Mr. Gordon, then the Lieutenant-Governor and commander-in-chief of the militia
of New Brunswick, His Excellency mentioned your name
to me with those of other commanding officers of militia
as a zealous and good officer, and one who had made himself well acquainted with infantry regimental drill, and,
had the militia continued under my command, I should
have felt it my duty to take into consideration your
claims, especially as your service in the militia appears
to extend over a period of twenty-eight years, although I
had myself no opportunity of judging of your capabili-
ties as you had not served under my immediate orders.

I have the honor to be, sir,

Your obedient servant,

(Signed)   HASTINGS DOYLE.

LETTER FROM HON. ARTHUR GORDON.

LONDON, 18 SPRING GARDENS, S. W ,
September 7th, 1868.

My Dear Sir:

I have to-day received your letter of the 18th ult., and I will not lose a post in sending you my reply, the tenor of which you will readily anticipate ; namely, that I have always regarded you as one of the best officers in the New Brunswick militia, and that it would give me most sincere pleasure to learn that you had received an appointment of importance in connection with the military force of the Dominion.

I think you especially well-suited for staff employment, the qualities which in my mind distinguished you among other good officers being an unusual power of combination, extreme accuracy and precision, and a perfect mastery of details without allowing them to master you. You were also remarkable for coolness and clearness of the head, and for an entire indifference to display, both qualities not often found in the civic soldier.

I cannot comprehend how any objections can be raised to you on the ground of seniority, as you were, I think, one of my first batch of lieutenant-colonels. But I think it only fair to state that it was altogether your merits which hindered your promotion, for I should have appointed you to the command of your battalion at even an earlier date had I not found that by so doing I should break up the fine volunteer company of which you were the captain.

You may make what use you please of this letter ; but I must in candor add that there is one officer (Colonel Anderson) who has, I think, even more claims to a permanent appointment than yourself ; and that there are one or two officers beside yourself who, if they asked for them (which they did not), would receive from me testamonials of nearly equal strength.

I remain,

Yours very sincerely,

(Signed)   ARTHUR GORDON.

P. S.—I should, I think, add that I know you to have made great personal sacrifice in improving the efficiency of the force under your command, and although this is not in itself a qualification for employment, it may, I think, *cæteris paribus* be taken fairly in consideration by the authorities.

A. G.

With the Honorable S. L. Tilley I had intimate business and social relations for many years. To him I enclosed these letters, with my application for the office of Brigade Major for District No. 8. I was aware that numerous applications had been made, and the strongest local influence brought to bear for others. I therefore waited with anxiety the result.

After a time I received a telegram from the Honorable S. L. Tilley, then a member of the Privy Council, asking my acceptance of the office of District Paymaster of Militia for District No. 8, the salary to be $600 per annum, with hotel and transport expenses paid when on duty; the salary to increase in the ratio of increase of duties. As there seemed at the time to be no alternative, I accepted, and on the 19th January, 1869, was gazetted.

I had just completed the organization of the

67th Battalion, Carleton Light Infantry,— a regiment I would have felt proud to command,— but which I was compelled reluctantly to resign, owing to my new appointment.

I at once entered upon my duties as Paymaster of District No. 8, with my office in Woodstock.

GEORGE.

Until George, our eldest son, had arrived at the age of eighteen years, he was almost continuously at school, and during the winter season for some years longer he applied himself to the study of the higher branches of an English education and the classics. Previous to the fire of 1864, he entered the shop to learn the drug business. In the fall of 1864 he passed at Montreal a preliminary examination for medical student at McGill College, and possessed over many other students the advantage of a practical knowledge of *materia medica*.

While a large number of candidates were awaiting in the hall admission to the rooms of the examiners, the face of each one as he returned was closely scanned to learn his fate. When George's name was called there came a voice from the crowd, "Hurrah! for New Brunswick!" It was young Roberts, of Fredericton,— long since a successful practising physician. These cheering words seemed to lift him above himself, and the passages in Latin and other subjects submitted seemed altogether too simple.

For three years he prosecuted his studies closely, in the enjoyment of good health. His summers were spent at home, assisting me in my business; walking and crossing the river each day to and from the farm, which was healthful exercise.

Having made good progress in his studies,—every facility for such being afforded by the professors, house surgeons and nurses, with whom he was a favorite,—he urged strongly the benefit he might derive from hospital practice, if he could remain during the summer. I had my fears for the result of his continued close confinement, but at last consented.

The excessive heat, and a double duty imposed by the absence of one of the dressers, whose work he undertook for him during a vacation, proved too much for his constitution; and, after some premonitory warnings, he made a visit home in the month of August, 1866.

On the journey by railway between St. Andrews and Woodstock, the train passed through a storm of hail. The day was excessively hot, and the windows of the car open. Fatigued with the journey, he slept through the storm and awoke chilled, and with a hoarseness from which he never recovered.

Arriving at home, his changed appearance startled me, and I was soon convinced that he was engaged in an unequal combat with the king of terrors.

In the fall of the year, his strength being considerably recruited, he resolved, contrary to the advice of his physician at Montreal, Dr. Drake, to return, with the hope of completing his studies that winter and obtaining his degree. The journey was, however, too much for him, and on the night of his arrival at Montreal he was prostrated by severe hemorrhage of the lungs. After some days rest and the kindest treatment by the nurses in the hospital he was enabled to return home.

George's medical advisers having recommended his living and sleeping in pure open-air on the sea or in the forest, I made arrangements for him to occupy during the winter a lumber-camp of William Murray, in Newburgh, about ten miles from home. A lumber-camp, well situated and appointed, is a most healthy abode; the winds are broken and tempered by the surrounding forest. The air you breathe is charged with a healthy aroma, arising from the fir or spruce boughs on which you sleep. The huge blazing log-fire in the centre of the camp, towards which your feet are placed, is ever bright and glowing; the healthy, well-prepared food, and the usual genial, good temper of the occupants,—present attractions which seem to more than compensate for hard work and an absence from home to the New Brunswicker. The cook, Henry Hartt, under whose special care

George was to remain, was a kind, good-hearted man, and an adept in his business.

The Christmas season having passed, in a pung, well-prepared and charged with many comforts, suggested or furnished by a kind mother, George and I started on our journey for Mr. Murray's camp. We arrived safely and found an excellent camp. We walked out a mile or so to where the crew of men were deftly felling with their axes the tall spruce and pine trees. We passed through a barren, sparsely covered with stunted spruce clothed with a crape-like moss, which had a most depressing effect.

From the moment of leaving home I did my best to appear cheerful, until at the camp door I said, "Good bye!" and turned my face homeward ; then, when alone, a sadness almost overwhelming seized me, the remembrance of which may never be effaced. We each thought what we dared not utter.

The invigorating influence of pure air, with daily exercise on snowshoes, sometimes in pursuit of large game, moose or caribou, had the effect of bringing him to within two pounds of his heaviest weight.

In the spring, at the breaking up of the camp, George returned home and amused himself as best he could during the summer, living as much as possible in the open air. The next winter he also spent in a camp, "Telfords," a mile or more north of the previous one, where he was fortunate in finding his old friend as cook.

During each of these winters I visited him frequently, and was sometimes accompanied by my wife or lady friends. We had also frequent opportunities of sending him nic-nacs, late papers or other reading matter.

The Newburgh Settlement being equi-distant from these camps, George made frequent visits to the houses of the settlers, who supplied him with milk, and among whom he exercised gratuitously his medical skill.

I had, some time previously, presented him with a lot of land, near "Meadow Brook," on the road to the Campbell Settlement. On one occasion, when visiting George at the camp, we tramped with one of the settlers about two miles to examine the lot. We found it pleasantly situated, — high land, well timbered and watered, and the road before mentioned crossing its northern extremity. We followed its eastern boundary, or side line, for some distance, where, on a large birch tree, George cut with a small axe his initials, which may still remain, while the hand that formed them has crumbled to dust.

Another summer having passed, the ever-present cough and other evidences showed but too plainly the ravages of consumption.

Letters from his uncle, Charles Shea, then in Kansas, U. S., described the climate as favorable to invalids of that class. Hoping for the best, in the fall of 1870 he left us for that distant country, visiting Montreal and college friends on his journey; thence by Chicago, where he had a severe attack of bleeding from the lungs, to Lawrence City and Quenemo, where he found his friends and a temporary home.

The high winds of that region and an unusually severe winter contributed nothing to his health; and in the month of April he set out on his journey homeward. Having reached St. Louis, where he found truly kind friends in the family of James Morse, formerly of Woodstock, he was stricken with fever and ague, which threatened his life; and from that city I received a telegram : "Come and take me home."

The despatch reached me in the evening, and at four the following morning I left Woodstock in the Houlton stage on my sad errand. A night having been spent at Mattawamkeag, I continued my journey by train to Boston; thence *via* the Lake Shore and Michigan Southern to Toledo, and thence to St. Louis, where I arrived on Sunday morning.

My feelings during this journey were most distressing, not knowing whether I should find my poor boy alive. Crossing the Mississippi in the ferry, the cab drove up to the "Plantation House," from which I hurried to the street and number I was seeking. Entering, I passed rapidly down the hall; rapped at the first door on the right, then at the second, which was almost instantly opened by dear George, and we fell into each others' arms, happy for the moment. "Oh, pa!" were his first words, "I was lying down, but knew your step!"

Under the treatment of a good physician, he had rallied from the attack of fever and ague, but he was advised to leave the city immediately.

On the following evening, the many kind friends and boarders of the house having said "Good bye," we started for home.

The Sabbath which I spent in St. Louis, being some great day with the Germans, I observed, in a short walk with Mr. Morse, their saloons open, and in such of the parks as I saw, crowds of German people were assembled, enjoying various games as on a week day. The scaffolding of the great Pacific railway bridge was being erected over the Mississippi River, just below where the steam-ferry crossed, and seemed to be a gigantic work of itself. Crossing the river toward the city, you pass from that which is clear water into that which is muddy, the line, as you look upward, being distinct. This is caused by the emptying of the Missouri some eight miles above. The wheat on the prairie land opposite St. Louis was about eight inches high, and apple trees at Rochester, New York, were budding into blossom.

Arriving at Portland, Me., on Thursday, we

were compelled to remain over till Friday noon, when we embarked on the Boston steamer for St. John, Mr. Morrow, of Oromocto, kindly surrendering his stateroom to us. We reached St. Andrews on Saturday, and were compelled to remain at a hotel until Monday, when we entered the train for Woodstock.

The journey home was comparatively an easy one, the waiters in the Pullman cars being very civil and attentive. Whether on the steamer or at the hotels, we experienced the utmost kindness.

Reaching Woodstock we crossed the river in a canoe at the ferry. On either shore the ice was piled to a height of ten feet or more; and in a short time George felt once more the endearing embrace of a loving mother.

After his return he gained considerable strength, but the various stages of the disease were to him quite evident. By using the most nutritious food, the use of cod liver oil in various forms of preparation, stimulants and opiates as required, life was sustained until the following February, when, after three years' battling with the last great enemy of our race, he died like a true Christian hero. He visited Woodstock with me for the last time on Christmas morning, when we attended divine service in the Methodist Church. While driving around a large air-hole in the river, as we returned, he knew and noticed many of the boys who accompanied the sleigh on skates, in which exercise he had himself been an expert.

The Rev. Mr. Addy, resident Methodist minis-ter, visited him frequently, and, on one occasion, administered to him the sacrament, his grand-parents and immediate connections partaking with him.

On the Sunday previous to his death, dressed and sitting unsupported in his bed, he looked unusually bright. With a calm serenity he turned over the pages of a Bible, — his companion in many journeys; then, pausing, he asked me to read the fifteenth chapter of 1st Corinthians, after which an earnest prayer was offered by his Grand-father Shea. There were several relatives and friends in the room, all of whom were overwhelmed with sorrowful emotion, he alone retaining his self-possession.

A few days before he died he called to his bed-side all the members of the family, and gave to each of his brothers and sisters Christian brotherly counsel. He also desired to see a faithful Chris-tian man-servant, a Swede, and a faithful woman-servant, giving them kindly words and a good-bye.

The following day the final dying struggle com-menced, and continued for three days, when, at five o'clock in the morning of the sixth of Febru-ary, 1872, his happy soul took its flight.

The day before his death, when sitting at his bed-side, I heard him say, " I hear the angels

singing," and repeated, with a joyous smile on his
countenance, the hymn, —

> Oh! happy day that fixed my choice
>   On Thee, my Saviour and my God;
> Well may this glowing heart rejoice,
>   And tell its raptures all abroad.

Our dear son had a most kindly disposition,
and was universally beloved.   After his death we
heard from many sources acts of disinterested
kindness prompted by a totally unselfish spirit.

"He being dead, yet speaketh."

Chapter xx.

Visit of the Governor-General to Woodstock.

[Taken from report in Carleton *Sentinel.*]

IN August, 1873, His Excellency Lord Dufferin, Countess Dufferin, Colonel Fletcher, Lady Fletcher, and Lieutenant Hamilton, brother of the Countess, visited Woodstock.

The party were met below the town by Colonel Baird, Honorable C. Perley, the high sheriff, and G. H. Connell, Esquire, members of the reception committee, and by Colonel Inches, who introduced them to His Excellency. Colonel Fletcher is not a stranger to this part of the country, as he passed through with the troops in 1862.

In the evening a large gathering was held in the Institute. Their Excellencies were received by a guard of honor. An address was presented by the Mayor, L. P. Fisher, Esq,, to which Lord Dufferin made a very appropriate reply. In the course of his address he said : " I assure you, Mr. Mayor and gentleman, that it has been a very great pleasure to me to visit this locality. Situated as Woodstock is upon the noblest river to be found between the St. Lawrence and the Mississippi, we have had an opportunity of observing as

we approach the town how civilization and industry are pushing farther back the old primeval
forest, and are assimilating the aspect of the
country to what is most dear to an Englishman,
a beautiful English county — the good cultivation,
the orchards, the hedge-rows — all combined to remind us that we were approaching thoroughly
English people.   Mr. Mayor, you have in your
address made an illusion to a domestic event
which naturally connects us in a very pleasant
manner with the soil of Canada.   This is the first
public occasion on which that event has been
alluded to, and, although I am afraid too young at
present to appreciate your kindness, I shall not
fail to remind the young lady, whenever she shall
be able to comprehend the meaning of my words,
that the first welcome she received in Canada proceeded from the inhabitants of Woodstock.   In
conclusion, Mr. Mayor and gentlemen, allow me
to thank you in Lady Dufferin's behalf, for the
kind wishes for our future happiness, with which
you have concluded your address."

Then followed the presentation by Colonel Baird
of the lady of the mayor, and several others, ladies
and gentlemen, noticeable among these the presentation of Captain William Skillen, who was recognized by the Countess, her brother and His Excellency, Captain Skillen having formerly lived on
the estate of the family of the Countess in "Kil-
lalee."   Subsequently the Countess requested an

interview with Captain Skillen, and presented her own and the Governor-General's photograph. The party left Woodstock the next morning intending to drive through to Grand Falls.

WOODSTOCK FIRE!

THE BUSINESS PORTION OF THE TOWN IN ASHES!

Loss over $275,000.

Eighty-five buildings destroyed by fire.

An area of six acres burned over.

(The above is the heading of a Woodstock paper, May 17th, 1877.)

About midnight on the 17th May, 1877, the church bell again rang out its ominous peal. The flames rose quickly, and we saw at a glance the direction of the fire.

John proceeded to get the horses, while I made all haste over the bridge on foot. Arriving at the Cable House, the flames were being driven across the street from Allan's corner, opposite ; and had, in the other direction, reached Lynch's store, a few doors from my place of business.

Entering the shop, I found Mr. Holyoke — his son was our clerk at that time — alone, placing articles of stock in large baskets prepared for this purpose. Friends coming in conveyed them to a place of safety.

There being no partition walls through the attics of the whole block, the fire swept with great fury, bursting, with a huge volume of flame, the large window in the photograph saloon over our heads. Fierce gusts of wind opened and closed the doors violently. Showers of sparks and sheets of flame threatened us as we went out and in, carrying such things as were readily seized and portable.

As the fire spread, nearly every one was engaged in saving what they could of their own; and it was almost impossible to obtain any assistance. The experience of previous fires prompted me to select first that which was most valuable and necessary.

While crossing the platform from the door on King street, and bent forward carrying something in my hands, I seemed to be passing through a shower of something, I knew not what. A man came running towards me saying, "My God! are you not killed!" A tall flue, some twelve or fifteen feet above the roof, had at that moment fallen. The leaf of my hat was cut and my elbow slightly injured by the falling brick.

King street, from the bridge on the south side, and from McCoy's on the north to the river, escaped destruction.

My sister kindly offered me one side of a large store she occupied in the Grover building on King street; and, the following morning, I lettered and nailed to the door my name and occupation, to be read from a new stand-point. Losing no time, I arranged the stock saved to the best advantage, and ordered more, thus continuing with but little interruption. For a time I controlled almost undivided the business, the destruction of the other drug stores being quite as complete as my own and were later in re-opening.

Paxton having returned from Newfoundland, and all arranged satisfactorily with the insurance companies, I turned attention to rebuilding.

Having purchased the freehold of the ground formerly held under lease, I decided to erect a brick building, two stories in height, to cover the ground on the corner of King and Main streets.

The insurance received on stock and building destroyed was applied to the liquidation of debts, which it nearly covered, and we commenced again with nearly a clean sheet. I say *we*, for a year or more previous to the fire, I had given my son, Henry Paxton, an equal interest in the business.

In November, 1878, I surrendered to him all my right and interest in the stock, together with the books and accounts connected with the drug business, and the management of the farm being given to our third son, John D., I was in a great measure released from the care and responsibility which for nearly forty years had rested upon me.

These arrangements appear to me to have been

made under providential direction, for scarcely had they been completed when I received from headquarters, Ottawa, an official letter informing me that in future the duties of District Paymaster and District Storekeeper would be discharged by one officer, and inquiring whether I would accept the appointment, and proceed to St. John and remain there.

My relations with Lieutenant-Colonel Cunard while connected with the brigade of garrison artillery, St. John, officially or otherwise, were always of the most friendly nature; but when, for purposes of economy, the government had amalgamated the offices as paymaster and senior officer, I felt compelled to accept. The change was not of my seeking or choice, as I would very much rather have remained in Woodstock, the difference in salary not compensating the increase of labor and cost of living, and the rupture of family and friendly associations.

Having accepted the new position with dual duties, ample time was given to make arrangements before proceeding to St. John; and during the interval I paid a visit to Ottawa.

Arriving at Montreal, I found my daughter, Helen, with her husband, then a medical student of McGill College, whom I persuaded to accompany me to Ottawa, at which place an Agricultural Fair was being held, and they might not again have so good a chance to see the Capital.

We left Montreal in the evening and arrived at Ottawa early the next morning.

We obtained after many difficulties lodging and a breakfast; then proceeded by coach to the fair, —the distance to the agricultural grounds was over four miles. I had seen in New Brunswick quite as good exhibitions of stock or produce, but the air of aristocracy was wanting. The Governor-General and Princess, gentlemen mounted on English thoroughbreds in jockey or hunting costume, English coaches with postillion, and wearers of foreign styles and accent, made up the difference.

Returning, we came down the Rideau Canal in a steamer, several of which were plying. Stepping on the deck of one when there was scarcely standing room, I feared a disaster, and at the last moment we stepped off on the wharf. Finding another, we again embarked, and had not proceeded very far when we passed the first steamer stuck in the mud, and were thankful for our deliverance.

This being my third visit to Ottawa in a period of some ten years, I saw vast changes as to the improvement in the Parliament and Departmental Buildings and grounds and the extension of the city. The Parliament Buildings are situated on a high cliff overlooking the Ottawa River and the Chaudiere Falls in the near distance.

The mills at these Falls have all the improved

appliances for the manufacture of lumber; some of the largest *pine* logs I had ever seen were at these mills. Immense piles of sawed lumber resembled in the distance blocks of buildings, forming as it were a village of no inconsiderable size.

I also witnessed here the manufacture of pails and matches, and was struck with the celerity and accuracy of movement which practice had given the *petite* manipulators.

On one occasion I walked across the river opposite the city on the ice to see Arthur Rankin and wife, from Woodstock, there comfortably and pleasantly situated, and imagined I was crossing at Woodstock, so close was the similarity of intervale and buildings opposite. In passing by a small grove of pine trees I observed, well-enveloped in blankets, a band of Indians, whom I afterwards learned were Chippewas, discussing their frugal meal.

On the occasion of my two previous visits I had entered my name on the books at "Rideau Hall," — once in Lord Dufferin's time, at the request of his private secretary, an old military friend of mine, Captain H. Moody. In the address presented to Lord and Lady Dufferin at Woodstock reference was made,—and the only instance in the Province, —to their daughter, the recent "young Canadian born," which seemed to touch them deeply, and, as remarked by Captain Moody, was the cause of a kindly regard for the people of our town.

The view of the surrounding country and exquisitely dressed grounds as seen from the dome of the Parliament Building is magnificent. Canadians may well be proud of these piles, either for situation, extent, beauty of architectural design, or finish within and without.

On two occasions I found the Parliament in session, and heard some of the debating talent—Sir John Macdonald, George Brown, and others. I had the honor also of being shown through the Senate chamber by Colonel the Honorable John H. Gray, of St. John, now a judge in British Columbia, meeting there several persons I knew from New Brunswick.

QUEBEC.

Leaving Ottawa for home, we returned by train to Montreal. On our journey down we found on board Mr. T. H. Hall and wife, whose kindness since our arrival at St. John I have pleasure in acknowledging.

Having spent a pleasant Sabbath at Montreal, I left on Monday morning by train for Quebec. Arriving safely after a tedious ride, and crossing from Levis on the steamer, cabby drove me through the narrow walled streets of the ancient city to the Union Hotel, kept by a genial Irish landlord.

Rising early the following morning, I walked

through a portion of the city, and visited the
Dufferin Terrace and the monument to Montcalm
and Wolfe near by.

Seeing a soldier in uniform hastening towards
the Citadel, I followed him, passing through the
gate and wall, thirty or forty feet thick, unchal-
lenged. Forming a part of the wall on the inside
were guard-rooms, from one of which a sergeant
issued, and I at once requested that a guide might
be sent to conduct me through the works. In a
few moments a soldier presented himself *cap-a-pie*
and saluting. I followed him over the parade-
ground by the platform near a wall where *bruin*
was cutting some antics ; passed by masses of shot
in piles, dismantled cannon, the building occupied
occasionally by distinguished visitors, etc., etc., to
the " Flag Staff Battery," the highest point in the
defensive works of the city.

While inspecting the Citadel and surroundings,
the officers and men of "A" Battery were assembling for inspection and monthly payment on the
parade ground within and opposite to the entrance
before named.

Dismissing my guide who had pointed out to
me on the parade an officer whose uniform was
familiar, I approached him, and soon found myself
taken in brotherly charge by Lieutentant Colonel
Forrest, D. P. and D. S. of No 7 District.

The battery was well equipped in men, horses,
and guns ; the uniform and trappings in excellent

condition ; and the discipline apparently as severe as in the regular service.

With Lieutenant Colonel Forrest, I visited his office and the club room ; the shortness of my stay preventing my accepting hospitalities generously offered.

I proceeded at once to the examination of the chief points of interest in and about the city, — Laval College, the interior of some French chapels, where fine pictures were exhibited, and Wolfe's monument I did leisurely and alone. I made in a memo book a rough sketch of Wolfe's monument, while reading thereon the inscription :—

"Here died Wolfe, September the 13th, 1759."

I tried to peer into the far past, and, by a spirit of incantation, reproduce the scene, which, on that spot, surrounded the dying hero ! The name of Wolfe must ever remain associated with Quebec,— the key or military pivot of the Dominion, — to whose indomitable energy and wonderful powers of combination, supported by the valor of British troops, we are indebted for the possession of a fortress called from its strength and position the Gibraltar of America.

In the afternoon my Irish cab-driver presented himself, and in a two-wheeled vehicle started for two dollars and fifty cents worth of driving, which embraced the city and Montmorency Falls.

The face of the rock, which the American General Montgomery attempted to scale in an attack on the city, was the first point of interest examined. Driving rapidly through one of the streets, a sudden jerk threatening dislocation of the neck, brought the horse suddenly to a halt in front of a low wooden building, the driver exclaming, "There's where they waked Montgomery, sir!" Words painted over the shingles announced the same fact, but it was the fate alone of the misguided officer that made the unpretentious building famous.

As we descended to the Lower Town, the localities of recent riots were pointed out, and scenes of frequent bloody frays between the populace and authorities described with rich Irish fervor.

Leaving the city, we descend the St. Lawrence *en route* for Montmorency Falls. The river which forms this magnificent cataract rises in the "Lac des Neiges." It precipitates its vast volume of water over a perpendicular precipice 240 feet in height, nearly 100 feet more than that of Niagara. Immense clouds of spray rise from the bottom in curling vapors and present an inconceivably beautiful variety of prismatic colors. The late Duke of Kent resided in a house close to the Falls, which commands a beautiful view of one of the most picturesque scenes in America.

Almost a continuous line of cottages, with small garden patches, line either side of the road, and the air was impregnated with the odor of onions, which the buxom female habitants, squatted on the ground, were busily gathering.

Several toll-bars during the journey forcibly reminded the passenger of ancient barriers which are happily unknown to provincials elsewhere in the Dominion.

The tolling of bells in Quebec seemed to be unceasing, and I was informed that from a chapel belfry near the hotel the death of every Catholic by night or by day was thus proclaimed.

Left Quebec on the morning of October 1st, 1879, for home. While crossing the St. Lawrence in the steamer to Point Levis, I heard my name called, and found near me a Frenchman named Rousseau, who had lived for several years in Woodstock. He worked as a machinist for R. Attay, and fitted up for Louis Coombes the first ferry-boat to cross the river at Woodstock, and erected for himself a saw-mill at Bull's Creek. He was an ingenious and intelligent man, and I was pleased to meet him.

Chapter xxi

Remove to St. John.

RETURNING to Woodstock, the order was received directing me to attend at the Store Department in St. John, to take over on the 15th of October instant the duties of storekeeper. The D. A. G., Lieutenant Colonel Maunsell, was the medium of transfer of stores, which were examined in my presence and handed over to my care and keeping.

The apartments in Store Building occupied as a residence were retained by Lieutenant Colonel Cunard until nearly a month later, which period I spent in private lodgings.

About the first of November I returned to Woodstock, where preparation had been made for our removal, and a day or two later we found ourselves on the train, *i. e.*, self, wife, niece, and grandson, together with our effects. Several members of the family and friends accompanied us to the Junction, where we parted,—turning our backs on a home of many joys and sorrows, and a town, where forty years previous, as a young man, I went to seek my fortune.

Arriving at Gibson, all was safely transferred

to the steamer "David Weston," where the captain made us as comfortable as possible. The following morning, November 5th, we sailed in a snow storm for St. John, and before six in the evening were in possession of our new quarters. The prison-like appearance of the building produced no prepossessing effect upon my wife, albeit the "Brown stone front" was offered as a consoling influence.

PERSONAL.

(From the St. John Telegraph.)

Of Lieutenant Colonel Baird, who has arrived in St. John to take up his residence here, to discharge the united duties of Paymaster and Military Storekeeper, the Woodstock *Sentinel* says :— " Losing Colonel Baird, this county loses a resident of forty years, he having come to Woodstock in 1839, when the town was yet in its comparative infancy, so that he has been closely identified with its changes, advances and reverses. Mr. Baird was always fond of and endeavored to encourage in others a fondness for manly sports, and constantly did what he could to cultivate a patriotic and military spirit. His present position in the military department he has fully earned by his efforts in the way indicated. In organizations as in agitations, having for their object the mental, social and political advancement of the community and the physical improvement of the town he was for many years an active and leading spirit, and his labors in these respects can only be appreciated by those whose living here has been contemporaneous with his. Our personal associations with Lieutenant Colonel Baird have for many years been so intimate that it is with deep regret we part with him as an every day friend and neighbor, and we feel assured that ours is a general feeling among at all events the older and longer residents of the town and country, and if the younger and more recent members of the community do not fully participate in this regret, it is only because from the very nature of things they cannot realize how much all are indebted to him. St. John receives from us an estimable and valuable acquisition, and we sincerely trust that in their present home Colonel and Mrs. Baird may find in new friends and fresh means of usefulness sources of happiness compensating them for those from which they are severed here."

In St. John I found many friends and many pleasant social ties were formed. On settling down to work there I became a member of the Mechanics' Institute. I also received the honor of election to honorary membership in the Natural History Society of St. John. I found the lectures of these societies, particularly the latter, exceedingly interesting and instructive. The learned and justly popular president of the society, Dr. Botsford, I knew as a resident of Fredericton and later

of Woodstock, which was his first field of practice
as an M. D.   I also took an active part in the work
of the temperance reform.   We attended the services and Sabbath school in Queen Square Methodist Church, where I became a teacher of a young
ladies' Bible class, and found it a service of much
profit.

SPARKS FROM A CAMP FIRE.

SUSSEX BRIGADE CAMP,
October, 1882.

The staff consisted of—

> Lieut.-Col. Taylor, D. A. G., Commandant ;
> Lieut.-Col. Crewe Read, Brigade Major ;
> Lieut.-Col. Baird, Paymaster ;
> Major Freeland (P.E.I.), Ass't Bri. Major.

I quote from a review of the camp the following
as touching the inspecting officer : " The camp at
Sussex unmistakably revealed the benefits which
General Luard is doing to the force.   From the
first to the last everything was done with the object of passing a creditable inspection."

For many evenings at this camp a huge windfall,—one of the denizens of the forest,—afforded
the staff and other officers of the camp light and
warmth.   The gentlemanly and courteous Brigade
Major, Crewe Read, from a well-stocked fund of
anecdote and wit, caused many to linger until a

late hour, while discussions on themes of military
and political import were engaged in by others;
and as a result some of the thoughts are crystalized
as follows :—

I.

Canvass, at this season of the year, is too much
of the refrigerator kind to cause one's thoughts to
ramble freely outside the regulation blanket or the
genial company surrounding the camp-fire. Blue-
nose boys never feel more at home than when
engaged in camp duty. It has been the highest
ambition of the country lad to attain to the age
and position of an axe hand in a lumber camp for
the winter, and the transition is an easy one to
camp-life *militaire.* The traditions of the country
all lead our youth in that direction. Their fore-
fathers having endured the hardships of "flood
and field" in battling for their country's rights,
were well fitted to endure the blast of a New
Brunswick winter, or a struggle for a foothold
with the native redman, the wolf or the bear.

The variety of employments in which the youth
of the country engage give full play to the powers, mental or physical, and, as an officer of high
rank once said, addressing six feet of a New
Brunswick man, produce a beau ideal of a soldier:
Ready in resource, patient under difficulties, and
possessing a spirit of bravery which the 104th
Regiment alone has had an opportunity to exhibit,

the yeomanry of New Brunswick might well be expected to take a front place at our country's call. The aptitude for drill, either as mounted or dismounted troops, and an erect bearing on the field, have caused favorable remark from General officers accustomed to reviewing the rank and file of English, Irish or Scotch recruits. With such material for soldiers, then,—and we believe the men, natives of the other Provinces of the Dominion, are but little if any inferior to the New Brunswickers,—what should be the duty of the government with regard to maintaining an effective force in the Dominion? The cry of "no danger!" from friends, politicians and others has acted as a brake upon the wheel of government military reform, and is even now threatening to extinguish the spark of loyalty in the country which the military spirit of the people has kept alive. The first condition of the existence of a thoroughly equipped militia force, embracing all arms of the service in the Dominion, would be its *necessity*, which I shall endeavor to show exists.

II.

The United States is generally acknowledged to be the great and apparently overwhelming Power with which Canadians on this continent may sooner or later have to battle for existence. The United States is but in its infancy compared with other nations of the earth. It has passed through

but one phase of testing stability. It has yet to
pass through its internecine struggles, the national
test applied by the historian Macauley, before being established or consolidated on a sound national
basis.   In other words it has its Scotland, its
Wales and its Ireland to win before being in
accord with the great family of nations.   Englishmen visiting the United States are overwhelmed
with its greatness, and often commit themselves to
print before recovering from their astonishment.
We have nothing to fear from the native Americans.   They are by blood, language and religion
our own, and in the great struggle it may be our
fortune to sustain their cause.   Having built the
great cities on the Atlantic coast and valley of the
Mississippi, they are following their red brethren,—
a second wave of humanity, moving westward.
Moreover, from the aversion of American women
to nursing children, the native element is said posi-
tively to be on the decline.   The increase of the
foreign element in the United States is rapid and
continued, and the bid of politicians during oft repeated elections for foreign national support, is
unconsciously giving a prominenee to parties whose
rivalry for the ascendancy may in the near future
shake the country from centre to circumference.

The civic government of New York, New Or-
leans, Chicago or St. Louis, are indices for the
future, the Sabbath desecration in any of which
would grieve the spirit of the Puritan fathers.

The sifting process has driven to the western borders many desperadoes whose artistic achievements in murders or railway robberies cast in the shade the most accomplished Italian banditti. These statements are not overdrawn. Cow boys and other organized bands of ruffians ride into towns, plundering and murdering the inhabitants, while the law seems powerless to inflict punishment.

The union of these discordant elements, under two or more leaders, will sooner or later produce anarchy and revolution, the end of which no man can forsee. Prophesying thus may be considered presumption, but nations are as surely punished as individuals for their sins.

If we are still feeling in Ireland the result of a spirit of lawlessness, let loose during the so-called "Southern Rebellion," how would this Dominion stand affected, should those scenes and deeds of horror be transferred to our own borders ?

Returning to England after his imprisonment in Kars, nearly the first words uttered by Sir Fenwick Williams were, "Woe be unto that country which in time of peace does not prepare for war."

Having now referred to the quality of our men as soldiers, and a possible contingency of their being employed, I will offer some suggestions as to who should lead them.

III.

England, now the first naval and military power on the earth, has had many commanders of armies, but few generals. The genius of an inferior officer, or the dogged obstinacy of her soldiers, has often turned defeat into victory. Her greatest generals have been those who best understood the instincts of the people against whom they were warring. "The courage and genius of Clive," says Hume, "converted an association of traders into a large and magnificent empire." This writer or clerk, one of the captives taken by La Bourdannas at Madras, decided the fate of India at Plassey, in the defeat of the Nabob's army of 50,000 men and forty pieces of cannon, with an army of 1,000 Europeans and 3,000 Sepoys, with eight field pieces and two howitzers.

Marlborough, son of a country clergyman, and page at the Court of Charles II., serving as a lieutenant in an English auxiliary force, in the reign of Louis XIV., under Turenne and Vauban, became so well versed in the tactics of those able French officers as to place Blenheim at the head of the list of English victories, and release his country from the condition of vassalage to a French monarch.

In 1758 the war waged in all quarters of the world, but the chief success of the year was achieved in Canada, where the plan of campaign was sketched out by Pitt himself. His plan of invasion was by three separate divisions, to unite at Quebec. In the appointment of commanders, ignoring claims of seniority, as well as those of aristocratic and parliamentary interest, Pitt was guided by merit alone ; and this was the secret of the success with which our armies were at this period attended. The gallant Wolfe, who had previously attracted the notice of the great statesman, was one of the chosen, and ascended the St. Lawrence with an army of 8,000 men.

A return to the system of making merit the passport to promotion has, in the person of Sir Garnet Wolsely, done much to retrieve the tarnished honor of our arms.

In generalship, the Crimean War was a failure : Alma, Balaklava and Inkermann being all battles of soldiers. Of the defeats which England has suffered through the incompetency of generals, none is more marked than that of "Sackett's Harbor," Sir George Provost in command, and in which battle our own 104th Regiment bore a conspicuous part.

The rivalry which exists naturally between people in the same condition of life sharpens the desire to obtain a knowledge which gives superiority. The tribal wars of this and other countries are examples ; and end only in a survival of the fittest. The condition of climatic and geographical obstructions are patent to the natives, and become their best barriers when assailed by others not to the manor born.

An infantry company skirmishing with precision of movement on skates would be a sight for the cockney on the Serpentine. Yet some of our readers have struck off left and right to the sound of the bugle, in the clear frosty air of a winter's morning. A chief surveyor, not a native, straying a little from his party, became lost in the woods on the Tobique River, and was, several days after, accidentally discovered on the Wapskahegan in a perishing condition. Two royal engineers, being driven through New Brunswick, saw a native woman with a large, back log on end, moving it diametrically to its destination. Her peculiar condition and employment attracted their notice, and with the best intentions they ordered the driver to stop, and went to her assistance. Alarmed at their approach, she let the log fall and retreated into the house. One officer at each end now tried to lift it, but failed ; and were compelled to admit that of the trio the woman was the best engineer.

IV.

The spirit of the men of New Brunswick in a military point of view cannot be considered mercenary. At the time of the border troubles with Maine, 1837-38, there existed corps of artillery, cavalry and infantry, drilled and uniformed at their own expense, and for physique could scarcely be excelled in any country. The promptness of these corps in volunteering for active service was warmly eulogized by the then governor, Sir John Harvey.

A knowledge of one's own country and that immediately beyond is important for stragetic purposes, and has been already referred to. In the late Franco-Prussian war the topographical maps of French territory, previously submitted by Prussian officers, forming a network of roads and railways, proved an important factor in the successes that attended the German invaders.

The purchase system, which for so long a period obtained in the British army, was a costly drain of blood and treasure upon the nation. The senior commanding officer, fit or unfit, led the army to battle, and it became a military proverb, "that the first year or two of the war would be to the English disastrous." When they came down to the middle strata, or hard pan, the solid sense and pluck of the nation asserted its supremacy.

The career of that veteran soldier, Sir Colin Campbell, is an illustration. In 1808, as a lad, an ensign in the 6th Foot, he saw the turning of a tide in human affairs — the opening of a mighty strife between column and line; saw the first of Napoleon's reverses, and the fame of Sir Arthur Wellesley beginning to dawn over Europe. With

Moore at Corunna; at Barossa; in the American war of 1812-14; the Chinese war of 1842; at Chilliawalla (see Kingslake, Volume I., page 524), —"after serving with all this glory for some forty-four years, he came back to England. But between him and the Queen there stood a dense crowd of families: men, women and children, extending farther than the eye could reach, and armed with strange precedents, which made it out to be right that people who had seen no service should be vested with high command, and that Sir Colin Campbell should only be a colonel." Upon the breaking out of the war with Russia, Sir Colin was appointed to the command, not of a division, but a brigade; and it was not until June, 1854, that his rank in the army became higher than that of a colonel.

The opportunities now afforded by the Dominion Government to young men for obtaining a knowledge of military science in military schools of gunnery, and as officers in the British army, will, we trust, soon present scores of Canadians qualified to fill any position, even that of major-general. The officer holding this distinguished position it may be wisdom for the British Government to appoint or approve, although it would be hard to give any very good reason for this, as Canadians occupying high positions have not proved recreant to their trust, although some of them the most trying, as at Kars and Lucknow.

Before extinguishing the last sparks of this

camp fire, I would suggest that plans of attack and defence, submitted by the general and staff, should be made a study for the officers at camps, with a view to intelligent action on the field ; and further, that a system of rapid transport and prompt connection by railway or steamboat should be inaugurated to and from given points, the necessity of troops *when and where required*, being as important in a choice of position as a knowledge of drill for its defence.

I trust that an abler pen may continue this theme until the claims of Canadians are recognized, and the same opportunity given to distinguish themselves in the *field* as in the *forum*, leaving open to them the highest military positions in their own land.

REBELLION OF HALF BREEDS IN THE NORTH WEST.

When the Dominion of Canada purchased from the Hudson Bay Company the large district known as the North Western Territory, it assumed the responsibility of assimilating or civilizing the various tribes of Indians embraced within its limits. Since the year 1670, when a charter was granted to the Hudson Bay Company, frequent intermarriages between the clerks or servants of the company in charge of factories or trading stations scattered over a large district of country and the native women have taken place. These were chiefly of Scotch and French origin ; and as an evidence of the truth of Lord Nelson's assertion that the dominant feeling between an Englishman and Frenchman is hate, so the French half breeds were the prominent leaders of the rebellion.

The wholesale destruction of animal life — their former means of subsistence — and the absorption and appropriation of land they believed by right and possession to be their own, to the simple minds of these children of the forest seemed a deep and grievous wrong.

Mutterings, too far off to fall distinctly on the political ear, had been frequently heard, and had the warnings of certain missionaries received the attention they deserved or an earnest desire on the part of the government been evinced to redress existing grievances, the calamity of civil war might have been averted.

If the *tactics* of either of the MacDougalls, father or son, had been adopted, there would have been fewer tears shed for brave men killed; a round million of dollars in the treasury; and a victory to boast of, not by force of arms, but by the higher force, which deals gently, honorably, nobly, with the weaker race we may chance to govern. Not a man of the tribes subject to the teaching of these reverend gentlemen was found in rebellion. With reference to the seeds of another rebellion now being sown, it is the duty of the government and people, to whom is entrusted the laying of the foundations of this new

Dominion, to see that they are established upon moral principles.

He is unworthy the name of statesman or honest man who will permit, sanction, or endorse the existence of an evil which, while it may advance his own party interests, degrades and destroys the instruments in trust formed for a higher purpose. There seems to be but one feeling representing the intelligence of this wide Dominion that spirituous liquors should by legal enactment be strictly, and under severe penalty for violation, excluded from the North West Territory. The pure, bracing and vitalizing air requires no stimulus to keep in full play the vigor and forces of animal life in this country, and the least indulgence often causes men to cross the faint line into lunacy, riot and bloodshed.

True Canadians were everywhere prompt in responding to the call for service in the North West. Such of the batteries or school corps as reached the front acquitted themselves nobly ; and the harrassing marches through slush and mud tested their soldierly qualities, and imparted to their commanders the confidence which ensures success.

If there were any refractory commanders with which the minister had to *deal*, they were not English or true Canadians ; but another illustration of the old adage that "blood is thicker than water." The fate of "Custer," like the incubus of a nightmare, anchored the force before Batoche ; but the dash of brave men, some of whom were *dropped* at each evening fusilade of Riel's sharpshooters, routed the enemy from cover and closed the war.

On the morning of the 18th of May, 1885, the Infantry School Corps, numbering ninety-six, officers and men, and a company of the 71st Battalion, under the command of Captain Howe, numbering forty-two, officers and men, marched, under the command of Lieutenant-Colonel Maunsell, from Fredericton, *en route* for the camping ground at Sussex, preparatory to the force there assembling being ordered to the Northwest. The company from the 67th Battalion, under Captain Baker, arrived at St. John at 6.30 in the evening.

Previous to the 62nd Battalion being ordered to the front, an inspection of the corps was made in the drill shed at St. John, where hundreds of prominent citizens, their wives and daughters, assembled to witness the inspection of the Fusiliers. The whole battalion was present in full dress uniform, with brass and relief bands. Animated and patriotic speeches were made by the Deputy Adjutant-General, Senator Boyd, Judge Tuck, J. V. Ellis and others.

BRIGADE ORDERS.

CAMP SUSSEX, May 18th, 7 p. m.

*Regimental Orders by Lieutenant-Colonel Maunsell,
D. A. G., commanding.*

In accordance with orders received from headquarters, a battalion is formed for active service
in the North West, composed of companies from
New Brunswick and Prince Edward Island, with
the following staff:—

Chaplain, Rev. G. G. Roberts.
Adjutant, Captain McLean, 62nd Battalion.
Quartermaster, Major Devlin, 62nd Battalion.
Paymaster, Major McCully, 73rd Battalion.
Sergeant-Major, Sergeant McKenzie, I. S. C.
Quartermaster-Sergeant, Sergeant Daniel, I. S. C.
Assistant-Sergeant Major or Staff Instructor,
    Sergeant Billman, I. S. C.
Instructor's Staff, Billman and Sloane, I. S. C.
Orderly Room Clerk, Sergeant Mayne, I. S. C.
Paymaster's Clerk, Sergeant Taylor, 62nd Batt.
Asst. Orderly Room Clerk, Sergt. Shea, I. S. C.

Company Officers, 62nd Fusiliers.

A Company—Captain Godard, Lieuts. Gregory,
Godard.

B Company—Captain Sturdee, Lieuts. Fraser,
Ruel.

C Company — Captain Hegan, Lieuts. Thompson, Lordly.

G Company — Captain Edwards, Lieuts. Churchill, McMillan.

67th Battalion — Captain Baker, Lieuts. Carman, Brown.

71st Battalion — Captain Howe, Lieuts. Loggie, Johnson.

74th Battalion — Captain Harper, Lieuts. McFee, Wedderburn, 8th Cavalry.

Infantry School Corps — Captain, Major Gordon ; Adjutant, Lieutenant Young ; Surgeon, T. Clowes Brown ; Lieutenants, Hanning, Russell.

Two companies of the Halifax Battalion, Major Walsh commanding, arrived at Saskatchewan — landing May 12th.

The battle of Batoche was fought on the 13th May ; Riel taken prisoner, and the rebellion ended.

The force in camp at Sussex was to be disbanded, and I received a note from Lieutenant-Colonel Maunsell to proceed to camp without delay for the payment of the troops there. I at once went to Sussex, examined the rolls with the assistance of Lieutenant-Colonel Cully, and issued cheques in payment, and the following morning the troops marched out of camp and returned to their homes.

OUR DOMINION ARMY.

In times of peace there is no service for which grants are so grudgingly made as the militia service. It is, therefore, all the more important that there should be a judicious expenditure ; the maximum of good for the minimum of cost.

It is a debatable question whether the expenditure of $45,000 per annum on an Infantry School Corps is a paying investment. Is it an improvement upon the schools of military instruction which obtained in this Province for a time under competent drill sergeants? The country is supposed to have at the end of three years one hundred trained men at a cost of $1,350 per man, ready for any emergency ; and in addition the knowledge that may have been obtained by such officers of the militia force as may have availed themselves of the instruction afforded by the schools.

In view of the federation of the British colonies the following may not be out of place : When Sir Leonard Tilley was provincial secretary in New Brunswick, there was submitted for consideration a scheme similar in some respects to that recently adopted in the establishment of military schools. The loss sustained by the British government from desertion, and the expenditure for apprehension and prevention of desertion, suggested the enlistment of our men for military service in British

America. Each Province was to organize and officer a regiment for three years' service from provincials. Those making the higher marks to be promoted and continued for a second or third term until the rank of liutenant-colonel had been reached; the officers and men when discharged to receive according to merit and position appointments in the militia. The garrisons, pay, food, arms, and clothing for the permanent force to be provided by the British government.

It is estimated that every British soldier landed in a colony is a cost to the government of £100 sterling. A regiment, therefore, of 1,000 men landed in New Brunswick would have cost the government £100,000. Had the suggestion, which I had the honor to submit, been acted upon, the cost of transport alone would have given a large margin; and, the distribution of provincial regiments triennially throughout the milltia, an available force ready for any emergency.

There might be some plan devised to retain in the country a large number of cadets receiving certificates of attendance at the schools. In some cases the allowance received has been applied to carry them out of the country. Sturdy young yeomen, who have property in the country, make undoubtedly the best citizens and soldiers; and from this class, where it is possible, a selection should be made.

No beer or intoxicating liquid of any description

should be sold or permitted within the barrack
enclosure ; the recruit should be *educated* to feel
that he is something more than a mere machine.

NEW BRUNSWICK REGIMENT OF CAVALRY.

Regi patriae que Fidelis.

The 8th Princess Louise, or New Brunswick
Regiment of Cavalry, is composed chiefly of Kings
county men, and has been for many years, considered from a militia standpoint, an efficient force.
Lieutenant-Colonel Saunders, a gentleman of leisure
and means, was for many years the commander,
and, ably supported by Majors Markham and
Otty, the corps attained to a fair degree of efficiency.

Kings being an agricultural county, men and
horses were readily obtained, and troops formed
within reasonable distances. From the infre-
quency of musters, either regimental or troop, a
good knowledge of cavalry exercise cannot be
expected. The steadiness of movement at inspections is, therefore, all the more remarkable as
exhibiting the intelligence of both the rider and
his steed.

It would be money judiciously expended to send
to troop or company headquarters for three months
of each year competent drill instructors. Not only
the officers and such of the men as could attend
would be benefitted, but a military spirit would be
imparted to the youth admitted as visitor, and a

home or national spirit aroused so necessary to the well being of the New Dominion.

The loyalty and ambition of the present commander, Lieutenant-Colonel Domville, to make the 8th Cavalry an effective force is never questioned, and should occasion arise to bring together in one place all the arms of the service, New Brunswick will have no cause to be ashamed of her soldiers.

FIELD BATTERIES.

The two field batteries in the 8th Military District are placed at opposite sides of the Province, Newcastle and Woodstock. Lieutenant-Colonel Call and Major Dibblee are good commanders and energetic men, else this important branch of the service would not have been so long and so well sustained.

It is a fine sight to see a field battery, or regiment of cavalry or infantry sweep by when fully equipped ; but few pause to consider the cost to the commander of reducing all the discordant elements of a volunteer force to that point of order and implicit obedience. The value of this arm of the service cannot be over estimated.

The work done by our brave New Brunswick men with their guns at Batoche paved the way for the brilliant and final charge of their brothers in arms, and together will form a red-letter page in the history of the Dominion. The names of

Peters and Drury stand prominent as good soldiers in this their first baptism of fire.

Lieutenant-Colonel Call generally secures men of good physique for his battery; while the horses of Carleton county cannot be excelled.

BRIGHTON ENGINEERS.

In the event of the Dominion forces being called into active service numerous ready-made corps of engineers would be found in New Brunswick. Under the direction of an energetic and skilled officer, costly appliances for transport, pontoons, etc., could be improvised, saving expense, valuable time, and adding much to the comfort of troops during a march. Major Vince is an excellent officer, jealous of the good conduct of his men, and when plans are submitted for field operations he is ably seconded by the genius and activity displayed in the work. I have several times seen a bridge thrown across a stream, over which troops four deep have marched in safety, the timber of which a few hours previous had been standing in the forest. In the instances referred to, the axe, the auger, and the spade were deftly handled by Major Vince's men, and any section ordered for the duty could apply intelligent labor. The advanced class of teachers distributed through our rural districts, are sending out young men possessing a fair knowledge of mathematics. Hence their

aptitude in discerning the point aimed at, and
alacrity in executing constructive works performed by engineer corps.

Sir Garnet Wolseley was not slow to discover
the peculiar trait in the native Canadian, from
whose book the navigators of the ancient Nile
have learned a useful lesson.   Major Vince volunteered the services of the Brighton Engineers for
Egypt, or other foreign active service, if required.

CITY CORPS—ARTILLERY, N. B. B. G., ST. JOHN.

The St. John Artillery Corps, as individual batteries or a brigade, have always been a presentable
force, either in point of numbers or efficiency in
drill.   The true spirit of the soldier was more
observable previous to confederation, when all the
expenses of volunteer corps were borne by the
officers and men.   But this was not all; they had
frequently to bear the taunts and sneers of the
less chivalrous but more grasping and money making portions of the community.

Growing out of this system, may yet be found
many officers in different sections of the Province
still honored as rendering effective service in their
day.   But many have passed away, only to meet
at the General Assembly.   Among these may be
mentioned of recent date Lieutenant Colonel S.
K. Foster of St. John, and Lieutenant Colonel
Hunter Peters of Carleton.   I knew them for

many years as personal friends, zealous officers and popular commanders. Lieutenant Colonel Lester Peters was also an excellent officer in this branch of the service; and many of his brother officers regretted his early retirement.

It is very difficult to select from the floating population of a city like St. John men who may be relied upon to complete their term of service. Hence an officer must endure the interminable A B C, or foundation drill of recuits, to keep his roll intact. To this end, the drill shed, before inspection, is in nightly requisition and the clear voice of the instructor heard at very late hours.

The artillery practice of the St. John and other batteries seaward from Fort Dufferin have earned favorable comment from the inspecting officers; and, with rifled cannon, should give a good account of an enemy's ships attempting to enter the harbor.

The present commander, Lieutenant Colonel Armstrong, is an energetic and painstaking officer, and the New Brunswick Brigade of Garrison Artillery, which he has just succeeded in organizing, is an honor to New Brunswick.

CITY CORPS—62ND BATTALION.

Semper Paratus.

The veteran commander of this fine corps, Lieutenant Colonel Blaine, is a sample of the energy and perseverance of the old time commanders of New Brunswick corps. *Semper Paratus* is not simply the motto of the corps, but its impress would be stamped on every officer by their commander.

This regiment had the honor of being called to the front at the threatened Fenian invasion, and went! They also marched out from their drill sheds under peculiar but pleasing circumstances for the North West.

New Brunswickers are proverbially loyal, and should the necessity arise, if properly led, will repeat the story of their fathers, the old 104th.

The march out of the 62nd, with its fine regimental band, is always a pleasing sight. It has, as General Grant said, when asked for his opinion of a British regiment, the swing of victory!

The damaging effect produced by the constant changing of men is still more felt when members of the band leave that branch. The finely strung nerves of musicians producing delightful harmony is a seeming paradox to the *discord* occasionally produced and demands the exercise of an oft-abused virtue by the commander.

The St. John Rifle Company, attached to the 62nd, is a fine company, in charge of Captain Hartt, a painstaking officer and crack shot. A thorough knowledge of light infantry or bugle drill, in which some of our rifle companies have been expert, would make this fine company still more effective.

COUNTRY CORPS.

The backbone of every army is composed of the solid yeomanry of the country, because of their number, powers of endurance, and the fields and hearths they represent. The men forming the greater part of the force of this Dominion are intelligent men; not mere machines. They have had the advantage of education; and but few rolls bear other than *bona fide* signatures of the English speaking volunteers.

The shortness of the season for farm work, and the varied employments in which they engage, in wood, field or river, give activity in motion and quickness of comprehension,—the peculiar attributes of good soldiers. From an experience of over forty years, as a commander of such men, I have always found that the officer who knew his duty and did it was respected. The man in the ranks who knows more than his officer is a dangerous man.

To appoint officers from the old country, of any rank, over these native-born soldiers, would be, in active service, to court disaster, as they could know nothing of the character of the country or the genius of its people. At Balaklava, when in a terrible wind the tents of the British officers were blown into the sea, a New Brunswick officer succeeded in holding his tent, not waiting for his servant, and was the first under cover.

As a police force to aid the civil authorities in the suppression of riots, the protection of property by fires, and their presence to check incipient rowdyism, the company of rural corps, stationed at the battalion headquarters,— generally the principal town of the county,— should be placed on a more efficient footing, *i. e.*, some compensation allowed for extra drill or services out of the ordinary course. If a money consideration were not available, a distinguishing mark might be given to such company as had attained to the highest degree of proficiency.

In frontier towns, like St. Andrews, where there is no military organization, or towns where the population is rapidly increasing, as Moncton, independent companies of rifles might be authorized, forming regimental corps or attached as the case may be. A company of rifles, well drilled men, was sustained in the town of Woodstock for more than twenty years, and during that period was ordered out on several occasions on active service.

In these days of communism, and the banding of men under various guises, whose object is disorder and strife, all intelligent and right minded men should give timely aid and support in establishing loyal organizations for the suppression of these enemies to peace and good government. "To be forewarned is to be forearmed."

Chapter xxii.

Work in St. John.

THE fire which destroyed the greater part of
the city on the 20th June, 1877, extended
its ravages to the barracks, which was completely
destroyed, and the large stone building containing
military stores was gutted and contents consumed.
The store building had been made fit for occu-
pancy, but the brick ruins of the guard house,
armorers' forge, *debris* from retaining walls, vaults
of garrison, and under-pinning of gun-sheds still
lay in unsightly heaps, or covered the grounds in
all directions.

The sanitary state of the old ruins compelled
me in self-defence to a necessary expenditure for
alterations, and as every vestige of outbuilding
and fence had been swept away, I erected necessary
buildings and fence at a cost of $150. I had been
led to believe that the amount obtained by sale of
debris, brick, stone, etc., would be allowed for
these necessary arrangements. This, however, was
not permitted. But I had the security that my
office was during good behavior, so that I would
have the enjoyment of their use for life.

When, at the confederation of the British Provinces, I applied for staff department as brigade major, I was requested by a member of the privy council, Sir Leonard Tilley, to accept as a personal favor the office of paymaster, at a salary of $600, to be increased as the duties increased, which would be a *permanent appointment*, while the office of brigade major, to which a higher salary was attached, might be done away with. *It was not then stated to me, nor did I learn until some time after, that the acceptance of either office had been left by the Privy Council at my own option.*

How these assurances have been carried out this narrative shows. The first increase of duty was, "annual drill and camp." When "camps of instruction" were authorized throughout the Dominion the district paymaster for the special service, under general orders issued annually, received an allowance of fifty dollars per month, covering two and in a few instances four months. This was continued until by a change of government Mr. Jones, of Halifax, was appointed Minister of Militia, when the allowance was cut off. From this time forward pay of rank only was allowed for this service and for the number of days actually in camp. With the establishment of "cavalry and infantry schools," the duties of paymaster were largely increased,—in District No. 8 by one-half.

Visiting Ottawa, when Sir Leonard was Minister of Finance, I stated in his office that paymasters in the upper provinces were in receipt of allowance withheld from me. In reply to which Sir Leonard said, "I shall insist on your being placed on as good a footing as any other paymaster in the Dominion." Notwithstanding, while paymasters of military schools in Ontario and Quebec have been receiving regularly an allowance of $200 per annum as payment for that service, the claim of the paymaster of District No. 8, for the disbursement of $45,000 annually to the Infantry School Corps of New Brunswick, has not been authorized by the Minister of Militia. The amount named is fully .equal to that paid to other schools, and why an exception should be made in favor of the upper provinces is not easy to comprehend.

To these increased duties was further added the audit monthly of the bank account, which embraced all moneys issued by cheque on militia account, amounting annually to about $80,000.

The monthly returns of the store department, requiring several days of close writing and many words being placed in a small compass, I began to feel after five years, work of this kind its bad effect upon my eyes. The department at Ottawa had been many times solicited to furnish forms with printed headings, as used in the regular service, but they came too late to prevent irreparable injury to my sight. When first attacked I was threatened with loss of sight in both my eyes, and asked to be retired with an allowance, which was refused. Why a man whose life may be placed in jeopardy by general order at any moment for the defence of his country has not the same intrinsic value as the civil servant enjoying a comfortable home, has yet to be explained.

The loyalty of the people of this country was doubtless taken into account when pay for militia service was being considered, else officers would have been placed on a par with persons employed in the civil service, who not only receive much higher salaries, but for whom an annual and respectable provision is made on retirement.

After several months' severe treatment by Dr. Coleman, to whom I feel grateful for constant and skilful professional attention, the progress of injury received was checked, and the nerve-power in one of my eyes fairly restored. In the meantime an allowance was given for a clerk, who made out the store returns only,—the paymaster's work I managed to get through with myself, and in this way everything seemed to progress satisfactorily for a period of two years more.

By instructions received from the director of stores, I made quarterly inspections of all the forts, batteries, magazines and militia properties situated within the military District No. 8. This involved quarterly visits to Fredericton, Forts Howe and Dufferin, Partridge Island, Red Head Battery ; also, Dorchester Battery and the drill shed at St. John, with an occasional visit to Fort Tipperary at St. Andrews. Full reports of the condition of all these properties were required to be made quarterly, and repairs or erections were frequently ordered under my supervision.

· Semi-annual inspections of the store department were made by the deputy adjutant general of the time and another officer, and to the credit of a faithful servant of the country, the foreman of the store department, James Emison, be it said, that not only during a period of fifty years as caretaker in the Imperial and Dominion service, had no charge been made against him, but on the contrary the fine condition of everything in charge was pointed to as a model for others in the department.

In the discharge of my duty as paymaster, during a period of twenty years under several ministers, I have no reason to think that at any time these duties were not performed in a manner satisfactory to all concerned. With the deputy minister, Lieutenant-Colonel Panet, and the director of stores, Lieutenant-Colonel Macpherson, I have recent evidence in my possession of the kindly feeling that has ever existed between us. No stores of any description have had to be accounted for, nor any explanation regarding the misappropriation of one cent of the public money during the whole period of my service.

The accountant, Mr. O'Meara, I ever found to be a courteous and painstaking officer, and in the death of Major Grant of the store branch, I felt that I had lost a personal friend.

RETIREMENT.

"The long and faithful services !" I had heard so many times iterated, and the promises of men who had the power to improve my condition, led me to hope that some change would take place for the better. But I had yet something to learn of the true inwardness of politicians, to whom the word *tuum* is a mere abstraction.

I had now been pursuing for some time the "even tenor of my way," without a ruffle to disturb the enjoyment of the approaching Christmas season, and as efficiently as ever performing the duties of my office. Returning with my wife from an afternoon visit to our daughter at Fairville, we met a friend on King street who said, "Have you seen the *Globe?* It is said that you are to be retired and your office given to another person." Information of so grave a nature received in this way, was certainly a shock for which we were not prepared. No dissatisfaction had ever been expressed at headquarters as to the manner of the discharge of my duty, and I felt there must be some mistake.

I was aware that a brisk canvass was going on in the city for the election of members to the Dominion Parliament. Dr. Barker was a candidate, and had also the patronage of the city. I had known the doctor for many years, and would see him and get an explanation. I asked the doctor if it were true that to effect some object in this election I was to be officially decapitated? He replied, *that he supposed that was what a soldier was made for.*

In this reply was a confession of cool and deliberate treachery. I felt at once that I was to be victimized, and awaited the course of events. I had certainly seen in a St. John paper, a few days previous, that at a conservative caucus held on the previous evening it had been said openly that, "Something must be done for Armstrong"; but it never occurred to me that there was a plotting for my removal.

A few days later the receipt of the following official letter removed every doubt:—

[Copy.]   14,960.

DEPARTMENT OF MILITIA AND DEFENCE,
Ottawa, 31st December, 1886.

SIR: I am directed by the Minister of Militia and Defence to inform you that an order in council has passed appointing Major Andrew Armstrong, of the New Brunswick Brigade Garrison Artillery, to the position of Paymaster and Superintendent of Militia Stores for District No. 8, and to request that you will be good enough to arrange with that gentlemen for the transfer of books, etc. The minister considering your long and faithful services has made an exception to the rule and recommended the council the granting to you of two years' salary ($1,400) as a gratuity, which recommendation has been approved of.

I expect to get a letter from you stating when Major

Armstrong will be ready to take up the charge of the office.
I am also writing to that gentleman to-day on that subject.

I have the honor to be, sir,

Your obedient servant,

Eugene Panet, Lieut.-Colonel,

Deputy Minister of Militia and Defence.

This letter confirmed what I had heard on the street. A proceeding so summary, endorsed by my chief, cut off any hope of appeal. Had it been Sir George Cartier, or some other Minister of Militia under whose *regime* I had served, I could have hoped for a demand being made to show cause why an old public servant, against whom no charge had ever been preferred, should be thus summarily dismissed; but "a new king had arisen who knew not Joseph," and cared not.

The condition or circumstances of the faithful officer or his family in spite of service rendered and still being given, of sacrifices made for party and country, of promises oft repeated,—all these things are of minor consideration to the candidate for a prospective seat in the House of Commons, or in the government or on the woolsack, for himself, though he is your professed friend. Without even a semi-official intimation of what was intended, left first to learn it from a friend on the street, then from the columns of the daily paper, and practically turned on the street in midwinter. Such a course is surely not the best calculated to encourage faithful service to one's country.

Some honorable man may be at this moment in a government office in the discharge of responsible duties, receiving a salary barely sufficient to maintain his family respectably, yet his office may be the subject of a treacherous negotiation to advance not the interests of his country but the personal or party political influence of some man or men.

The following extract from a letter received from a gentleman in St. John, after the election, seemed to be also the expression of public opinion: "The only qualification for his successor was the active membership of a society whose influence the government candidate hoped to get, and who had by running an election in which, though defeated, the party was anxious to put out of the way,—and thus, for a local political exigency a militia officer of fifty years' service is turned out of his office in midwinter without justification whatever to offer for it, save and only that his office is wanted by another man. The government, largely through the intervention of manipulators in this election and for political reasons fearing the loss of votes, has made an additional grant of $100 per annum to the salary of your successor."

The election was not however won, even though such means were used to secure a majority, and the government candidate was left in a minority of votes to ponder the uncertainty of position in the public service.

The following is from the St. John *Telegraph*, of February 12th, 1887 :

FIFTY YEARS' SERVICE.

The Honorable Military Career of Lieut.-Colonel William T. Baird, late District Paymaster and Superintendent of Stores.

The *Canada Gazette*, for February 5th, contained the following announcement :

MILITIA GENERAL ORDERS.

District Staff.

Major A. J. Armstrong, from the N. B. B. G. Artillery, has been appointed paymaster and superintendent of stores for military District No. 8, from 1st February, 1887, *vice* Lieutenant-Colonel William T. Baird, who has been permitted to retire retaining his rank of lieutenant-colonel.

In these formal and simple terms is chronicled the close of the active military career of an efficient officer and honorable gentleman. Few men — in New Brunswick at any rate — can count as many years of continuous service as he can, and none other perhaps has done so much towards bringing our militia forces to a high degree of perfection. It was fifty years ago when Colonel Baird's career began by his volunteering as a member of the Fredericton Rifles, and he saw his first service during the boundary line troubles and

in the so-called Canadian rebellion. Three years
after, in 1841, he aided in organizing a rifle company in Woodstock, and was commissioned lieutenant. During the Orange riot at Woodstock, in
1847, he commanded the guard for the defence of
the town. In 1849, he was made, by general
order, captain commanding the Woodstock company, and his performance of the duties so well
justified the choice that to-day every old resident of
Woodstock remembers the proficiency and activity
of Captain Baird's men. The year 1859 saw the
company ordered out by the Lieutenant-Governor
to suppress the railway riots,—and they were suppressed. In 1860 and 1861, Captain Baird's service was of a more peaceful and pleasing nature,
for in the former year he commanded the guard of
honor to the Prince of Wales at Fredericton, and
in the latter the guard to Prince Alfred at Woodstock. The four years following, however, brought
him sterner business. In 1862, he organized and
commanded the post service on the frontier for the
prevention of desertion in connection with the
"Trent" affair. The posts were located at Woodstock, Florenceville, Tobique and Grand Falls, and
here he was occupied for three months. On the
first of January, 1863, he received the merited
honor of being gazetted lieutenant-colonel,—and
June 8th of the same year, he was gazetted deputy
quartermaster general, in which capacity he went
with the company assembled in 1865, under orders

of Colonel Anderson, commanding on the frontier, to proceed to St. Andrews to repel the Fenian force.

In 1865, by a general order, Colonel Baird was placed in command of the 62nd Battalion service militia, twenty-six days in camp at Fredericton. The brigade was composed of the 15th Regiment under command of Colonel Cole; the 1st Battalion commanded by Lieutenant-Colonel Wilmot, and the 2nd Battalion by Lieutenant-Colonel Baird. It was inspected July 8th, 1865, by General Doyle, who bore strong testimony to the discipline of the camp. In 1866, Colonel Baird again proved his efficiency as an officer by organizing and commanding a battalion 400 strong, which was detailed for frontier service at the time of the Fenian raid. It was inspected by the governor, Hon. Arthur Gordon, and Lieutenant-Colonel Maunsell. In 1868, Colonel Baird organized the 67th Battalion Carleton Light Infantry. During the same year he commanded at the guard of honor to Prince Arthur at Woodstock. In 1869, Colonel Baird was appointed paymaster of Military District, No. 8, and in 1879 was made district storekeeper in this city.

Now, after the fifty years of faithful service set forth above, Lieutenant-Colonel Baird has been retired on a gratuity of two years' pay—the paltry sum of $1,400.

In reply to notice of removal dated 31st December, the following was respectfully submitted to the Deputy Minister :—

St. John, N. B., January 6, 1887.

Sir,—

I beg to acknowledge the receipt of your letter 14,960, dated December 31st, informing me that Major Armstrong had been appointed in my place, and requesting that I will arrange with that gentleman for the transfer of books, etc. I am also informed that an order in council has been approved granting me a gratuity of two years' salary, $1,400. A letter is also expected from me stating when Major Armstrong will be ready to take up the charge of his office.

In reply, I have the honor to state that this information was a shock to me, because unexpected, and without plan or prospect for a future living or employment. If my salary were not supplemented by allowances each year from district camps, I could not have subsisted, and have now bills in arrears for actual necessaries of life. It was, therefore, impossible to lay by anything from my salary with a view to future possibilities. The minister, considering my "long and faithful service," has been pleased to recommend a gratuity of two years' pay, $1,400.

It is just possible that ministers and council may not know the work and responsibility of the office of paymaster, which I have had the honor to hold since confederation of the British Provinces, and beg to submit the work of the year 1886, viz., cheques received for services and amounts, as follows :—

General service.............. ....$17,210 78
A Company, Infantry School........ 45,300 00
Annual drill..................... 19,633 36

                                    $82,144 14

This does not include the amount paid to troops at
Sussex ordered to the Northwest.

The disbursement of this amount, computed at the
ordinary rate allowed by banks or on commercial account,
would largely exceed the amount received as a salary. I
have herein made no reference to the various duties of
superintendent of stores, for which duty my predecessor
received $700 per annum, and which duty I have per-
formed for the last seven years.

I have presented through you, as Deputy of Minister,
several petitions and requests, asking that the amount of
$200 per annum, received by paymasters of infantry school
corps in the upper provinces, be allowed to me as paymaster of the Infantry School Corps at Fredericton, which
duty I have performed for the past three years, but without avail.

The notice may involve a removal of my family at an
inclement season of the year, from rooms on which money
and labor have recently been expended by me to make
them comfortable for the winter. There have been erections and improvements made at my expense on the
grounds, the cost of which will be submitted in detail;
also, for rent or cost of *office furniture*, all of which I have
supplied, and on which 1 have paid taxes and insurance
during the past seven years. (See claim for desk, $37.)

In view of the facts herein stated, I have earnestly to
request that you will submit for the favorable consideration of the Honorable the Minister of Militia and Defence
the following, viz.:

I. Increase of gratuity to....................$2,000 00
II. Allowance as ˌPaymaster Infantry School
    Corps, three years' service, at $200...... 600 00
III. Payment for value of improvements..... 110 37
    Also, cost or rent of office desk.......... 37 00
IV. Permission to occupy dwelling apartments in Store
    Building and use of fuel until the spring opens,—
    my wife being an invalid.
V. Continuance of salary or subsistence until the
    first of May, or time of removal from St. John.
VI. Expenses of removal from St. John to Woodstock,
    from whence I came, and the cost of removal
    hither,— which was paid by me.
VII. Permission to retire with my rank.

My services as a volunteer commenced in 1837–38, and
has been continuous until the present time. (See public
records and General Orders.)

    I have the honor to be, sir,
        Your most obedient servant,
            W. T. BAIRD, Lieutenant-Colonel,
                D. P. and S. of S.

LIEUTENANT-COLONEL PANET,
    Deputy Minister of Militia and Defence,
        Ottawa.

In addition to the foregoing claims was one for
twenty-four days' service from the first of February—the date of my release as Paymaster and
Superintendent of Stores,—authorised as follows,
by telegraph :

        Dated OTTAWA, Ont., February 2, 1887.
To Paymaster, St. John:
Major Armstrong has been notified to assume duties of
District Paymaster from first instant. Please complete

payments of services up to thirty-first ultimo, as per credit
provided, and notice forwarded to you by mail.

> J. MacPherson, Lieutenant-Colonel,
>   Acting Deputy M. of M. and D.

The above telegram was confirmed by official
letter received later.   Note in the address, "*Late
D. Paymaster of St. John*":

> Department of Militia and Defence,
>   (Account Branch),
>   Ottawa, 1st February, 1887.

Lt.-Col. W. T. Baird, Late D. Paymaster, St. John, N. B.
   Sir:

Major A. J. Armstrong having been notified to assume
the duties of Paymaster of Military District, No. 8, from
the 1st inst., you will please complete the payments of
the services up to 31st ultimo, as provided by credits
notified to you in the ordinary printed forms or notices
and authorities forwarded to you by mail up to that date.

Having completed these payments you will please hand
over to Major A. J. Armstrong all cash, books, ledgers,
cheque books, and public papers you hold in connection
with the office of paymaster of the district.

You will please forward the usual accounts and vouch-
ers up to the 31st ultimo, and send a statement on Form
No 42, showing the balance of your accounts at the bank,
and giving the number, date, to whom payable, and
amount of each cheque unpaid by the bank at the date of
rendering such account.

You will please then refund by separate deposit receipts
the balance at credit of each account as shown by your
ledger.

> (Signed)   J. Macpherson, Lieutenant-Colonel,
>   Acting Deputy Minister M. and D.

My services as paymaster having ceased on the 1st February, also the customary monthly allowance, here was plainly an authority from the government to perform a service for which I would be entitled to receive pay of rank, and so said a staff officer, to whom at the time I submitted the authority; but this, with all other claims for services rendered, have up to this time not been paid by the authorities at Ottawa, although some at least have been admitted correct and just. The validity of at least some of these claims is substantiated by the following letter from His Honor Sir Leonard Tilley:

Government House, Fredericton,
February 18th, 1888.

My dear Sir Adolph:

Colonel Baird writes me that he is about to make some claims upon your department for extra services rendered and money expended on buildings at St. John. during his residence there, and asks me to say a word to you in favor of his application. He has sent me a synopsis of his claims, and to me some of them seem quite reasonable. Of the others I am not in a position to express an opinion; but I would ask for his application the most favorable consideration that can be given it. He needs every dollar that can fairly be given him.

Knowing your appreciation of the services of the men who have devoted their lives to the perfecting of our militia service, I have every confidence that you will take a liberal view of his case.

I feel strongly for Colonel Baird, because I have an intimate knowledge of the great sacrifices he made in maintaining our militia force before Confederation, when government did but little to reimburse the active officers for work performed. Under all the adverse circumstances with which our officers had thus to contend, *he* was always active, giving his time and his money in the interest of his service. In fact, he and a few others were mainly instrumental in the reorganization of our militia after it had been permitted to die out. It is my appreciation of his valuable services then rendered that makes me feel anxious for a generous consideration of his present claims. I know you gave him on retiring two years' salary; but with that his means are limited, and he finds it hard to get along.

Yours sincerely,

(Signed)   S. L. TILLEY.

Sir ADOLPH CARON, Minister of Militia, Ottawa.

On the first day of March, 1887, wearied with packing and preparation for the journey home, the mercury at zero, we left the apartments occupied by us in the store building, St. John, and the service of a government *professedly conserving* the best interests of the country.

Various attempts having been made through influential men to impress favorably the Minister of Militia regarding my claims. The Minister of Marine and Fisheries having expressed himself favorably during the election canvass in St. John as to the payment of at least one of the claims, viz., "For improvements on store grounds," and also having given an explicit assurance if found just the other claims would be paid; that they would be liberally and generously dealt with, and would be all right, I addressed to that gentleman, as a representative of this Province in the Dominion, a letter as follows :

Woodstock, N. B., June 15, 1888.

My dear Sir :

Before the last session of Parliament, I made up a full statement of my claims against the government, which, supported by letters from Sir Leonard Tilley and others, were, I believe, submitted to the Minister of Militia by Mr. Hale, the representative of this county.

"I cannot see that any objection should be made to my claim for transport expenses to and from my post of duty when acting under orders. See Regulations and Orders for the Militia of Canada, 1883, par. 141. 142 : "When any officer of the District Staff is *relieved* from duty or is transferred to another station," etc. 142. "On reporting for duty, etc., beside actual personal transport and hotel expenses *en route*, an allowance is provided for transport of luggage, 1,000 pounds, *and a sum of money equal to two months' pay* to cover all other *personal claims and expenses incident to his removal.*"

The Staff of a District is composed of the following officers, viz., Deputy Adjutant General, Brigade Major, Paymaster and Superintendent of Stores. These are statutory provisions approved by the Governor-in-Council, December 17th, 1883.

With the claims referred to was submitted a statement by Mr. Fairweather, an architect in St. John, of the value of a building, fence and other improvements erected and paid for by me on the government grounds adjoining the store building in St. John, which valuation was made in the year 1887. The building, etc., is now used by and in possession of my successor, Major Armstrong, from whom, nor from any other person, have I received anything as payment for the expenditure.

I certainly had no authority to make these improvements, but they were a necessity, as everything had been swept from the premises in the great fire of St. John ; and had I been permitted to remain in occupation and discharge my duty as paymaster, etc., as promised when I first accepted the office at Confederation, "to be held during good behavior or ability to discharge the duty," the claim in all probability would never have been presented. I cannot remove those improvements, and am slow to believe that the government will determine to appropriate for the public service personal property, the cost or value of which I now so much need.   I was instructed to remain and complete the work of the year during the month of February, for which service I have received nothing.

There being no gas on the premises, my claim for light and fuel for kindling coal fires in the public service is a just one.   For three years as paymaster of the Infantry School at Fredericton, I disbursed all moneys paid on that account.   Other paymasters received $200 per annum, while in New Brunswick the paymaster received *nil*. These claims are fair and honest.

I now earnestly and respectfully request that you will examine them in the office of the Minister of Militia, or I will send you copies, and give me your opinion and reasons if any, why moneys expended by me in the public service, when acting under authority, should not be refunded and payment for services rendered authorised.

I am, sincerely yours,

W. T. Baird, Lieutenant-Colonel.

Hon. G. E. Foster, Minister of Finance,

Ottawa.

To this was received only the usual brief, evasive, polite acknowledgment of receipt. Up to the present time the results are about as satisfactory as when that note was received. The claims still remain unsettled.

Chapter xxiii.

Squa-took Lakes, Upper St. John, N. B.

FTER sundry assurances given by the cautious Deputy Minister of Militia, Lieut.-Colonel Panet, that the public service would not be permitted to suffer in consequence of my absence, I gladly closed my desks, and, leaving the warlike stores in charge of the old and faithful foreman and caretaker, Emison, entered one fine morning Dan's coach for the New Brunswick train. The delights of a school boy in his holiday enjoyment is approached in the "leave of absence" from the desk of routine of duty by the government official. The pure air of wood or lake, the sense of liberty and freedom from the daily cares and responsible duties that may devolve upon him are enjoyed as phases of a new existence.

A few days spent at the old farm and home near Woodstock, my wife and I leave for a brief visit to Bairdsville, my early wilderness home. Arriving at the station, directly opposite, an old friend and well-known lumberman on the St. John River, William Kilburn, kindly fixed his canoe and set us over. Reaching the highway by an old and steep road from the river, the creek, lake, and once familiar spots present themselves.

Among the comfortable and neatly painted buildings composing the residence of Henry Baird, Esq., I spied one diminutive, unpainted and retiring from view, as if unfit to associate with its more modern and artistic brothers. But to me it was the loveliest of all. Within its rude walls I had slept the sleep of youthful innocence and contentment; it had been to me a palatial residence; it had been the home of a dear mother, and it had sheltered us from wintry storm and blast.

The visit was one of mixed joy and sadness—memory was busy with the past. But the wonderful progress which stamped every object was a cause of rejoicing. Instead of a small patch of clearing, the whole farm, a mile in depth, was denuded of trees and under good cultivation; an excellent turnpike road, a church, a school-house, well dressed people, fine horses and carriages and the whistle of the railway, exhibited a moral and material development I had never expected to witness in that section of the county.

On Monday, August 10th, 1885, Paxton having arrived by train, we join him at Kilburn's, and continue the journey to Tobique, where we meet our Indian guides, Steve Loler and John Thomas, with their barks. All aboard! We pass swiftly through the pleasantly situated village and over fine table land to the Restook. Above the Tobique and Restook rivers,—important tributaries of the St. John,—the main river becomes narrower, with higher banks and lofty hills or mountains in the near distance.

Passing the " Ranger" Settlement, an old settlement composed of disbanded British soldiers, — and Salmon River, on which is a new Danish settlement, — we reach Rapid de Femme, at which place is located the salmon hatchery, one of the most useful institutions established by the Dominion government. After an exchange of passengers at Grand Falls, we proceed to Edmundston, where we arrive at half-past eight.

The platform at the station was too high to make a step down, and a leap in the dark must always be at somebody's risk. In this case Paxton touched bottom, minus a portion of epidermis from a lower limb. Inexcusable thoughtlessness; in this case a sloven loaded with iron crossing the pathway, often causes us to *shin* what we should *shun*.

Leaving the guides to remove their canoes to the shore and pitch the tents, I cross the Little Madawaska River to "Babin's Hotel." Finding several official letters which demanded attention, the Indians are despatched at early morn, to be joined by us later, with wagon containing all necessary supplies for our journey. For some distance above Edmundston, from the road which skirts the Little Madawaska River, towering hills of curious form arise, at the base of which cosy residences of town officials nestle. For the greater part of the distance to the Temiscouata Lake, this beautiful

river winds its way through farms gently receding
on either bank or through the primeval forest, which
claims every inch to the water's edge. The driver,
pausing for a few moments at the iron post which
marks the boundary between New Brunswick and
Quebec, I deposit for a third time, through a de-
fective opening, the date and names of the party,
which, if ever read or by whom, none can tell.

About one in the afternoon we arrived at Big
Creek where our stores were dumped, and we
awaited in a friendly shade the arrival of the Indians. The beautiful barks soon rounded a bushy
point near us, and all being transported to the
opposite side of the river, preparation was made
for dinner. O'Brien, with his son and two horses,
soon after put in an appearance and commenced
preparation for our conveyance to Mud Lake.
With the facility and genius of a native, O'Brien
constructed two sleds or extensions of the ordinary
winter sleds, on which small poles, longer than the
canoes, with grass pillows, forming a spring bed,
were placed to carry our barks and camp equipage.
To the uninitiated I may say that all the tools
required for general purposes in the woods are an
axe and an augur. The material for construction
is everywhere present.

While at dinner a brisk shower drenched everything; and the repeated baptisms from the thick
leafy bushes as we proceeded were, we fear, not in
all cases accidental. An attempt to leap with a

pole over mud holes was for a time attempted ; but after a few slips we accepted the inevitable and trudged on through thick and thin. We reached the camping ground at Mud Lake, a distance of four miles, about dark. A rousing fire was soon kindled, and the bushes adjoining were ornamented with saturated linen or woollen garments.

We were fortunate in obtaining two of the most expert canoe-men and intelligent guides on the St. John. Whether making a tent comfortable or a meal palatable they cannot be excelled. Any directions were altogether unnecessary. On the contrary, wants of even a trifling nature were anticipated. Their knowledge of the haunts of the finest "finny" was to us invaluable.

Refreshed and suffering no inconvenience from the delays and tramp of the day previous, we entered our canoes, which had been prepared for us in Beardley's, *alias* Mud, Lake. A slab of cedar against which to recline, a seamless bag filled with fine wild hay for a cushion, floating on a silver lake in a tight canoe, and a trusty red-skin behind you at the helm, — is a position that cannot be fully appreciated until once enjoyed. The dam at the outlet of the lake being reached and passed, we arrive at the second dam, when the Indians make a halt to *shoe* the canoes, — the low condition of the water making this necessary to protect them while being dragged over the stony beach.

Leaving us on a smooth grassy plot they enter enter the woods. The sound of the axes are cheering, and in an hour they return, each drawing after him three pieces or strips of cedar sixteen or eighteen feet in length, five inches in width, and about three-quarters of an inch in thickness. A strip of the tough cedar bark is passed through the upper edge, and over the top of each piece of shoeing a bow, centre and stern, reaching up the sides and being tied to the cross bars inside of the canoe. The straps or harness, for drawing the canoe, are also made of the rough cedar bark, and attached to the first bar, thence over the shoulder and breast.

The scrape of the previous day and sundry grimaces, drew attention to Paxton's injured limb, now seriously inflamed from the wet and muddy tramp. But John, the medicine man, was equal to the occasion. Superior skill and medicine were both available. Bathed, and dried with the soft fleshy leaf of the maple within reach, he caused to drop upon the wound fir balsam pressed from the fresh bark. Over this was dusted the light ash from cedar bark, which formed a perfect dressing, and remained until the wound was perfectly healed.

Dinner being speedily prepared, a few trout we had just taken gave zest to the meal. After a heavy drag of three miles we reached the alders, which quite met in the now very narrow stream, and through which we fought our way. No fencer,

however skilled, could have done this *a la mode.*
They were to the right, left, and in front. Now
taking off a hat, now a smart slap, or scooping
from the canoe a portion of its contents. Poles or
paddles were useless—pulling, pushing, liftiug, or
twisting of the thickly interwoven bushes was the
manner of our proceeding.

At five in the afternoon we cut the wither, leaving our shoe appendage behind, and shot out into
the clear, cold, beautiful river, Squa-took. A
spurt, aided by a swift current, brought us to good
fishing ground at the entrance to the lake.
Speckled beauties, a pound and over, rose *every*
time to our flies, and as we reeled up from the last
throw a look into the basket dispelled all doubt
of success.

Entering the lake at night-fall, we pull for the
left shore, where, behind a barrier of massive trees
and other drift on a level spot, our tents are soon
pitched. Time hangs heavily on the hands of a
hungry man,—but sometimes it pays to wait.
Reader, I must confess my inability to describe
the enjoyment, mentally and physically, of that
evening's repast. Seated on a cushion ; by your
side a firkin, from the top of which arises in curling fumes the aroma of pure mocha, with sugar
and condensed milk to taste ; a plate with a pound
trout beautifully browned ; another with a flour
pancake light and fluffy, well buttered and heavily
coated with finely scraped maple sugar ; a mealy,

smoking *pomme de terre* with pork gravy ; and an appetite such a day's work only can give ! What gourmand's palate could refuse or what poetic genius express the ecstatic enjoyment of that moment.

The adventures of the day having been discussed, the warriors sit in the light of the camp fire smoking the calumet of peace. "Every leaf is at rest, and we hear not a sound." But, hark ! A splashing on the smooth lake near by ! We instinctively reach for our rifles. Has some denizen of the forest been attracted by the light and now rushing to his doom ? But the spell is broken. The sound of a human voice falls upon our ears, and two men emerge into the light. A Philadelphian, camping on the opposite side of the lake, tenders a greeting. He is a good shot, and his object the large game—moose, caribou or bears which abound in these wilds. He was a pleasant, gamy fellow, and adds one point in the retrospection.

At early morning we are again afloat, and the number of fine fish "out of water" considerably increased. Taking all in all, this,—the reach of water approaching the first lake in our descent, bounded by a large area of wild meadow and covered with pond lilies, excepting a channel through the water,—was the most beautiful and best fishing ground discovered in the route. The water is exceedingly cold, coming from the deep recesses of the forest and mountain shades, where ice or snow may be found the greater part of the year. The name, Squa-took, is Indian, signifying "last one" of the series of five lakes commencing at the Temiscouata.

Breakfast over and all snugly packed, we launch our barks and continued our journey. A stiffish breeze has sprung up, and we encounter rough water as we pass from headland to headland. A large and fine fish, called "Tuladie," are taken at certain seasons in those lakes, sometimes by trawling, which, in this day's sail we tried, but failed to catch.

Having accomplished five miles,—the lake is eight or nine miles in length,—we land, on a smooth rock in a shady cove, for dinner. This despatched, we pull on for the outlet, where there are some good places for fishing, but the roughness of the water prevented an attempt.

Rounding a point a romantic scene was presented to our view. A beautiful quiet harbor, an old camping ground, with smooth grassy plots and poles of tents still in. At the narrowest place of egress, poles were standing in the water and remains of fish traps erected by the French, when barrels of fine fish are often secured.

In the descent of the stream which we have now entered are many falls or rapids, which require skilled men to navigate safely. With wonderful acuteness the Indian discovers in a ripple or bulge a hidden danger, and by instantaneous action averts the destruction of his frail craft. To prevent abrasion or brooming, the end of the pole is pointed with steel or iron. In this passage we narrowly escaped what might have been a serious accident. The end of my Indian's pole became fixed in a fissure of a rock in the bottom of the stream. In swift water, if shallow, he could jump out and hold the canoe until the pole was extracted; but the water was deep and swift. If there were no boulders in front of us, he could have let her run until shallow water was reached. The third and only remaining alternative was successful. With almost superhuman strength and skill, he broke and twisted the pole clear from the part fixed in the crevice without apparently checking the speed of the canoe, and planted it in time to prevent a smash-up on a dangerous rock we were approaching.

Recent marks of moose and caribou passing over muddy or soft places on the shore were frequently seen; and in one instance was floating a branch the berries from which had been recently plucked by a bear. Later we ascend the "Jam," around which the canoes, etc., were carried, and in a short time another halt was made to chop and clear a passage through more drift. These jams are formed by the standing of trees and other drift in shallow places; and from continued contributions caused by the undermining of banks or slides during the spring freshets, become formidable obstructions to navigation.

As night was approaching, we pushed on vigorously and reached Little Squa-took, the second lake. A black and heavily charged cloud, travelling in a parallel line on our left, began to pour out streams of liquid fire upon the earth and belch forth a fearful cannonade. Our objective point was an island on which to camp for the night. The sullen stillness of the past hour was now broken by sudden gusts, dashing the spray and threatening to overwhelm our gallant barks in the lake which we had now entered.

Reaching the island in safety the tents were pitched with all speed and stores protected with cover. After a few moments of perfect stillness, we seemed to be suddenly enveloped in a darkness that might be felt. Then the batteries of heaven seemed to open over our heads; vivid flashes of lightning illuminated the mountain, "Squa-took," towering high above us on the mainland; then a deluge of rain that seemed to occupy space and make breathing difficult. A fracture of the tent poles, from the extreme tension of the cords, was threatened and immediately relieved.

In keeping with the terrors of the night and during a lull in the storm would be heard the weird cry or screech of the loon. Committing ourselves and absent dear ones to Him whose "voice is in the clouds," we slept to awake refreshed and to examine, like Robinson Crusoe, the curiosities of the island. Our rubber blankets, etc., had been spread over a mass of fruit and foliage, — blueberries of a size and quality such as we had never before seen. The island is a mass of rock ; the few trees on which afford but little shelter.

The Squa-took mountain is lofty and in form bears some resemblance to that mountain of flesh, "Jumbo." I have been told that from its summit a view of 150 miles may be obtained. A long tramp through wet bushes prevented our attempting an ascent.

While at breakfast the flock of loons that had made night hideous sailed by. Steve saluted them with a breech-loader, but not having adjusted the sight the bullet missed its mark. At ten in the morning, with a clearing sky, our barks are again afloat, and after a pleasant sail enter another of the rivers which unite the chain of lakes. We had a smooth flow of current, and scenery that the ladies would call "just lovely."

The peculiar appearance of some foliage led us to examine it, and we found the white willow, which, under cultivation, attains to a large size. We also found clam shells four and five inches in length. About noon we entered the fisherman's *el dorado*, the famed Horton branch. We passed through a grove of Balm of Gilead trees of enormous size, the tops from either side completely shading the river and filling the air with perfume.

Spaces here and there through masses of pond lilies resembled artistic walks in a flower garden, or again carry you to some fairy bower of flowers or wild grasses that strew the shore. The song of a melodious divinity alone was wanting to cause one to linger forever in this wilderness of beauty. The land or singing birds that frequent the haunts of men in this country were not seen in this region, and the crane, wild-duck or king-fisher but rarely.

We arrived at our camping ground near the "Big Jam" at two in the afternoon. Our tents had just been pitched and a fire lighted, when a thunder shower passed over, making uncomfortable, an hour later, the passage through the bushes and tall brakes. A bend in the river gave easier access from this point to the head of the Jam, which was a half mile in length.

The portage being easier on the opposite side, our Indians first crossed over, taking chips out of the slippery timber here and there with their axes to make sure footing when they carried their canoes. Following the Indians, we find it necessary to pick our steps. The rushing of the water and the many open spaces into which a mis-step would cast you demanded constant watchfulness.

Passing the first jam, we proceed but a short distance, when we reach another but smaller obstruction. This also passed, we have reached the objective point, the *ultima thule* of our hopes and desires. Several casts are made, but no response. Night is approaching. In an attempt to reach a promising cove my flies became entangled in overhanging bushes. The canoe is wheeled about for Steve to extricate them. On looking down, he cried out, " Oh, my ! I never see such big fish. Tousands ! tousands !" I said, " Drive them out with your pole !" He did so, and in a moment the water seemed to be alive. Trout weighing one and two pounds were taken from the hooks as rapidly as possible. Our lines and rods were sometimes tested by too heavy and active fish. While we could see the flies on the water the sport was continued. I never saw anything like it before. The water was splashed as if by a young duck, several fish running at once to seize the flies.

With increasing darkness, looms up in our imagination the passage over the " Big Jam," which, however, is accomplished in safety ; and reaching our resting place, sit down, happy but hungry, and await with satisfaction further developments.

August 15th. — At half-past four we aroused the Indians and sallied forth. A half-hour later we were switching over the water which seemed alive with fish the previous evening, but without getting a rise. Ascending the stream, we entered the mouth of a creek, and were rewarded by seeing a fine school of trout, three of which Steve soon had in the canoe, by a piece of pork which he used for bait. Trying the plan of the previous evening, three gamy fish about two pounds each,—making thirty in all at this place,—were added to my basket ; Paxton about the same number.

Perfectly satisfied that the reputation of the fish and fishermen had been fully sustained at Horton Branch, we returned to camp for breakfast, and to reload our canoes for the journey homeward. Several inscriptions quite readable, in pencil, noted visitors of years past. Our names were added on a fresh *blaze* made for the purpose on a tree ad-joining our tent. At 9.20 in the morning we turn our prows for the Toledi. The sail down is charming with foliage—almost uninterrupted—to the water's edge.

At one in the afternoon we touched the shore on Little Toledi Lake for dinner. For many miles above the water was nearly level with the surface of the land. We here found a slight elevation, where were growing hazel-nuts, cranberries and wild gooseberries. In less than five minutes, with split cedar and birch bark, a fire is blazing around the frying pan, which soon emits a fragrant odor, and from bacon though it be, most inviting to the appetite. Asking after dinner who gives us all good things, Steve replied, "Heseolup," Milecite for God.

At 2.20 we re-enter our canoes, and with a clear sky and westerly wind paddle along the Little Toledi Lake. Mountains skirting the Big Toledi

Lake are directly before us in the distance. All this part of the country having been overrun by fire, tall, dry trees stand thickly among the second growth. On the top of one of these, Steve pointed out the nest of a large fish hawk, six feet in circumference, made of roots, sticks and grass. At 4.30 in the afternoon we ran the rapids. The water being very low, the canoes were passed over the worst pitch by line and hand.

Paxton tried a fly at the foot of the falls, but there was no response, and without further delay we resumed our journey. At 5.45 having passed all the rapids safely, we entered the Temiscouata, passing inward along its eastern shore. It appeared to us like an inland sea, and white caps were quite visible in the distance. A long rolling swell made the sailing more pleasant than otherwise. At seven in the evening we reached the point of land opposite a cheerful village, and a large chapel came in view as we entered the lake.

Our tents were soon pitched, and we read in the smooth waterworn pavement many familiar names of New Brunswick, some of whom have since obtained a local distinction of soldier or statesman. The night being cold, our sleep was a disturbed one. A five o'clock the clear loud tone of the chapel bell, a mile distant, ushered in the Sabbath morn.

After breakfasting, "we folded our tents and silently stole away." The sound of the Notre

Dame or lake chapel bell, softened by the distance, pursued us for many miles. Our reflections on this morning and under the circumstances would naturally be solemnized in a review of the past week, — the scenes of wild grandeur through which we had passed, the wonderful works of the Creator, and his protecting care over us through many perils.

Passing a large raft of cedar *en route* for Edmundston, we again entered the little Madawaska River, making nearly a complete circuit of one hundred miles. A few miles below the "Degele" our guides land under the friendly shade of a Balm of Gilead for the midday meal. In a cool spring near the landing were two bright tins, and following a path we were led through a meadow to the house of a *habitan*. A pleasant and sturdy "madame" was engaged in the toilet of a nearly nude *garcon*, while four others stood by like steps in the family ladder. Retiring to the tins at the shore, she added a bowl of milk to the boiling coffee, and to our surprise a neighboring Frenchman arrived with a plump *poulet* nicely roasted.

Dinner disposed of and again afloat, we pass a fine farm owned by Mr. Hickson, of the Grand Trunk Railway. This farm had been our headquarters two years previous, and Birch River our fishing ground, where some fine trout were taken.

We arrived safely at Edmundston at six in the

evening, August 16th, 1885 — the round trip of
the lakes having been made in six days. After
tea and a hasty toilet at Babin's, where my valise
had been left, I listened with pleasure, and, I
trust profit, to a sermon in the Episcopal Church,
by the Rev. Mr. Armstrong, to a small but select
congregation, from some of whom I received after
the service — the reverend gentleman included,—
a friendly greeting.

THE SEA! THE SEA!

From the upper windows of our residence in the
store building, we had an uninterrupted view of
the harbor from Navy Island to Red Head Battery; also, of Partridge Island, Fort Dufferin, the
Beacon light, and the buoys marking the course of
the Bay channel. During a heavy blow from the
south the breaking of the sea over the huge boulders forming the Breakwater was a magnificent
sight. Very near to us, at the Ballast Wharf,
huge swells would mount to a height of thirty or
forty feet, dashing as many more over the railway
track and falling into the slip.

We experienced while in that building many
terrific gales of wind. One vessel was swept over
the rocks and high on the shore just below the
Hospital, another wreck occurred in Courtenay
Bay, but without loss of life in either case.

After the erection of the Exhibition Building,

the weird Eolian chords produced by the whistling of the wind through the halyards of the flag
staffs, with the heavy roll of ocean on Courtenay
or Carleton shores, impressed one with the majestic
force and sublimity of the ocean's waves, heightened by a sense of comparative immunity from
their effects.

The entrance of large ships under full sail was
of almost daily occurrence; yet from a sight of
which one never tires. Sometimes following the
sinuosities of the channel, — stately, unguided, as
if imbued with life ; again, with heavy hawser attached to the puffing, plunging, gallant little tug,
which often disappeared, but as often rose again
from the trough of the huge wave, pluckily to pursue its course. I have seen in the harbor at one
time eight or nine staunchly built iron steamers,
loading with timber, chiefly for European ports.
The lurch or lop-sidedness of some of the heavily
deck-laden timber ships would seem to make one fear
for their safety in a storm, but it is supposed that
the load is shifted to balance after sailing. Coast-
ers, or small sailing vessels, are continually passing
in and out of the harbor, and the value of short or
sawn lumber carried by them must be immense.

I saw the plank drawn for the last time from
the wharf at St. John on board the "Cedar Grove,"
and the last words uttered were, " Boy, did you
bring that *three gallons of brandy on board?*"
Alas ! " Cedar Grove ! "

FORT LA TOUR.

Under instructions received from the Director of Stores, I visited Carleton to ascertain the position of and report upon certain land claimed by the Dominion Government. To this end I examined the position of Old Fort or "Fort La Tour." Mr. Harding, of Carleton, kindly accompanied me, by whom I was introduced to Mr. Belyea, for seventy-three years a resident of the fort. He remembered it as "Fort Frederick," enclosed by a palisade, and of hearing the bugle call and drilling of the detachment in charge. He showed me the outline of earthwork and embrasures, the elevation and slope of which is yet in many places well defined.

When abandoned as a fort, several persons squatted thereon, building houses which they occupied for many years. The British Government ordered their removal; they resisted by legal defence; but finally compromised by paying the government £1000, when possession was given and boundaries established by iron pins or stakes. These were placed under what is known as the "Keleher" survey, some of which are yet visible. I examined the plan, which gives the names and allotments, also the amounts paid.

The land sought for, and which I subsequently found, proved to be an elevated position in Carleton, "Blue Rock." It embraces a full square, a plan and measurement of which were made by me and duly forwarded to the ·Department. Fort La Tour occupies the point of land in Carleton directly opposite Navy Island, and commanded the mouth of the St. John River.

Chapter xxiv

Return to Woodstock.

ON leaving St. John for Woodstock I found I was leaving many friends behind, and not the least gratifying token received was from the Sunday School with which I had been so pleasantly associated. The following is from the columns of a local paper :

PRESENTATION.

During his residence in St. John, Colonel Baird taught a large class of young ladies in the Queen Square Methodist Church, by the members of which, as well as by the whole school, he was held in high esteem. On his departure to return to Woodstock he was presented with a flattering address, accompanied by a neatly executed group of the young ladies of his class, photographed by Notman, in St. John, but enlarged to 24 x 28 and finished at Montreal. The frame is heavily gilt of floral design, with interior border of plush. The colonel may well feel proud of this beautiful souvenir, as well as of the complimentary address.

Returning to Woodstock after an absence of eight years many changes were noticeable, showing a marked improvement in the extension of the town, the character of the buildings, and the increase and prosperity of its inhabitants. The upper part of the town, which only a few years previous had been destroyed by fire, had been rebuilt, and many recent erections exhibited good taste in the adoption of a modern and improved style of architecture.

Situated upon a river which Lord Dufferin spoke of as "the noblest river to be found between the St. Lawrence and the Mississippi," and in the centre of a district called the garden of New Brunswick,—Woodstock presents more than ordinary attractions to the tourist or lover of what is beautiful in nature. From the hill-top beyond the river and opposite to the town a view may be obtained which for scope, richness and variety of scenery is scarcely excelled in any country. Excellent carriage roads radiate in every direction from the town, affording inviting drives into the country. Through Jacksontown one has a choice of level roads, by farms and houses presenting a well cultivated and populous district.

From points on the highway road through Richmond to Houlton may be seen, northward, "Mars' Hill," and westward "Mount Katahdin," with intervening spaces of wilderness or clearings, covering a distance of more than 100 miles. A favorite drive is for five miles along the bank of the St. John below Woodstock. It is for that distance almost a dead level. The old elms, the receding natural terraces, and the beautiful and comfortable homes recall the scenes of an early conquest of mind over matter by the first loyalist occupiers, to whom all around was a rude wilderness.

From the highway road to the Upper Corner, or through Northampton on the opposite side of the river, are visible many extensive orchards and nurseries, which, for quality and variety of fruit, enjoy a more than provincial fame. Its inhabitants are probably as pushing and energetic as those of any other town in the Province, and its history, in spite of numerous disastrous fires, has been one of steady progress.

In 1847 the town of Woodstock contained 600 inhabitants. There were then 120 dwelling houses. In 1857 the population was 1581, with 215 inhabited houses. In 1881 the population was over 3,000.

Courts of Session governed the town and county previous to its incorporation. The magistrates gathered from all parts of the county, sometimes with interests differing from the town. It was thought the town could best look after and manage its own business, and an Act of Incorporation was obtained.

The first election for mayor and councillors took place May 12th, 1856. There were three candidates for the office of mayor, viz., Messrs. L. P. Fisher, James Robertson and George W. Cleary. The trial of strength, however, was between the two first named, consequently Mr. Cleary only received a few votes, Mr. Fisher, the mayor-elect, receiving 146 votes, Mr. Robertson 126. The following were elected councillors : Ward 1—William T. Baird, 61 ; Hugh McLean, 53. Ward 2—Wm. F. Dibblee, 50 ; W. W. Hammond, 48. Ward 3 —John Bradley, 42 ; Edward Smith, 26.

In 1854 the first telegraph line was built to Woodstock. Mr. Torney, from Quebec, visited the town, and a public meeting was held in the Institute and stock subscribed for. Later on he visited Fredericton, where the stock list was increased, and the line,—one of the earliest built in New Brunswick,—was opened to Woodstock.

In 1868 the railway from St. Andrews was built into Woodstock, and in October, 1871, the line of the Western Extension was extended to Vanceboro, giving railway connection with the United States. The opening of this line was made the occasion for a large gathering of people from the United States and Lower Provinces. Gentlemen occupying high positions, civil and military, on either side of the line, were present. Representing the United States were General Grant, its President, the Postmaster General and George W. Loring ; the Dominion of Canada by Lord Lisgar, Governor-General, L. A. Wilmot, Governor of New Brunswick, and Sir S. L. Tilley. The reputation of the gentlemen named as orators was well sustained in words of kindly greeting and in picturing the future of the two great countries, now joined not only by bands of iron but by the stronger and more imperishable bond of commercial and social intercourse, which make enlightened nations great and glorious. Ladies and gentlemen to the number of a thousand or more enjoyed hugely the sumptuous dinner prepared for them, and left for their homes impressed with the cordial good feeling which marked the whole proceeding.

The railway to Fort Fairfield in Maine was opened in 1875. The warmest interest was manifested by the people on both sides of the "Line," and this dovetailing of the two nations along the boundary may prove too strong to be broken by any political faction.

In 1876-77 the first bridge was built across the river at Woodstock by the New Brunswick Railway Company, connecting the railways on the east and west sides of the river; giving also as a part of the railway bridge the first bridge for horse and foot passengers between the Grand Falls and St. John. The first train crossed the bridge April 4th, 1877.

To a business man, the length and frequency of the trains passing over the roads, is a sure indication of the extent of its trade as a distributing centre. Its business establishments are proof of its energy and business push. Good hotels and livery stables, with every necessary appliance for convenience and comfort, are found in the town. The electric lights meet you everywhere as you enter the town ; and a substantial iron bridge across the Meduxnakic gives evidence of the wisdom of an enlightened legislature.

The rebuilding of Woodstock after a nearly total destruction by fire on two or three occasions; the contribution by its inhabitants of $40,000, to make it the terminus of the first railway projected in the Province; and the erection of a complete system of water works for its use and protection should give its people a name and fame worthy of record in the future annals of this country.

As the settlement of the country progresses, discoveries are being made of valuable minerals. Silver, gold and iron ore of superior quality exist in great abundance. From its natural advantages of position, the fertility of its soil, the value of its forests and minerals, its facilities for travel by rail and river, and the energy of its people, there is every reason to expect a bright and prosperous future for the district of which it is the centre.

ERRATA.

On page 4, 1st line, for "French" read "Trench "
"   "   4, 19th "   "   "Cowan"   "   "Gowan."
"   " 11, 4th "   "   "sisters"   "   "sister."
"   " 15, 12th "   "   "at"   "   "on."
"   " 52, 23rd "   "   "Craig"   "   "Coffin."
"   " 99, last "   "   "militia"   "   "military."
"   "104, 17th "   "   "seen"   "   "scene."
"   "121, 4th "   "   "Tyler"   "   "Fyler."
"   "136, 7th and 12th lines, for "Commissioner"
                              read "Commander."
"   "138, 17th line, for "Sundy's" read "Lundy's."
"   "146, last "   " "naval"   "   "navy."
"   "153, 11th "   " "to"   "   "by" the
                              commander.
"   "155, 27th "   " "sincerity" "   "severity."
"   "156, 14th "   " "when"   "   "where."
"   "159, 9th "   " "possession" read "proces-
                              sion."
"   "205, 18th "   " "sheds"   "   "sleds."
"   "216, 2d   "   " "when"   "   "where."
"   "312, 1st   "   " "department" read "ap-
                              pointment."